Penguin Books

The Little Aussie Fact Book

Margaret Nicholson was
Newcastle, NSW, in 193
graduating from Sydney T
College, she taught Eng
numerous city and country s
over thirty years, retiring in
now lives on the shore of be
Macquarie, south of Newca
and has an extended fam
children and ten grandcl

Breathes there the man, with soul so dead,
  Who never to himself hath said,
  'This is my own, my native land!'
                    —*Sir Walter Scott*

This book is for my husband and our family,
and they all know the reasons why.

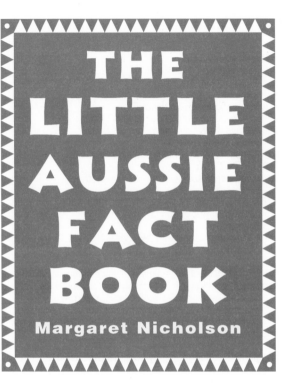

THE LITTLE AUSSIE FACT BOOK

Margaret Nicholson

Penguin Books

Penguin Books Australia Ltd
487 Maroondah Highway, PO Box 257
Ringwood, Victoria 3134, Australia
Penguin Books Ltd
Harmondsworth, Middlesex, England
Viking Penguin, A Division of Penguin Books USA Inc.
375 Hudson Street, New York, New York 10014, USA
Penguin Books Canada Limited
10 Alcorn Avenue, Toronto, Ontario, Canada M4V 3B2
Penguin Books (N.Z.) Ltd
182–190 Wairau Road, Auckland 10, New Zealand

First published by Pitman Publishing Pty Ltd, 1985; 4th edition 1988
Published by Penguin Books Australia 1993, 1995
10 9 8 7 6 5 4 3 2
Copyright © Margaret Nicholson, 1985, 1993, 1995
Illustrations Copyright © 1995

Made and printed in Hong Kong by Longman Asia Limited

National Library of Australia
Cataloguing-in-Publication data:

Nicholson, Margaret (Margaret Alice),
The little Aussie fact book,

6th ed.
ISBN 0 14 024869 2

1. Australia – Miscellanea. I. Title.

994

Contents

Preface

This is a book about Australia, one of the most beautiful and fascinating countries on earth. It is a country always in a state of change, always incredibly diverse, always challenging yet surprisingly accommodating and protective. Its people enjoy a lifestyle equal to any in the world and acceptance and tolerance is the rule rather than the exception.

In 1985 when the first edition of *The Little Aussie Fact Book* was published, my intentions were to compile a practical and condensed book of essential facts and figures about Australia, a book for perhaps young Aussie travellers going overseas who needed to have a small touch of home in their backpack or jacket pocket. However, over the many editions since, it has proved to be of value not only to travellers abroad, but to new settlers to the country hungry for information, to school children with their projects, to business people needing readily accessible facts and figures and to the average Aussie family who find the words to songs and poems or the answers to essential questions about Australia elusive and difficult to find.

One of my greatest joys came in 1994 when a visiting Russian gentleman insisted on meeting me. He had landed in the country with only a smattering of English and found it difficult to communicate. My enterprising brother gave him a copy of my book. Some weeks later, my brother met up with him and commented on how well he had mastered the language. 'It's the little book' he cried. 'You know – the little book – I study it day and night!'

I hope this sixth edition gives you pleasure and enjoyment, and, whether you are a resident or a visitor, that you find Australia, with all its colour and excitement, a stimulating and vibrant country.

Margaret Nicholson
1995

Foreword

It is understandable why this book sells so well. It is as down to earth in its approach as the Australian character – it is colourful and easy to understand.

Australians are at last realising how little we know about ourselves. This book is a brilliant way to start the wonderful path to rediscovering what it is to be Australian. Our Ambassadors would do well to study the contents thoroughly. Personally, I am learning all the 'Did You Know?' items first.

John Williamson

Past

Prehistory

During the ice-age, perhaps as early as 70 000 years ago, peoples and animals of the northern hemisphere began to drift southwards to escape the intense, advancing cold, as well as to find new food supplies. As a result, more southerly groups were pushed even further south, causing a chain reaction of migration.

The ice had built up in the waters of the sea to form massive ice caps, lowering the level of the water (estimated to be 70–90 metres lower than it is today). This uncovered bridges between land masses, nearly joining islands and making migration possible. People in crude craft were able to 'island hop', and perhaps it was possible for the first human inhabitants of Australia unknowingly to enter the great southern continent.

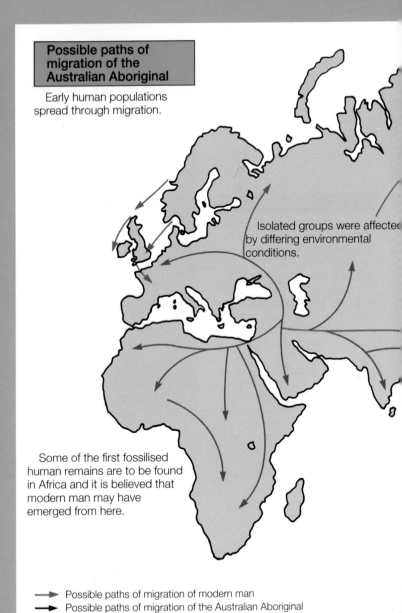

Possible paths of migration of the Australian Aboriginal

Early human populations spread through migration.

Isolated groups were affected by differing environmental conditions.

Some of the first fossilised human remains are to be found in Africa and it is believed that modern man may have emerged from here.

→ Possible paths of migration of modern man
→ Possible paths of migration of the Australian Aboriginal

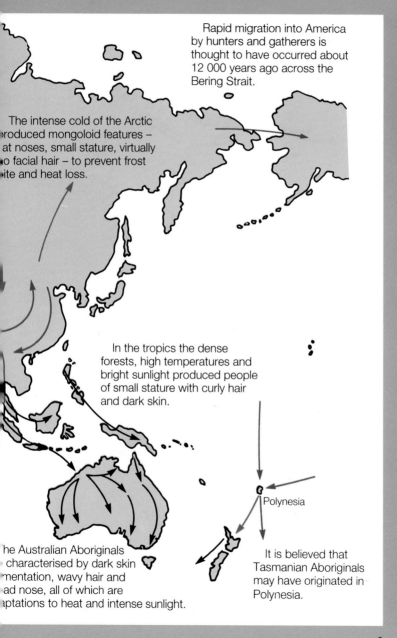

Rapid migration into America by hunters and gatherers is thought to have occurred about 12 000 years ago across the Bering Strait.

The intense cold of the Arctic produced mongoloid features – flat noses, small stature, virtually no facial hair – to prevent frost bite and heat loss.

In the tropics the dense forests, high temperatures and bright sunlight produced people of small stature with curly hair and dark skin.

Polynesia

The Australian Aboriginals are characterised by dark skin pigmentation, wavy hair and broad nose, all of which are adaptations to heat and intense sunlight.

It is believed that Tasmanian Aboriginals may have originated in Polynesia.

Aboriginal history

Some Aboriginal tribal regions

Tiwi

Larrakia | Yoingu
Mildjingi
Dalabon Gumatj
Kakadu
Ingaladdi   Lar

Wandjina

Nyulnyul

Warramanga

Gurindji

Kalkadoo

Karadjeri   Walbiri

Pintubi

Wilgie Mia   Wenamba   Aranda
Pitjantjatjara Matuntara

Dieri

Nakako

Wongkongu

Wirangu

Kaurna

Whadjuk

Archaeological sites found

● More than 30 000 years old
||| 15 000–30 000 years old
⊙ 10 000–15 000 years old

Wik-mukan

Kongkandji

Kabikabi

Walawaka

Bigambul

Jagara

Galibal

Bandjalang

Kumbainggiri

Kamilaroi

Awabagai

Worimi

Dharug

Wiradjari

Kameraigal

rna

angan

Mooroopna

jari

Tjapruwong

nne-

keer

Panninher

Peeberrangner

Leetermairremener

Mouheenner

Then and Now

In my dreams I hear my tribe
Laughing as they hunt and swim,
But dreams are shattered by
*   rushing car,*
By grinding tram and hissing train,
And I see no more my tribe of old
As I walk alone in the teeming
*   town.*
I have seen corroboree
Where that factory belches smoke;
Here where they have memorial
*   park*
One time lubras dug for yams;
One time our dark children played
There where the railway yards are
*   now,*
And where I remember the
*   didgeridoo*
Calling to us to dance and play,
Offices now, neon lights now,
Bank and shop and advertisement
*   now,*
Traffic and trade of the busy town.
No more woomera, no more
*   boomerang,*
No more playabout, no more the
*   old ways.*
Children of nature we were then,
No clocks hurrying crowds to toil.
Now I am civilized and work in the
*   white way,*
Now I have dress, now I have
*   shoes:*
'Isn't she lucky to have a good job!'
Better when I had only a dillybag.
Better when I had nothing but
*   happiness.*

                    Oodgeroo of
              the tribe Noonuccal
              (formerly Kath Walker)

5

Aboriginal culture

Australian Aboriginals existed in almost total isolation for over 40,000 years. They had no written history so only fragments of Dreamtime stories, cave paintings and etchings remain to record their remarkable past. Only in the last few decades has a systematic investigation revealed the rich and complex culture that they possessed.

It was, and still is, a culture based on strong spiritual ties which link them inexorably to the ancient land – a gift from the creator of the Dreamtime. It is believed the people are born of the spirit which inhabits the land, and on dying, return to the soil to be re-born. Each person is thought to be descended from either a plant or an animal and this becomes their 'totem', with its own taboos and rules of behaviour.

Before white settlement, most of the continent was occupied. Although their cultural and language patterns differed, the 600 or more scattered tribes existed in comparative harmony. They each occupied and hunted a recognised tract of land where sacred sites were protected and boundaries, designated in the Dreamtime, were crossed only by invitation.

Tribal elders who, because of their wisdom were considered suitable for making decisions, upheld the laws. Every occasion demanded proper behaviour and breaches of law brought severe penalties.

The economy was based on relentless daily activities of hunting and fishing by the men and the gathering of seeds by the women. Drought and famine were interpreted to mean that the spirits were displeased and that 'man must make amends'. All made and repaired spears, boomerangs and digging sticks which were mainly made of wood. As well, Aboriginals used ground-edge tools made of stone 10,000 years before their European counterparts.

Aboriginal society was a creative one and art, music, song and dance were integrated into both daily routine and spiritual ritual. The elders prescribed the form of ceremonial life, particularly the initiation, marriage and burial rites in which the rest of the tribe, including song men and artists, were totally involved. Also, corroborees and cave paintings reflected the powers of the Dreamtime. Symbolic designs were etched into most objects from tools to the sacred Dreamtime stone, the *Tjurunga* (see p. 117).

Sorcery was not a daily occurrence although no one doubted its power. 'Pointing the bone', the most dreaded magic used, projected the power of evil hidden in the bone into the victim's body.

As the Aboriginals confronted European settlers, the whole fabric of this fragile society was shaken. Early contact was usually made on the outskirts of towns where the materialistic values of white man clashed with the co-operative sharing of the Aboriginals. The myth that this was an uninhabited land when Captain James Cook discovered it, gave the European settlers of the 18th and 19th centuries *carte blanche* to move into areas regardless of the consequences. This erosion of frontiers continued unheeded for over two centuries. Many Aboriginals separated from their spiritual place and stable environment became dispossessed.

By 1850, concern was felt and segregation laws were passed to protect the Aboriginals from the poverty to which they were now exposed. Many were confined to missions and reserves run by white officials with extensive power and control. Some were used as a cheap source of labour by landowners, who although benevolent, still held great power. Others dwelt in a 'twilight zone' on the fringe of white society with little hope of recognition, where health, housing and education became endemic problems.

Changes in attitudes of both black and white peoples came after World War II. White society began to recognise the appalling lack of understanding of the Aboriginal and Aboriginals became more aware of their national identity. In 1962 they were granted the vote in Federal elections and were included in the census for the first time in 1967. National health services began to improve and housing and education services were made a priority. Sacred sites and land rights became issues and by 1977 the Aboriginal Land Trust had lodged claims and were granted title to 114 former Aboriginal reserves. In 1992 the High Court of Australia handed down the controversial and far-reaching 'Mabo' judgement. It ruled that Aboriginals who could prove unbroken occupancy of land were able to lodge claims to that land.

Much has been achieved in the last fifty years towards reconciliation and recognition of the human rights of the Aboriginals, however, monumental problems still remain to be solved.

Aboriginal children

Terra australis incognita

European explorers and cartographers had long referred to a great land mass in the Southern Ocean as 'Terra australis incognita' (the unknown southern land). It was thought that to balance the large continental mass in the Northern Hemisphere a land mass must exist in the south.

Many explorers, spurred on by trade and constant reports by Chinese and Malays who were frequent visitors to the area, sailed to the Southern Ocean, braving the vagaries of the weather and the uncharted seas to discover the Great Southland.

In 1606 William Janszoon gave European navigators the first certain knowledge that 'Terra australis' existed. In the seventeenth century the western section was called New Holland, and in the eighteenth century the British established the penal colony of New South Wales on the east coast. It was not until the early nineteenth century, when it was established that these two sections were part of the same land mass, that the navigator Matthew Flinders suggested the Great Southland be called Australia.

Thévenot's Map of 1663 of Terra australis incognita

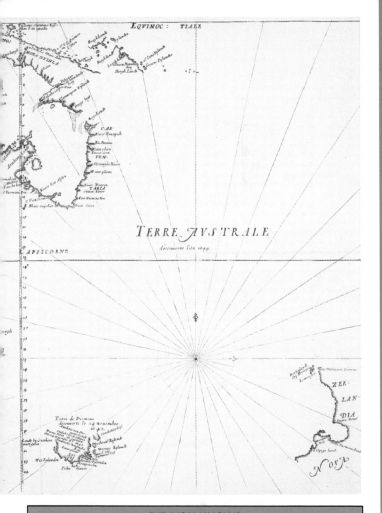

DID YOU KNOW?

Dame Enid Lyons (wife of prime minister Joseph Lyons 1932–39), mother of twelve children, became Australia's first woman federal parliamentarian in 1943, and in 1949 she became Australia's first woman cabinet minister.

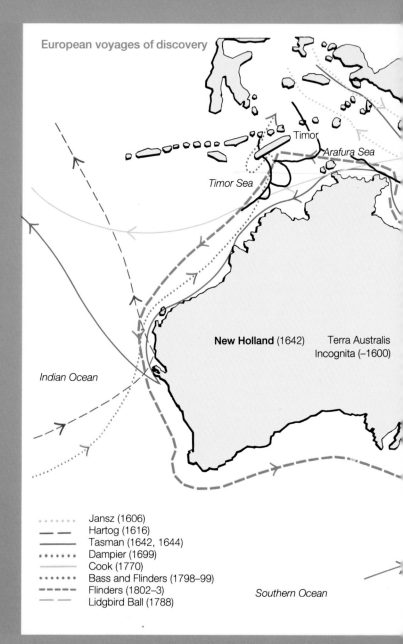

European voyages of discovery

Timor

Arafura Sea

Timor Sea

New Holland (1642)   Terra Australis
Incognita (–1600)

Indian Ocean

.... Jansz (1606)
— — Hartog (1616)
——— Tasman (1642, 1644)
•••••• Dampier (1699)
——— Cook (1770)
•••••• Bass and Flinders (1798–99)
— — — Flinders (1802–3)
— — Lidgbird Ball (1788)

Southern Ocean

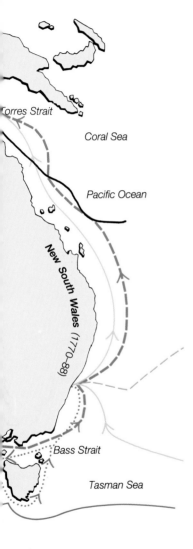

Torres Strait

Coral Sea

Pacific Ocean

New South Wales (1770–88)

Bass Strait

Tasman Sea

Famous explorers

George Bass 1763–1808

A ship's surgeon; together with Matthew Flinders he circumnavigated Van Diemen's Land (Tasmania) in 1798, proving that it was an island.

Gregory Blaxland 1778–1853
William Charles Wentworth 1793–1872
William Lawson 1774–1850

These three men were inland explorers. In 1813 they crossed the Blue Mountains west of Sydney and so opened up the fertile western plains to the colony.

Robert O'Hara Burke 1821–61
William Wills 1834–61

Burke, a policeman, and Wills, a surveyor, were the first Europeans to cross the continent from south to north. In 1860 they trekked from Melbourne to the Gulf of Carpentaria. On their return journey, because of exhaustion and lack of food, they slowly starved to death at Cooper Creek.

James Cook 1728–79

Cook landed in Botany Bay in 1770. At Possession Island, Torres Strait, he claimed the eastern coast of Australia in the name of King George III of Great Britain, and named it New South Wales.

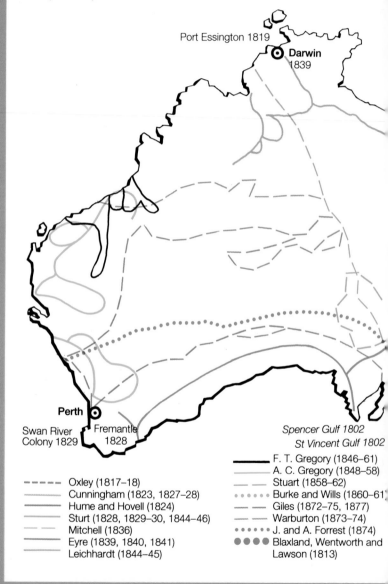

European exploration of Australia

Port Essington 1819

Darwin 1839

Perth
Swan River
Colony 1829
Fremantle 1828

Spencer Gulf 1802
St Vincent Gulf 1802

----- Oxley (1817–18)	—— F. T. Gregory (1846–61)
—— Cunningham (1823, 1827–28)	—— A. C. Gregory (1848–58)
—— Hume and Hovell (1824)	— — Stuart (1858–62)
—— Sturt (1828, 1829–30, 1844–46)	••••• Burke and Wills (1860–61)
– – Mitchell (1836)	— — Giles (1872–75, 1877)
—— Eyre (1839, 1840, 1841)	—— Warburton (1873–74)
—— Leichhardt (1844–45)	••••• J. and A. Forrest (1874)
	●●●● Blaxland, Wentworth and Lawson (1813)

Port Bowen 1802
Brisbane 1825

Port Macquarie 1818

Newcastle 1804
Sydney
Port Jackson 1788

Melbourne
1835

ort Phillip 1802

Hobart 1804

William Dampier 1652–1715
A British privateer who visited the western coast of Australia in 1688 and again in 1699.

Edward John Eyre 1815–1901
An inland explorer, he crossed the continent from Streaky Bay, South Australia, to Albany, Western Australia, in 1839–41, a trek of almost 1600 kilometres.

Matthew Flinders 1774–1814
A British naval officer, he circumnavigated Australia in 1801–3, thus allowing the coastal mapping of Australia to be completed.

Dirk Hartog c. 1570
A Dutch navigator who landed on an island off Western Australia in 1616, later named after him.

Hamilton Hume 1797–1873
Australia's first native-born explorer forged a route across the Great Dividing Range at Razorback, from the south coast of NSW to the fertile areas of Goulburn and Yass in 1814–21.

Willem Jansz c. 1550
A Dutch sea captain, he gave European navigators the first certain knowledge that Australia existed. In 1606 he landed on the west coast of Cape York Peninsula.

Ludwig Leichhardt 1813–48

He explored inland from Brisbane to Port Essington, Northern Territory, in 1844, a 3200 kilometre trek. In 1848 he and an entire expedition disappeared without a trace, while trying to cross Australia from east to west.

Sir Douglas Mawson 1882–1958

Antarctic explorer and geologist who made many expeditions to the cold continent between 1907 and 1924. He was largely responsible for Australia gaining sovereignty over Antarctica between the 45° and 160° eastern meridians.

John McDouall Stuart 1815–66

He finally crossed the continent from south to north in 1862, after three attempted journeys into the interior.

Charles Sturt 1795–1869

An inland explorer who discovered and named the Murray River in 1829.

Abel Tasman 1602–59

A Dutch navigator, he discovered Van Diemen's Land (Tasmania) and Statenland (New Zealand) in 1642.

Sir Hubert Wilkins 1888–1958

He travelled beneath the arctic ice cap in 1931 in the US submarine *Nautilus* to within 1000 kilometres of the North Pole.

The intrepid explorers

'No country can possibly have a more interesting aspect . . . if a further trace into the interior is required . . . I respectfully beg leave to offer myself for the service. I see no end to travelling'. This was a request by explorer George William Evans, in a letter to Governor Macquarie in 1815.

It has often been asked just why men are gripped with the compulsive drive to explore. The Australian desert explorer Ernest Giles wrote: 'An explorer is an explorer from love and it is nature, not art that makes it so.'

The explorers were a diverse band. Some were highly educated government officials with scientific knowledge or surveying skills, others were fine bushmen with a natural talent for exploration, but the overriding love for the Australian landscape was common to all. It was said of Charles Sturt, the overland explorer, 'he quested because of his love for the interior of the continent and his ambition was to reach its very heart.'

Whatever their reasons, many explorers endured dreadful suffering in regions of impenetrable jungle or merciless desert. Colonel Peter Warburton, finding water at last after a particularly tortuous desert crossing, wrote in his journal, 'If we press on we risk

Sturt's Party at the junction of the Murray and Darling Rivers, 1830

losing our camels and dying of thirst. If we stand still we starve'.

Robert O'Hara Burke and William Wills were stranded with no food at Cooper Creek, after their incredible trek from the Gulf of Carpentaria. Exhausted and starving, they gave up hope and waited for death. Burke's last diary entry read, 'weaker than ever . . . my legs and arms are nearly skin and bone.' The only survivor of his party was a man named King. He was found in the care of Aboriginals by Alfred Howitt. His rescuers wrote, 'we found King sitting in a hut which the natives had made for him. He seemed exceedingly weak and we found it difficult to follow what he said'.

In retrospect, we can see that their judgement was sometimes questionable. For instance, in 1770 Captain Cook reported to the British Admiralty that Botany Bay was 'capacious, safe and commodious'. In 1788 Governor Phillip found it to be too exposed, and speedily moved the infant colony to Port Jackson, which he considered 'the finest in the world, where a thousand sail of the line might ride in the most perfect security.' When the Surveyor-General, John Oxley, described land in southern New South Wales as 'uninhabitable and useless for all purposes of civilized man', he would never have dreamed that the 'country south of 34 degrees west of the meridian 147.30 east' would one day become the fertile Murrumbidgee Irrigation Area. Again, Francis Gregory, the leader of the first expedition into the mineral-rich Hamersley Range in Western Australia, commented in his journal, 'Of minerals I was unable to discover any, except iron.'

Many explorers took great pleasure in the beauty of the surrounding countryside. Sir Thomas Mitchell wrote of the Nandewar Ranges of New South Wales as 'a beautiful variety of summits', while the Polish explorer, Sir Paul Strzelecki, described Mount

Landing of Captain Cook at Botany Bay 1770 by E. Phillips Fox

Kosciusko, our highest mountain, as 'a craggy, scenic cone cresting the Australian Alps'. It was also with obvious pleasure that Mitchell, exploring the south of the continent, wrote, 'It was not without some pride as a Briton, that I gave the name of the Grampians to these extreme summits of the southern hemisphere.'

The urgency to open up the interior was to enable the colony to expand beyond the confines of the coastal settlements. Although it took place in an atmosphere of excitement and challenge it was mainly for the purpose of gain, a reason for which we may be dubiously proud. However, there is reason to be proud of the intrepid explorers who, with passion and drive, journeyed into the unknown to open up new lands for the eager pioneer settlers.

Early European discovery and settlement

1642	Van Diemen's Land (Tasmania) discovered
1770	Botany Bay discovered
1774	Norfolk Island discovered
1788	Port Jackson (Sydney) settled; Lord Howe Island discovered
1802	Spencer Gulf and St Vincent Gulf discovered
1802	Port Phillip discovered
1804	Newcastle and Hobart settled
1818	Port Macquarie settled
1819	Port Essington discovered
1825	Brisbane settled
1828	Fremantle discovered
1829	Swan River Colony (Perth) settled
1835	Melbourne settled
1836	Adelaide settled
1839	Port Darwin discovered

DID YOU KNOW?

Between 1788 and 1856, 157 000 convicts were sent to Australia. This is only one-third of the total sent to the United States.

Development of a nation

From 1788 to 1850 the government of the colony was in the tight control of New South Wales. Resentment ran high when laws passed by the New South Wales Legislative Assembly affected newer parts of the colony, hundreds of miles away. In 1850 the *Australian Colonies Government Act* was forced through parliament, resulting in responsible government for each of the states. Each state now had its own governor.

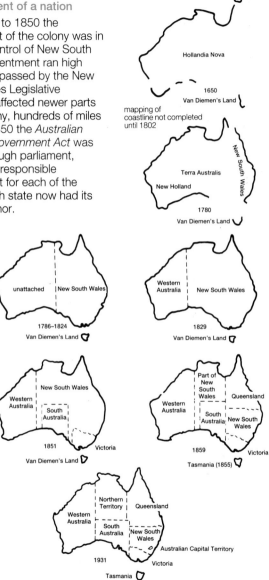

Hollandia Nova

1650
Van Diemen's Land

mapping of coastline not completed until 1802

New South Wales

Terra Australis

New Holland

1780
Van Diemen's Land

unattached | New South Wales

1786–1824
Van Diemen's Land

Western Australia | New South Wales

1829
Van Diemen's Land

Western Australia | New South Wales | South Australia

1851
Van Diemen's Land | Victoria

Part of New South Wales | Queensland
Western Australia | South Australia | New South Wales

1859
Tasmania (1855) | Victoria

Western Australia | Northern Territory | Queensland
South Australia | New South Wales
Australian Capital Territory

1931
Tasmania | Victoria

A helping hand with Australian history

'Terra australis incognita' was inhabited by its Aboriginal people who had their origins in remote antiquity.

1606 Willem Jansz lands on west coast of Cape York, Queensland.

1616 Dirk Hartog lands on the island later named after him, off the west coast of Australia.

1642 Abel Tasman discovers Van Diemen's Land (Tasmania) and Statenland (New Zealand).

1770 Captain James Cook lands at Botany Bay. He calls the eastern coastline New South Wales in the name of Britain.

1788 Beginning of European settlement as a penal colony. Arrival of Governor Arthur Phillip and First Fleet, at Botany Bay, 18 January, and at Port Jackson on 26 January, when Phillip formally takes possession of the whole of the eastern part of the continent, including Tasmania.

Hobart Town Gazette, 1843

1793 First free settlers arrive.

1796 Discovery of coal at Newcastle.

1797 Introduction of merino sheep by John Macarthur.

1798 George Bass and Matthew Flinders circumnavigate Van Diemen's Land (Tasmania).

1802 Discovery of Port Phillip, Victoria, and of Port Bowen, Queensland, by Lieutenant John Murray, and St Vincent Gulf and Spencer Gulf, South Australia, by Matthew Flinders.

DID YOU KNOW?

Ten thousand years ago both the Europeans and the Australian Aboriginals were hunters and gatherers. However, over-population in Europe forced agricultural development, whereas the Aboriginals, with plenty of land, did not have to change their ways.

1804 Lieutenant David Collins establishes settlement at Hobart.
1807 First shipment of sale-able wool to England.
1808 The Rum Rebellion. Deposition of Governor William Bligh.
1813 Crossing of Blue Mountains by Gregory Blaxland, William Charles Wentworth and William Lawson.
1814 Matthew Flinders suggests the name Australia instead of New Holland.
1817 The first bank, Bank of New South Wales (now Westpac), is established.
1819 Lt Phillip King discovers Port Essington, Northern Territory.
1822 Establishment of penal settlement at Macquarie Harbour, Van Diemen's Land.
1823 Brisbane River discovered by John Oxley and three convicts.
1825 Separation of the administration of Van Diemen's Land from New South Wales. Establishment of settlement of Brisbane.
1828 First census taken: 36 000 convicts and free settlers, 2549 military personnel. No Aboriginals counted.
1829 Foundation of settlement at Swan River, Western Australia. Perth founded.
1834 First settlement at Twofold Bay, New South Wales. Henty brothers form settlement at Portland, Victoria.
1835 Foundation of Melbourne, planned by Governor Sir Richard Bourke.
1836 Settlement founded at Adelaide under Governor Sir John Hindmarsh.
1838 Captain James Bremer establishes Port Essington, Northern Territory.
1839 Port Darwin discovered by crew of the *Beagle*.
1840 Abolition of convict transportation to New South Wales.
1841 New Zealand proclaimed as a separate colony.
1842 First elected council in New South Wales.
1847 Melbourne proclaimed a city.
1850 Sydney University founded. Representative government granted to

Attempted escape, Darlinghurst Gaol, 1855

Victoria, Van Diemen's Land and South Australia.

1851 Edward Hargraves discovers gold at Lewis Ponds, New South Wales. The Port Phillip District is created a separate colony, named Victoria.

1852 Abolition of convict transportation to Van Diemen's Land (Tasmania).

1854 Eureka Stockade riot at Ballarat, Victoria, sparked off by goldminers' objections to high mining licence fees.

1855 Van Diemens' Land renamed Tasmania, commemorating its discoverer, Abel Tasman. Responsible government granted to New South Wales, Victoria and Tasmania.

1856 Responsible government granted to South Australia.

1857 Granting of the right to vote to adult males in Victoria.

1858 Granting of the right to vote to adult males in New South Wales.

1859 Queensland proclaimed a separate colony.

1863 Northern Territory taken over by South Australia. Discovery of gold at Kalgoorlie, Western Australia.

1864 First sugar made from Queensland cane.

1869 'Welcome Stranger' gold nugget found at Dunolly, Victoria.

1872 Trans-continental telegraph completed. First cable message from Sydney to London.

1876 Death of Truganini, last full-blooded Tasmanian Aboriginal.

1878 First telephone in Australia.

1880 Ned Kelly, bushranger and rebel, captured.

1883 Silver discovered at Broken Hill, New South Wales.

1885 New South Wales contingent sent to Sudan, Africa. Broken Hill Proprietary Silver Mining Company (BHP) floated.

1889 Sir Henry Parkes's 'Tenterfield Address' on federation.

DID YOU KNOW?

The first ration list in 1788, per person per week, included 7 lbs (3.17 kg) of bread or flour; 7 lbs of beef or 4 lbs (1.81 kg) of pork; 3 lbs (1.36 kg) of peas; 6 oz (170 g) of butter, and $\frac{1}{2}$ lb (225 g) of rice.

1899	First Australian contingent sent to Boer War in South Africa.
1900	Federation: on 17 September Australia announced its intention to become independent from Great Britain.
1901	1 January – the first day of the new century – the Commonwealth of Australia was proclaimed. First Federal election. 1901 census – white population 3,773,801. Aboriginals not counted.
1902	Granting of the right to vote in federal elections to women.
1908	Canberra chosen as the site for the federal capital.
1910	First Commonwealth bank notes issued.
1911	Mawson leads expedition to the Antarctic.
1913	First Commonwealth postage stamps issued.
1914	First World War declared, 20,000 troops embark for overseas – devastating losses in battle of the Somme. German raider, *Emden*, sunk by HMAS *Sydney* in Indian Ocean.
1915	BHP opens in Newcastle. ANZAC (Australian and New Zealand Army Corps) troops land at Gallipoli on 25 April, evacuated on 18 December.

1917	Completion of transcontinental railway.
1918	First wireless message from London to Sydney. Armistice with Germany, 11 November. Australia House, London, opened by King Geoge V.
1919	Return of Australian troops from Europe. Ross and Keith Smith make the first flight from England to Australia. Influenza epidemic sweeps Australia.
1920	Queensland and Northern Territory Aerial Services (QANTAS) formed by Hudson Fysh. White population 5 411 300.
1922	Queensland is the first state to abolish the death penalty.
1923	Sydney Harbour Bridge commenced.
1926	Auction sales of wool begun.
1927	Seat of government moved from Melbourne to Canberra.
1928	Kingsford Smith flies from America to Australia in *Southern Cross*. Flying Doctor service begun. First traffic lights in Australia installed in Melbourne.
1929	Beginning of Depression. Fall in exports. Commonwealth government mobilises gold reserves.

1932 Sydney Harbour Bridge opened. Lang government in New South Wales dismissed.

1933 BHP takes over steel works at Port Kembla, New South Wales.

1935 Kingsford Smith lost without trace near the Bay of Bengal, flying from England to Australia. Ansett Airways set up by Reginald Ansett.

1936 Hume reservoir completed.

1938 Coca-Cola is first made in Australia.

1939 Second World War declared. The last grain clipper race to England held.

1940 20 000 Australian troops embark for service abroad. Introduction of food and fuel rationing.

1941 Sinking of HMAS *Sydney* and HMAS *Canberra*. Australian troops besieged at Tobruk.

1942 Darwin and Katherine bombed. Fall of Singapore. Battle of the Coral Sea. Japanese midget submarines in Sydney Harbour.

1943 Industrial conscription introduced.

1944 Pay-as-you-earn taxation begun. Japanese prisoners of war attempt mass breakout at Cowra, New South Wales; 234 killed.

1945 Second World War ends; demobilisation of 500 000 men and women begun.

1946 United Nations grants trusteeship of New Guinea to Australia.

1947 Commonwealth Arbitration Commission established. Arthur Calwell's immigration drive begun.

1948 Forty-hour week established. First Holden car made by General Motors-Holden. Meat and clothes rationing ends.

1949 The right to vote granted to certain Aboriginals. Snowy Mountains Hydro-Electric Scheme commenced. An attempt to nationalise banks defeated. Prime Minister Ben Chifley deposed. Liberals come to power under Robert Menzies.

1950 Petrol rationing ends. Australian troops join United Nations force in Korea.

1951 Melbourne becomes an international airport.

1952 ANZUS Security Treaty signed in Washington. Discovery of uranium at Rum Jungle, Northern Territory. Nuclear experiments begun at Australian National University.

1953 Atomic Energy

Commission established. Television Bill passed. Atomic weapons tested by United Kingdom at Woomera, South Australia. Wool prices drop after four-year boom. South-East Asia Treaty Organisation (SEATO) founded.

1954 Queen Elizabeth II makes the first visit to Australia by a reigning monarch. Uranium discovered at Mary Kathleen, Queensland. Troops withdrawn from Korea. 'Petrov Affair': accusations of Communist espionage in Department of External Affairs. Petrov defects.

1955 Opposition Labor Party splits. Severe floods in eastern Australia cause havoc.

1956 Olympic Games in Melbourne.

1958 The first nuclear reactor opened at Lucas Heights, Sydney.

1960 Aboriginals become Australian citizens and so become eligible for social service benefits. Reserve Bank established.

1961 Huge iron-ore deposits found at Pilbara, Western Australia.

1962 Standard-gauge railway track opened between Brisbane, Sydney and Melbourne. Aboriginals granted the vote. Australia grants approval to the United States to build communication base at Exmouth, Western Australia, and space tracking station at Tidbinbilla, near Canberra.

1964 HMAS *Voyager* sinks after collision with HMAS *Melbourne*; 82 lives lost. First flight of Blue Streak rocket launched at Woomera, South Australia.

1965 Australian infantry battalion sent to Vietnam. Australia imposes economic sanctions against the Smith regime in Rhodesia.

1966 On 14 February decimal currency introduced. Aboriginals appeal to the United Nations for human rights. Prime Minister Sir Robert Menzies retires. Gough Whitlam becomes leader of the Labor Partyi The phasing in of the metric system of weights and measures begun.

1967 Prime Minister Harold Holt disappears at Portsea, Victoria. John McEwen acts as prime minister. Aboriginals included in census figures for the first time. Demonstration in Melbourne against the hanging of Ronald Ryan, the last person to be hanged in Australia.

1968 First Australian heart transplant performed. John Gorton becomes leader of the Liberal Party and prime minister.

1969 HMAS *Melbourne* collides with USS *Frank E Evans* with the loss of 74 lives. Indian–Pacific railway completed. Poseidon company announces a find of nickel; as a result, share prices soar. Robert Hawke is elected president of the ACTU. Arbitration Commission grants equal pay to women for work of equal value.

1970 Vietnam Moratoriums: large-scale demonstrations against Australian and United States involvement in Vietnam war. Mineral shares boom ends. Tullamarine airport opened in Melbourne.

1971 Australia ends fighting role in Vietnam. Lake Pedder in Tasmania is flooded as part of a hydro-electric scheme.

1972 Australian Labor Party wins victory under the leadership of Gough Whitlam. Withdrawal of troops from Vietnam. Formal ending of White Australia Policy.

1973 Eighteen-year-olds are granted the right to vote in federal elections. Queen Elizabeth II to be known as Queen of Australia.

1974 Cyclone Tracy hits Darwin, Northern Territory (Christmas Day). Bankcard is introduced. Fully elected assemblies set up in the Northern Territory and Australian Capital Territory.

1975 Dismissal of Whitlam government by Governor-General Sir John Kerr. Return of Liberal–Country Party coalition to power under leadership of Malcolm Fraser. Papua New Guinea becomes independent. No-fault divorce introduced. The MV *Lake Illawarra* collides with the Tasman Bridge, Hobart. Five Australian journalists are killed in East Timor.

1976 Flexitime is approved for federal public servants.

1977 Granville train disaster; 81 die.

1978 Northern Territory becomes responsible for its own administration.

1979 Aboriginal Land Trust by now gains title to 144 properties, all formerly Aboriginal reserves.

1980 Campbell Inquiry into Australian financial

system. Nugan Hand Bank collapses. The disappearance of baby Azaria Chamberlain at Ayers Rock.

1981 Severe drought affects large areas of Australia.

1982 New South Wales introduces random breath testing. Franklin Dam controversy rages in Tasmania. Lindy Chamberlain found guilty of the murder of her daughter, Azaria. Devastating floods in Western Australia.

1983 Robert Hawke leads Labor Party into office after Prime Minister Malcolm Fraser is granted a double dissolution of parliament. Ash Wednesday bush fires devastate South Australia and Victoria. America's Cup victory by *Australia II*. Conservationists win battle against Franklin Dam project.

1984 Prices and Income Policy Accord reached. Control of Ayers Rock (Uluru) given to local Aboriginals. Milperra bikie massacre – 7 people shot dead. World's first test-tube quads born in Melbourne.

1985 McClelland Royal Commission into British nuclear tests in Australia.

High Court Justice Lionel Murphy charged with allegedly having conspired to pervert the course of justice. Federal Treasury allows banking licences for 16 foreign banks.

1986 Queen Elizabeth II signs a proclamation which finally severs some of Australia's historical, political and legal ties with United Kingdom – Australia Act of 1986 comes into force. Lindy Chamberlain released on licence from gaol. Russell Street Police Headquarters, Melbourne bombed. Kevin Barlow and Brian Chambers convicted of drug trafficking and subsequently hanged in Malaysia. Fringe Benefits tax introduced. High Court landmark ruling against Australasian Meat Workers' Union in dispute over wages and conditions at Mudginberri Abattoirs in Western Australia. Pope John Paul visits Australia. Justice Lionel Murphy dies.

1987 Northern Territory Government grants a pardon to Lindy and Michael Chamberlain which is not acceptable to them. Four men found guilty and one pleaded guilty of murder in the Anita Cobby trial. The Milperra massacre trial – the longest-running in NSW legal history – ended with 7 men being found guilty of murder, 21 guilty of manslaughter and 31 guilty of affray. The Australian share market collapses. Sir Joh Bjelke-Petersen resigns as Premier of Queensland. 14 people shot dead in Melbourne's Clifton Hill and Queen Street massacres. Vietnam veterans march in long-overdue 'Welcome Home' parade.

1988 At Bicentenary celebrations, Queen opens new Parliament House in Canberra. Alice Springs devastated by record floods. Charges against Lindy and Michael Chamberlain quashed.

1989 Decline in living standards follows high interest rates. Human Rights Commission estimates 50,000 children homeless. Collapse of National Safety Council in Victoria. Queensland police and politicians are flayed by Fitzgerald corruption report. 17 people killed in two ballooning disasters in the Northern Territory. 56 die in Australia's two worst coach crashes. Airline pilots' strike ends after 17 crippling weeks. Destructive earthquake in Newcastle – 12 dead. Environmentalists' victory over Wesley Vale pulp mill, Tasmania. Corporate failures emerge as result of 1987 share market collapse.

1990 ANZAC contingent attend 75th Anniversary of the landing at Anzac Cove, Gallipoli. Record low prices for grain. Australian Navy represented in Gulf War. Worst recession for 40 years has widespread effects. HMAS *Voyager* survivor receives compensation after 26-year battle with government. Collapse of Bond Corporation and Pyramid Building Society. Australian hostages return from Baghdad. Fairfax Group placed into receivership.

1991 Sydney hit by severe storms. Devastating Queensland floods. Banks affected by widespread losses. After 17 years of reserve pricing, Wool Corporation adopts free marketing system. Tariff barriers and import quotas reduced. Sweeping reforms for Aboriginals held in custody. Mining of uranium at Coronation Hill, Kakadu, banned. Heart transplant pioneer Dr. Victor Chang murdered. Strathfield Shopping Plaza massacre – 9 dead. Paul Keating becomes prime minister.

1992 1c and 2c coins phased out. Chelmsford victim receives landmark settlement. Chamberlains granted $1.3 million compensation. Unemployment 11.3%. Anglican Synod allows ordination of women priests. Sydney Harbour tunnel opens. Armed Forces accept homosexuals. Appointment of QCs ceases in NSW. Landmark Mabo High Court decision enables Aboriginals, with unbroken occupancy of land, to claim title.

1993 Lowest inflation rate in 3 years. Highest unemployment ever. Record fifth successive term for ALP. Exmouth tracking station abandoned. The Unknown Soldier interred in the Hall of Memory, Canberra. Sydney wins Year 2000 Olympic Games.

1994 Four people die in NSW devastating bushfires. One dies in horror NCA bombing in Adelaide – insufficient evidence to obtain conviction. Unemployment steady at 9.5%. Alexander Downer becomes Liberal leader. Man charged with Belanglo backpacker murders. 9 dead in Seaview air crash. 12 die in Queensland bus crash. El Nino cycle brings devastating drought which blankets Australia. Labor Conference agrees 35% of winnable seats to go to women. Move to extradite Skase fails. *Endeavour* replica leaves Fremantle.

1995 Papal visit – the beatification of Blessed Mary McKillop. One bale of ultra super-fine merino wool brings over $1 million. Pay TV launched. Unemployment falls to 4-year low. Balance of Payments deficit histori-cally high. Drought still grips eastern Australia. Controversy rages over rugby super league. Landmark 'Right to Die' law passed in Northern Territory. NSW Police Royal Commission into corruption has wide-spread ramifications.

Controversy over French nuclear testing in the Pacific. Devastating salinity rises in Murray Basin.

The Pinnacle Desert, Nambung National Park, W.A.

Dread, doubt, despair, brutality, horror, sadism, the lash, injustice, famine, hangings, murder, revolt, floggings, disease, pestilence, depravity, thieving . . . a worthy scenario for a modern horror movie? In actual fact it is a list of words often used to describe our history since 1788. From the very first, when Governor Phillip desperately sought better supplies and conditions for the 'wretched felons' from the overcrowded British prisons, who were about to make the hazardous journey to New South Wales, the story was one of desperation and brutality.

The struggling infant colony began with bitter disappointment. Lack of food, constant sickness and indolence seemed to set the pattern for the years to come. The country appeared to be a huge and empty land, hostile to British ideas and ways. The colony also had conflicting obligations. It had to contend with the commercial demands of the British government as well as with the needs of a new penal colony. There were no encouraging signs for anyone to feel that the foundation of a prosperous nation could be made from such a hopeless beginning.

Gradually, the tenacity of the colonists and their improved understanding of the land, led to better times. At the same time, explorers blazed tracks into the interior and people began to spill out of the overcrowded towns and cities and into the country. Terms such as pioneers, squatters, emancipists, chain gangs, currency lads, new chums, cattle duffers, honest battlers, bolters, free selectors and bushrangers, all became part of Australian phraseology, and a spirit of self-reliance seemed to flourish in isolated communities. Compared to the confines of the English countryside there was space to breathe in this far-off colony in the antipodes, and the people liked it.

'The days of gold', from the 1850s to 1880s, brought an uninterrupted boom to the colony, and tradesmen, clerks, shepherds and sailors all headed for the goldfields gripped by 'gold fever'. Any kind of order in the towns or cities was disrupted, and although 'great excitement prevailed' and 'whole towns were in hysterics', Lieutenant-Governor La Trobe of Victoria contemptuously remarked, 'The whole structure of society and the whole machinery of government is dislocated.' Though trouble intermittently flared up on the goldfields, due to various injustices and persecutions, the only major rebellion of the period and of the whole of Australian history, took place at the Eureka

Stockade near Ballarat in December 1854.

Towards the latter part of the 19th century, railways and improved roads brought the country closer to the city and a new feeling of nationalism was born. Constitutionally, there was no such thing as an Australian citizen or an Australian nation,

Horse-drawn carriage, 1870s

Arrival of first railway train at Parramatta, from Sydney

Sydney Cove, Port Jackson, 1788

but people from both town and country wanted to be counted as one.

In his Tenterfield Oration of 1889, referring to the joining of all States in a federation, the revered statesman, Sir Henry Parkes said, 'Surely what the Americans have done by war, the Australians could bring about by peace without breaking the ties that hold them to the mother country . . . We ought to set about creating this great national government for all Australia.'

The Commonwealth of Australia was proclaimed on the first day of the new century, 1 January 1901. Sir Edmund Barton, the first prime minister of Australia, remarked, 'For the first time in history we have a continent for a nation and a nation for a continent.'

A nation coming of age (1900–93)

Although the young Commonwealth began the new century on a note of cautious optimism it was obvious that it needed to be awakened to the demands of such a monumental experiment as federation.

To establish a new identity was the main concern of most Australians, but the old loyalties and demands of Britain were strong. Australian 'soldiers of the Queen' marched off to fight the Boer War in South Africa, one which many saw as 'the most iniquitous war ever waged'.

Nevertheless, times were rapidly changing. The Commonwealth had blundered into a new century and progress came at a bewildering pace. In 1905 the Pure Foods Act ensured quality and purity of food, substantially reducing infant mortality. Electricity had replaced gas lights, trams, trains and cars had superseded the horse, and the new inventions of wireless, cash registers and typewriters all led to an increasing demand in skill. This was the machine age, and opportunity was everywhere, demanding that everyone become literate. The workers backed trade unions, and a five and a half day week and a £2 2s ($4.20) average weekly wage was introduced. Change was in the air worldwide, and Australia was making great strides in coming of age and keeping up with the rest of the world.

Yet loyalty to Britain persisted. When war broke out in 1914, Australians again fought thousands of miles away from home. On 25 April 1915 the ANZACs began the bitter campaign against the Turks in Gallipoli, and a shocked nation learned of the long casualty list. All told, 416 809 men volunteered for the war, of which 59 258 were killed or reported missing in action.

Times were confusing for the returning 'diggers'. They were years of uncertain prosperity, followed by the Great Depression of 1929–32. The disaster affected all Australians: at one stage 30% of the workforce was unemployed, and those lucky enough to keep a job had restricted working hours or cut wages.

Although suspicions of Japan's intentions in 1939 were mounting, it was the troubles in Europe again which plunged Australia into the Second World War. By 1945, 993 000 persons had enlisted. As the casualty list grew, news from such places as the Middle East, Greece, North Africa, Tobruk, was eagerly sought. On 8 December 1941 the Prime Minister, John Curtin, announced that Australia was at war with Japan. Singapore, Borneo, Java, New Guinea, the Kokoda Trail, Coral Sea, Rabaul, Owen Stanley Range and Changi prison, became hushed household words. In 1942 Darwin was bombed with a loss of 238 lives. The war in Europe ended in May 1945, and under the threat of a widening of atomic warfare, after the bombing of Hiroshima and Nagasaki, the Japanese surrendered on 14 August 1945.

The post-war years brought growth and prosperity. With the signing of the ANZUS pact, Australia was at last making decisions without reference to Britain. In the 'cold war' atmosphere of the 1950s, Australian troops joined the British Commonwealth Brigade in Korea. Increased production and labour shortages brought full employment, and the rural and home building industries flourished. A forty-hour week was introduced and the basic wage was £5 16s ($11.60). A new immigration drive resulted in a more tolerant attitude towards Europeans and their cultures, and public awareness of the plight of Australian Aboriginals grew. Education became more readily available, and there was more time for leisure and cultural pursuits.

During the 1960s there was a time of affluence and prosperity with the mineral boom. Few people took notice of the war in Asia. However, the government argued that to retain the United States' protection through the newly formed SEATO alliance, Australia must support the United States in Vietnam. Over 50 000 troops served in the war, with 400 deaths and 2000 injured. A moratorium clearly demonstrated that the majority of Australians were against our involvement, and after world-wide pressure, the USA ceased hostilities.

General dissatisfaction in the 1970s and 80s saw political parties come and go, with a new wave of unrest sweeping the country. The White Australia Policy was dropped, and Asian migration was encouraged. Australia was at last overcoming the feelings of isolation from Europe and finding a place in the Pacific region. Automation dramatically changed technology, and workers displaced by computers saw traditional jobs disappear, requiring them to retrain for new skills, or join the list of the unemployed.

The race into the 1990s brought great change. Fiscal deregulation, the 1987 stockmarket crash and recession forced Australia to review its world position. Improvement of standards was essential to keep pace with the highly competitive nations of Asia. As well, multiculturalism through migration, a greater awareness of indigenous Australians and the proposal for a republic began to change the Australian character.

The grand experiment begun in 1900 with federation, embraced a vision for the future of a cohesive nation. Now, even though enormous difficulties have and still are to be overcome and harsh realities faced, great triumphs and achievements have been gained. Australia has become a more independent nation enabling it to enter the 21st century with confidence and dignity.

Kids afloat: Rhododendron Festival: Blackheath New South Wales

DID YOU KNOW?
The expected life-span for Australian males is 72.9 years, for Australian females 79.5.

Place

Geography

Location

Australia consists of two land masses: mainland Australia, and Tasmania. It lies on and extends south from the Tropic of Capricorn in the southern hemisphere between latitudes 10°41' and 43°39' S and longitudes 113°9' and 153°39'E. It is bounded by the Pacific Ocean to the east, the Indian Ocean to the west, the Arafura Sea to the north, and the Southern Ocean to the south. The nearest neighbour is Papua New Guinea, 200 kilometres north. Timor is 640 kilometres to the north-west, New Zealand is 1920 kilometres east, and Antarctica is 2000 kilometres due south.

Area

The area of Australia is 7 682 300 square kilometres. Australia is about the size of the mainland states of the United States, excluding Alaska, and approximately twenty-four times the size of the British Isles.

Distances

Mainland east–west, 3983 kilometres; north–south, 3138 kilometres. Coastline, including Tasmania and off-shore islands, 36 735 kilometres.

Average monthly rainfall and temperature around Australia

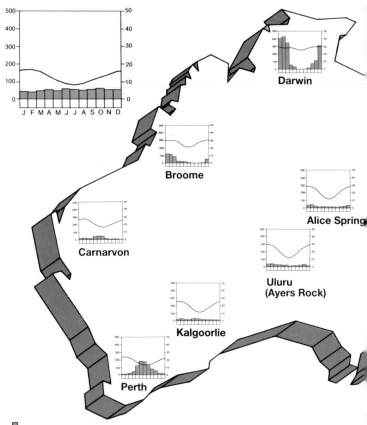

■ Blocks show rainfall in millimetres

‿ Curves show temperature in degrees Celsius

DID YOU KNOW?

The highest recorded temperature of 53.1°C was at Cloncurry Queensland, on 16 January 1889. The lowest recorded temperature of minus 23°C was at Charlotte Pass NSW on 28 June 1994.

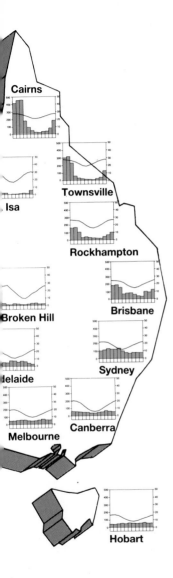

Climate

Australia is considered to be one of the driest continents on earth, however, because of its insular position and lack of natural features such as high mountain ranges, there are generally no great extremes of climate. Climate varies because of the size of the continent. The temperature ranges from 23–26°C above the Tropic of Capricorn to 38°C in the arid plateaus and deserts of the interior. The southern areas are more temperate, although subject to wide variations, such as high rainfall, great heat and irregular flooding and drought.

El Nino – Spanish for Christ child – was named by early Peruvian fisherman, who noticed the Pacific Ocean currents off Peru becoming warmer every few years around Christmas. Australia is affected by the same El Nino weather cycle in reverse. High pressure cells build up over Northern Australia and the air pressure is low in the central Pacific. The waters off the east coast become cool while those off the west coast of America become warm. This combination turns trade winds away from Australia towards the central Pacific, resulting in a reduced cloud build up, less rain and consequent drought for eastern Australia.

Landform

Australia is one of the oldest continents, and because of the effects of 250 million years of erosion it has become the flattest land mass on earth.

The shape of Australia was defined by the separation and rifting of the Australian continent from the super-continent Gondwanaland about 70 million years ago. It is considered to be the most stable land mass in the world, being free of any major mountain building events for the past 80 million years. Even so, Australia has a wide variety of landforms, mostly consisting of vast ancient crustal blocks: the western plateau is approximately 300 metres above sea level, the central eastern portion (a lowland which formed the bed of ancient seas), and the eastern highland running north and south along the eastern coastline. The lowest elevation is Lake Eyre (16 metres below sea level) and the highest peak is Mt Kosciusko (2228 metres above sea level).

The Three Sisters, Katoomba, N.S.W.

DID YOU KNOW?

The weather reports in Western Australia can take up to 15 minutes to deliver because of the number and diversity of climatic zones. They have ranged between 50.7°C at Eucla on 22 January 1906 and −6°C at Booylgoo Springs on 12 July 1969.

Time zones

There are three time zones within the Australian continent. The eastern states – Queensland, New South Wales, Victoria and Tasmania – are 30 minutes ahead of South Australia and the Northern Territory (including Broken Hill), and they are two-hours ahead of Western Australia.

New South Wales, Victoria and Tasmania follow Eastern Summer Time (Queensland has decided against Summer Time), and South Australia follows Central Daylight Time. These are subject to change, but the period usually falls between the months of November and February, and can extend for up to two weeks on either side. Tasmania has extended daylight saving to six months, from early October to late March.

Time zones within Australia

Standard time zones

0°   30°   60°   90°   120°   150°

gain a day

United Kingdom

Germany
France
Italy
Spain
Greece
Gibraltar
Turkey
Algeria
Iraq Iran Pakistan
Libya Egypt
Saudi Arabia
India

Commonwealth of Independent States

Manchuria
China
Japan

Bangladesh
Hong Kong

Ethiopia
Uganda

Sri Lanka
Singapore
Malaysia
Bornee
Philippines

Papua New Gu

Nicobar Is
Indonesia

Zimbabwe
South Africa

Mauritius

Cocos Is
Christmas Island
Australia

Norfolk Is

Cape of Good Hope

Indian Ocean

McDonald Islands
Heard Island

New Zea

Universal Time Constant

noon

−10	−9	−8	−7	−6	−5	−4	−3	−2	−1	0	+1
2 am	3 am	4 am	5 am	6 am	7 am	8 am	9 am	10 am	11 am	12	1 pm

hours later than Universal Time Constant

DID YOU KNOW?

The world's largest cattle station, 30 028.3 square kilometres, is Strangeray Springs in South Australia. It is almost the same size as Belgium.

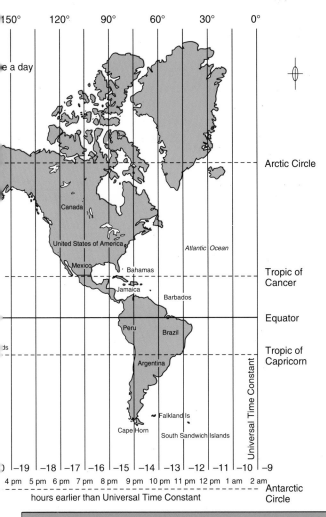

150°   120°   90°   60°   30°   0°

e a day

Arctic Circle

Canada

United States of America

Atlantic Ocean

Mexico   Bahamas

Tropic of Cancer

Jamaica

Barbados

Equator

Peru

Brazil

Tropic of Capricorn

Argentina

Falkland Is

Cape Horn

South Sandwich Islands

Universal Time Constant

) |−19 |−18 |−17 |−16 |−15 |−14 |−13 |−12 |−11 |−10 |−9

4 pm 5 pm 6 pm 7 pm 8 pm 9 pm 10 pm 11 pm 12 pm 1 am 2 am

Antarctic Circle

hours earlier than Universal Time Constant

DID YOU KNOW?
Protective trade tariffs were first introduced in Australia in 1901.

The Commonwealth of Nations

Commonwealth nations

DID YOU KNOW?
Of all coloured peoples, the Australian Aboriginals are
ethnologically most akin to Caucasians.

Australia in the Commonwealth

The Commonwealth of Nations is a world-wide association of nations and their dependent territories, which recognises the British monarch as its titular head.

The members share many customs and traditions because of their association with the former British Empire, of which all formed a part. These include parliamentary systems of government, judicial systems and educational institutions which are similar to those of the United Kingdom. Although English is the official language, it is used widely in only eight member countries.

The main function of the Commonwealth is to encourage communication, exchange ideas, and develop mutual aid between its member nations.

Canada

Bermuda
· Bahamas
Jamaica
St Vincent
Barbados
Grenada Dominica
Trinidad and Tobago
Guyana

St Helena

Falkland Is

South Sandwich Islands
South Shetland Islands
South Orkney Islands

DID YOU KNOW?
Australians can trace their ancestry to any one, or a mixture, of more than sixty nations.

Members of the Commonwealth of Nations and their dependencies

Member nations with dependencies	Status of dependency	Member nations with dependencies	Status of dependency
Australia		Pakistan	
Australian		Papua New Guinea	
Antarctic	Territory	St Lucia, St Vincent	
Christmas Is	Territory	& the Grenadiers	Associated state
Cocos Is	Territory	Seychelles	
Coral Sea Is	Territory	Sierra Leone	
Heard &		Singapore	
McDonald Is	Territory	Solomon Is	
Lord Howe Is	Territory	Sri Lanka	
Macquarie Is	Territory	Swaziland	
Norfolk Is	Territory	Tanzania	
Bahamas		Tonga	
Bangladesh		Trinidad & Tobago	
Barbados		Tuvalu	
Belize		United Kingdom	
Botswana		Anguilla	Colony
Brunei		Antigua	Associated state
Canada		Barbuda	
Cyprus		Bermuda	Colony
Dominica		British Antarctic	
Gambia		British Indian	
Ghana		Ocean Territory	Territory
Gibraltar		British Virgin Is	Colony
Grenada		Cayman Is	Colony
Guyana		Dominica	Associated state
India		Falkland Is	Colony
Jamaica		Gibraltar	Colony
Kenya		Hong Kong	
Kiribati		Montserrat	Colony
Lesotho		Pitcairn	Colony
Malawi		St Helena	Colony
Malaysia		St Christopher-Nevis	
Maldives		South Georgia	
Malta		South Sandwich Islands	
Mauritius		St Kitts–Nevis	Associated state
Nauru		Turks & Caicos Is	Associated state
New Zealand	Territory & associated states	Uganda	
Niue & Tokelau Is		Vanuatu	
Cook Is		Western Samoa	
Ross dependency		Zambia	
Nigeria		Zimbabwe	

Australia in the western Pacific

DID YOU KNOW?
Because of the combustible nature of eucalyptus forests, Australia is considered to be one of the most explosive and fire prone countries on earth.

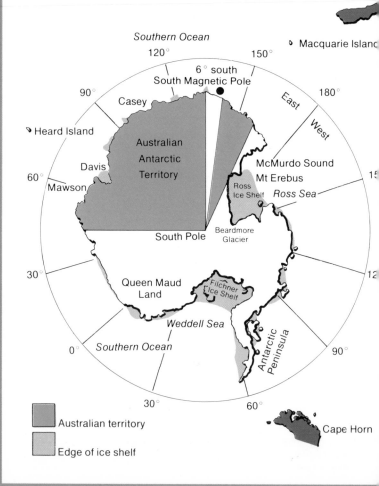

Australian Antarctic Territory

Australia

Tasmania

New Zealand

Macquarie Island

Southern Ocean

120°

150°

6° south
South Magnetic Pole

90°

180°

Casey

East

West

Heard Island

Australian
Antarctic
Territory

McMurdo Sound
Mt Erebus

Davis

Ross
Ice Shelf

Ross Sea

60°

Mawson

South Pole

Beardmore
Glacier

30°

Queen Maud
Land

Filchner
Ice Shelf

Weddell Sea

0°

Southern Ocean

90°

30°

60°

Antarctic Peninsula

Australian territory

Edge of ice shelf

Cape Horn

Australia in Antarctica

Location

Antarctica lies in the southern hemisphere below the latitude of 60°S and is 2000 kilometres due south from Melbourne. Mawson, Australia's first Antarctic station, is 5200 kilometres south-south-west of Perth.

Landform

Ice comprises more than 95 per cent of the total surface and the other 5 per cent is bare rock. The greatest rock exposures are in the Antarctic Peninsula and the Trans-Antarctic Mountains. Antarctica has enough ice to cover the whole of Australia with a mantle of snow nearly 2 kilometres thick.

Climate

Antarctica has one of the most hostile environments on earth: it experiences the coldest temperatures, the strongest winds and the largest deserts. In coastal areas at 1000 metres, the mean annual temperature is minus 12°C, while in high parts, near 4000 metres, it falls to minus 60°C. The high plateau receives very little precipitation at all and is the world's largest and driest desert. A little more snow falls in the lower areas and is equivalent to an annual rainfall of 5 centimetres – half as much as is experienced by places like Birdsville, Queensland. The quantity of ice present has been formed by the accumulation of snow over millions of years.

In winter it is so cold that the surrounding sea freezes to 200–300 kilometres off shore, and in summer the ice breaks to form pack ice. Under the influence of winds and tides it is distributed widely in the Southern Ocean, exerting a major influence on the world's weather patterns. During mid-winter it experiences twenty-four hours of darkness, and during mid-summer there are twenty-four hours of daylight.

Population

There are no permanent inhabitants but world scientists are continually studying this vast continent; few stay longer than two years.

Australia maintains four scientific research stations, namely Casey, Davis and Mawson in Australian Antarctic Territory and Macquarie Island in the sub-Antarctic.

DID YOU KNOW?
An international embargo on mineral exploration in the Antarctic will be enforced until the end of the century.

Flora and fauna

Because of intense cold and dryness, only simple algae, lichens and mosses, and a few tiny animals, such as mites, live there the year round. Many birds and animals breed on the fringes of the continent during summer, but move northward for the winter. These include penguins, albatross, snow petrels, various species of seals and whales. The ocean around the Antarctic has a distinct fish fauna of about 100 species, 75 per cent of which are Antarctic 'cod' (not found in other seas) and hag-fishes, skates, squid and small eel-pouts.

Southern Ocean, Western Australia

DID YOU KNOW?
Sir Douglas Mawson was the first Antarctic explorer to use morse code radio. It was his only link with the outside world when he and five companions were stranded during the long winter of blizzards in 1913 in Antarctica.

Australia in proportion to Europe

Estimated world population for 1995

Country	Estimated population (million)	Surface area (km²)	Population density (per km²)
Australia	18.0	7 682 300	2
Belgium	10.2	30 513	325
Brazil	153.4	8 511 965	17
Canada	28.5	9 916 139	3
China	1238.3	9 569 961	113
France	56.1	551 500	101
Germany (including GDR)	81.3	357 010	246
India	800.0	3 287 590	238
Indonesia	201.5	1 904 569	89
Italy	57.9	301 268	190
Japan	125.9	377 801	323
Malaysia	20.1	329 749	50
Netherlands	15.5	40 844	359
New Zealand	3.6	270 986	12
Norway	5.0	323 895	13
Pakistan	115.2	796 095	128
Philippines	58.9	300 000	191
Singapore	2.9	618	4 228
South Africa	33.8	1 221 037	27
Sweden	8.8	440 945	19
Switzerland	6.8	41 293	158
UK	57.4	244 100	233
USA	250.0	9 372 614	26

DID YOU KNOW?

Between the towns of Ooldia and Nurina in Western Australia is the world's longest straight stretch of railway, 478.4 kilometres long.

Profile

Population

The Australian population in 1995/96 is estimated to be around 18 million. Because of the arid interior, the relatively recent settlement and the fertility of the coastlines, 88 per cent are urban dwellers. Although it is considered to have one of the highest degrees of urban concentration in the world within the cities, the density of population is low by international standards, with an average of two persons per square kilometre. A striking feature of Australia's population is the large number of immigrants who have settled here since the Second World War. At present, one in every four persons is either a first- or second-generation settler.

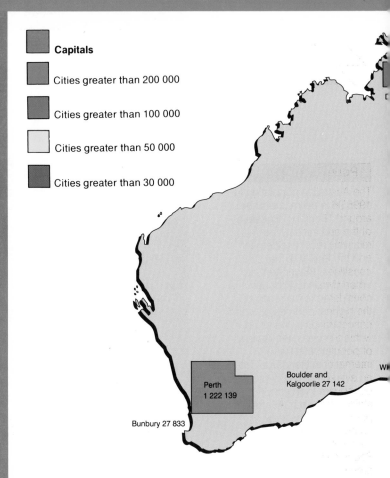

Perth
1 222 139

Boulder and
Kalgoorlie 27 142

Bunbury 27 833

DID YOU KNOW?

The average number of persons per household has
decreased from 3.31 in 1971 to 2.64 in 1995 due to a
change in social attitudes leading to a reduction in the
size of families.

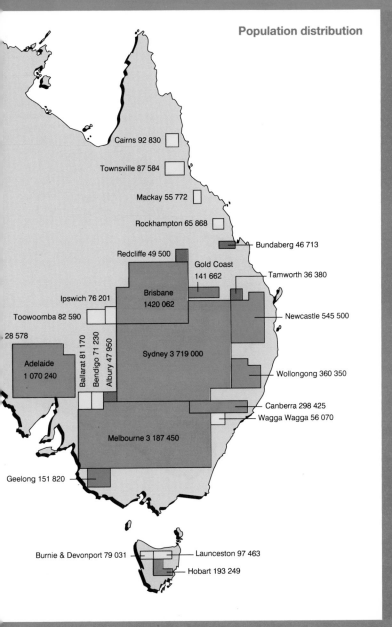

Population distribution

Cairns 92 830

Townsville 87 584

Mackay 55 772

Rockhampton 65 868

Bundaberg 46 713

Redcliffe 49 500

Gold Coast 141 662

Tamworth 36 380

Ipswich 76 201

Brisbane 1 420 062

Toowoomba 82 590

Newcastle 545 500

28 578

Ballarat 81 170

Bendigo 71 230

Albury 47 950

Adelaide 1 070 240

Sydney 3 719 000

Wollongong 360 350

Canberra 298 425

Wagga Wagga 56 070

Melbourne 3 187 450

Geelong 151 820

Burnie & Devonport 79 031

Launceston 97 463

Hobart 193 249

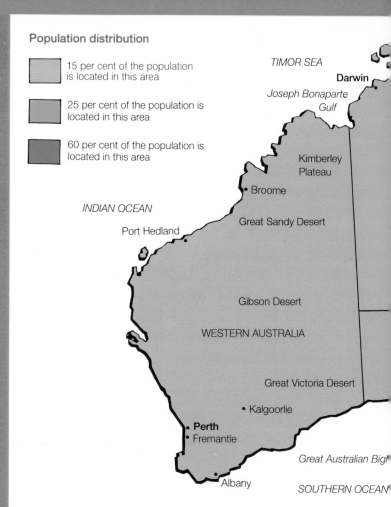

Population distribution

15 per cent of the population is located in this area

25 per cent of the population is located in this area

60 per cent of the population is located in this area

TIMOR SEA

Darwin

Joseph Bonaparte
Gulf

Kimberley
Plateau

• Broome

INDIAN OCEAN

Port Hedland

Great Sandy Desert

Gibson Desert

WESTERN AUSTRALIA

Great Victoria Desert

• Kalgoorlie

Perth
• Fremantle

Great Australian Bigh

Albany

SOUTHERN OCEAN

DID YOU KNOW?

Marital figures for Australia (1995) show 6.4 marriages per 1000 people. Median age for brides is 26.4 years. Median age for bridegrooms is 28.8 years.

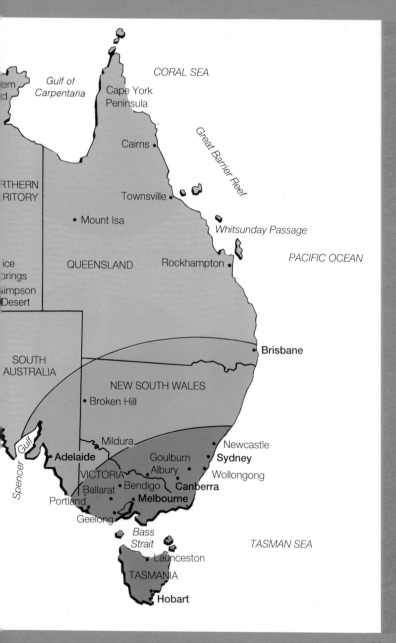

CORAL SEA

Gulf of Carpentaria

Cape York Peninsula

Cairns •

Great Barrier Reef

em
d

RTHERN
RITORY

Townsville •

• Mount Isa

Whitsunday Passage

PACIFIC OCEAN

ice
prings
Simpson
Desert

QUEENSLAND

Rockhampton •

SOUTH
AUSTRALIA

Brisbane

NEW SOUTH WALES

• Broken Hill

Spencer Gulf

Mildura

Newcastle •

Adelaide

Goulburn • **Sydney**
Albury •

Wollongong

VICTORIA
Ballarat • Bendigo **Canberra**
Portland •
Melbourne

Geelong •

Bass Strait

• Launceston

TASMANIA

TASMAN SEA

Hobart

53

Population changes since federation

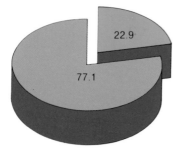

▲ % of people living in Australia, but born elsewhere
▲ % of native-born Australians

22.9
77.1

1900, total population 3 765 300

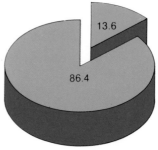

13.6
86.4

1930, total population 6 500 800

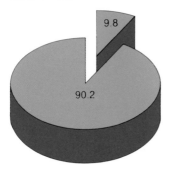

9.8
90.2

1947, total population 7 579 400

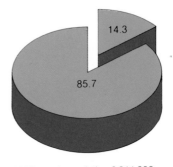

14.3
85.7

1955, total population 9 311 800

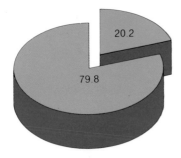

20.2
79.8

1971, total population 13 067 300

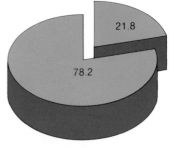

21.8
78.2

1981, total population 14 923 300

Total Australian population (est.)
18 000 000 as of 1995–96.

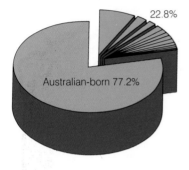

22.8%

Australian-born 77.2%

U.K. and Ireland	6.93%
Italy	1.50%
Former Yugoslavia	0.98%
Greece	0.82%
Germany	0.68%
Netherlands	0.58%
Other European	3.58%
Vietnam	0.77%
China	0.52%
Philippines	0.48%
Malaysia	0.46%
Other Asian	1.92%
New Zealand	1.62%
Africa	0.98%
Americas	0.98%

Birthplace of overseas-born

United Kingdom
England, Wales, Scotland, Northern Ireland.

Europe
Albania, Austria, Belgium, Bulgaria, Czechoslovakia, Denmark, Estonia, Finland, France, Germany, Greece, Hungary, Italy, Latvia, Lithuania, Malta, Netherlands, Norway, Poland, Portugal, Republic of Ireland, Romania, Spain, Sweden, Switzerland, Ukraine, Russia, Yugoslavia.

Middle East
Israel, Lebanon, Syria, Turkey, Egypt.

Asia
China, Hong Kong, India, Indonesia, Japan, Malaysia, Myanma, Pakistan, Philippines, Singapore, Sri Lanka, Vietnam.

Africa
Mauritius, South Africa.

Americas
Canada, South America, United States, West Indies Federation.

Pacific Islands
Fiji, New Caledonia, New Zealand, Vanuatu.

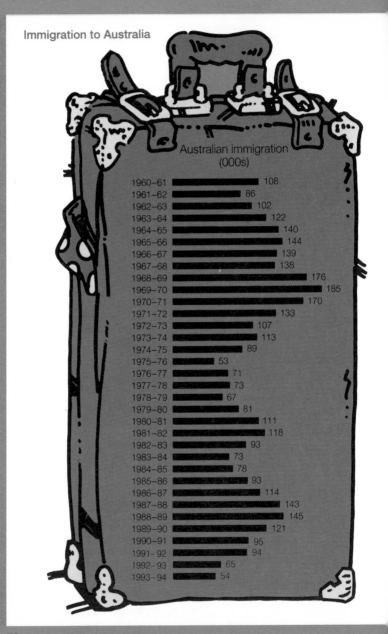

Immigration to Australia

Australian immigration
(000s)

Year	Value
1960–61	108
1961–62	86
1962–63	102
1963–64	122
1964–65	140
1965–66	144
1966–67	139
1967–68	138
1968–69	176
1969–70	185
1970–71	170
1971–72	133
1972–73	107
1973–74	113
1974–75	89
1975–76	53
1976–77	71
1977–78	73
1978–79	67
1979–80	81
1980–81	111
1981–82	118
1982–83	93
1983–84	73
1984–85	78
1985–86	93
1986–87	114
1987–88	143
1988–89	145
1989–90	121
1990–91	95
1991–92	94
1992–93	65
1993–94	54

Comparison of Aboriginal and European populations

	Aboriginal population	European population (census estimates only before 1967)	
1788	300 000	1 030	
1860	22 200	1 145 600	
1900	93 300	3 765 300	
1910	80 100	4 425 100	
1920	71 800	5 411 300	
1930	80 700	6 500 800	
1947	76 000	7 579 400	
1960	84 500	10 391 900	
1966	100 000	11 000 000	

In 1967 the Australian Constitution was changed to stop the specific exclusion of Aboriginals from the census. In 1971 Aboriginals were included in the census for the first time.

	Aboriginal population	European population	Total
1971	106 300	12 961 000	13 067 300
1981	144 600	14 778 700	14 923 300
1985	220 000	15 531 500	15 751 500
1986	227 000	15 681 755	15 909 400

Torres Strait Islanders included in census for first time

	Aboriginal population	European population	Total
1991	257 333	16 742 667	17 000 000
1993	265 459	17 234 541	17 500 000
1995–96 (est.)	288 086	17 711 914	18 000 000

Aboriginal population

Because of the difficulty of obtaining accurate counts, until 1930 only estimates were made. An estimate of the number of Aboriginals in Australia at the time of European settlement was thought to be 300 000, but current research suggests that the figure could have been as high as 500 000.

With European settlement, the Aboriginal population declined drastically due to the introduction of disease (to which Aboriginals had no natural immunity), alcohol and violent conflict.

By the early 1920s the Aboriginal population had decreased to just over 70 000. With increased expenditure on welfare and health, the population decline had reversed by the 1960s.

DID YOU KNOW?

Australia is the world's second largest inhabited island and the smallest continent. It is also the largest continent occupied by one nation and the least populated.

The national flag

The red ensign

Flags

For many years the Australian Blue Ensign was regarded as the official flag. This was a plain blue flag, with the Union Jack in the upper corner of the hoist, together with the seven-pointed Commonwealth star beneath. It also contained the five-starred Southern Cross. However, it had not been clearly established that any particular flag was the national flag. In 1951 King George VI approved a recommendation by the government that the Australian Blue Ensign be proclaimed the national flag, and the Australian Red Ensign be the proper colour for merchant ships registered in Australia. The *Flags Act* was passed in 1953 by the Commonwealth parliament, making these the official flags of the Commonwealth.

The state flags are based on the plain Blue Ensign with the particular badge of each state added. The Northern Territory flag is based on colours found in desert regions, and the Territory's badge is added.

Coat of arms

The present coat of arms was granted in 1912 by King George V, following approval of substantial alterations by the Commonwealth government. It consists of a shield composed of six parts, each containing one of the state badges. These are

The national coat of arms

surrounded by an ermine border, signifying the federation of the states into the Commonwealth. The shield is supported by two Australian animals, the kangaroo and the emu, standing on ornamental rests, behind which are small branches of wattle. The crest consists of the seven-pointed Commonwealth gold star, a symbol of national unity. At the base of the shield is a scroll on which is printed the word 'Australia'.

Anthems

The royal anthem, 'God Save the Queen', is used in the presence of Her Majesty the Queen or a member of the royal family.

The vice-regal salute, which consists of the first four and last four bars of the tune 'Advance Australia Fair', is used in the presence of the governor-general.

The national anthem 'Advance Australia Fair', is used on all other ceremonial occasions. For the words of Australia's national anthem, see p. 201.

Colours

Green and gold are the national colours of Australia, and are used on all appropriate occasions, such as the Olympic Games.

National floral emblem: golden wattle Acacia pycnantha

National animal emblem: kangaroo

DID YOU KNOW?

The oldest skeleton found in Australia was at Lake Mungo in south-west New South Wales. It is believed to be 38 000 years old and is the skeleton of a female. It has traces of ceremonial ochre (a sign of culture), which is thought to be the oldest sign of ochre use ever discovered.

Public holidays and special days

| January | 1 | New Year's Day |
| | 26 | Australia Day (public holiday on Monday following, except New South Wales which celebrates on the day) |

March
First Monday	Western Australia: Labour Day Tasmania: Eight-Hour Day
Second Monday	Victoria: Labour Day and Moomba Parade
Third Monday	Australian Capital Territory: Labour Day

April
| First full moon after equinox (may fall in March) | Easter holiday begins on Good Friday and continues until following Monday (in some states Easter Tuesday is also a public holiday) |
| 25 | Anzac Day |

| May | First Monday | Queensland: Labour Day |
| | | Northern Territory: May Day Holiday |

June
| Second Monday | Queen's Birthday (except Western Australia) |

| August | 1 | Wattle Day (some states) |
| | First Monday | New South Wales: Bank Holiday |

| September | 1 | Wattle Day (some states) |

October
First Monday	New South Wales and Australian Capital Territory: Labour Day
6	Western Australia: Queen's Birthday
Second Monday	South Australia: Labour Day

November
| First Tuesday | Melbourne, Victoria: Melbourne Cup Day |
| 11 | Remembrance Day |

December	25	Christmas Day
	26	Boxing Day (except South Australia)
	28	South Australia: Proclamation Day

Powers

Australia's official name is the Commonwealth of Australia. Its form of government is a constitutional monarchy. The head of the state is Queen Elizabeth II of the United Kingdom of Great Britain and Northern Ireland, who is also Queen of Australia. She is represented in Australia by the governor-general. The head of government is the prime minister, leader of the party or coalition of parties holding a majority in the federal parliament.

Australia is an independent self-governing member of the British Commonwealth of Nations, and a foundation member of the United Nations. It is in alliance with the United States of America and New Zealand in the ANZUS pact, and a member of the South-East Asia Treaty Organisation (SEATO).

It is a federation of six states, with two internal federal territories – the Australian Capital Territory and the Northern Territory – and a number of external territories – Norfolk Island, Cocos Island, Christmas Island, Lord Howe Island, Macquarie Island, Australian Antarctica between 45° and 160° longitude – under its control.

Levels of government

Federal

Australia chose its executive form of government, consisting of a prime minister and cabinet, mainly from the British Westminster system. As well, some minor aspects of the United States congressional system were adopted.

The Australian federal parliament is generally responsible for matters of national importance. These include defence, external affairs, customs and excise, communications, foreign trade, social services, treasury, and immigration. In addition it shares mutual responsibilities with the state legislatures. These include education, agriculture, energy services, health, and law enforcement.

The Australian constitution, a document agreed to by the separate colonies in 1901 at federation, limits the power of the federal government. To maintain strict control, the constitution can be altered only by a referendum.

There are two houses in the federal parliament, the House of Representatives (lower house) and the Senate (upper house).

The House of Representatives

This is often called the people's house as the 148 members are voted in directly by the people of Australia, with each member representing about 70 000 voters. The House consists of a government and opposition, it sits for 70–80 days each year, and is limited to a three-year period. However, it may be dissolved sooner by the governor-general on the advice of the prime minister. Its main function is to debate and discuss bills, which are proposed new laws. The political party or coalition of parties holding majority support in the House has the right to form the executive government, with the leader of the party (or

---

DID YOU KNOW?
Australia is the only English-speaking country to have made voting compulsory in federal and state elections. It results in a voter turn-out of 95 per cent.

senior party) becoming prime minister. The official opposition consists of the major party or coalition of parties opposed to the government.

The Senate

This is virtually a house of review, where the procedures are designed to allow debate on the merits or defects of any bill passed by the House of Representatives. The Senate can request amendments to, and can reject, any bill. There are 76 senators, 12 being elected from each state, regardless of population size, thus enabling the less populous states a greater weight in the political system. Senators from states are elected for a six-year period. Every three years half the senators retire, but may stand for re-election. Senators from the territories are elected for three years.

The Ministry

This consists of members of the government who are responsible for a particular area of policy. Most ministers are members of the House of Representatives and a few are from the Senate. They have specific departments of the public service to help them administer their portfolios. The prime minister is, by convention, always a member of the House of Representatives. Members

who are not ministers or leading members of the opposition are called back-benchers.

The Cabinet

This is an inner council and consists of the leading figures (those with senior portfolios) of the government and the Senate, with the prime minister as chairman. Junior ministers attend cabinet meetings only when matters affecting their departments are being discussed.

The Executive Council

It has the task of advising the governor-general of major political decisions affecting the nation which have been made by meetings of the Cabinet.

The Governor-General

He is the Queen's representative in the Australian parliament, and is appointed by the Queen on the advice of the prime minister. All laws made by parliament finally depend on his assent.

Voting

Compulsory preferential voting is the most common system used in Australia. In voting for the House of Representatives, one candidate only from any one party is selected to represent each electorate. The voter must vote for all the candidates in order of preference. If no candidate

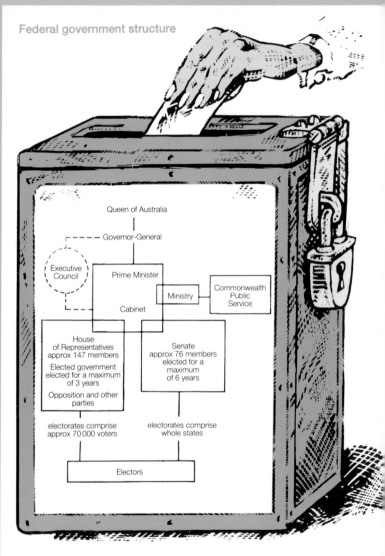

Federal government structure

Queen of Australia

Governor-General

Executive Council

Prime Minister

Cabinet

Ministry

Commonwealth Public Service

House of Representatives approx 147 members

Elected government elected for a maximum of 3 years

Opposition and other parties

Senate approx 76 members elected for a maximum of 6 years

electorates comprise approx 70 000 voters

electorates comprise whole states

Electors

All Australians over the age of 18 are eligible to vote.

Voting is compulsory for everyone except Aboriginals. Aboriginals may choose whether or not to register; if they register, they must vote.

receives an absolute majority, then there is a distribution of preference votes.

Distributing Preference Votes

All votes are sorted according to the voters' first choice and then counted. The candidate with the least number of votes is eliminated and his/her votes are distributed according to the voters' second choice. All votes are then re-counted and for the second time the candidate with the least number of votes is eliminated and his/her votes distributed according to the voters' next choice of candidates and so on. The first candidate who finally reaches 50% or over of the votes, wins.

The number of members of the House of Representatives depends on the population of each state. In 1995 there were 147 members: 50 for New South Wales; 38 for Victoria; 25 for Queensland; 12 for South Australia; 14 for Western Australia; 5 for Tasmania; 2 for the Australian Capital Territory; and 1 for the Northern Territory.

Proportional representation is the other major electoral system in Australia. It is used in the Senate and in some state elections. Each Senator represents a whole state; as the electorate is so large, more than one candidate is elected for each state. In 1995 there were 76 senators; 12 for each state, and 2 for each territory.

Procedures

A *double dissolution* of parliament is the dissolving of both the House of Representatives and the Senate due to a deadlock arising over the passing of a bill. This necessitates a general election of both houses.

The unusual procedure of a *joint sitting* of parliament occurs when a party wins a majority in the House of Representatives but not in the Senate, after a double dissolution. Both the House of Representatives and the Senate may sit jointly to work out a solution if a deadlock still exists.

Supply is the money granted by the passing of legislation before the end of the financial year in order to proceed until the next budget is passed. *Appropriation bills* authorise the use of revenue collected by the government.

DID YOU KNOW?

The Australian Labor Party, the oldest surviving Labor Party in the world, celebrated its centenary in 1991. The first meeting was held under a gum tree at Barcaldine, Queensland, in 1891.

Each state (except Northern Territory and Australian Capital Territory) has an executive council consisting of the governor, premier and selected ministers.

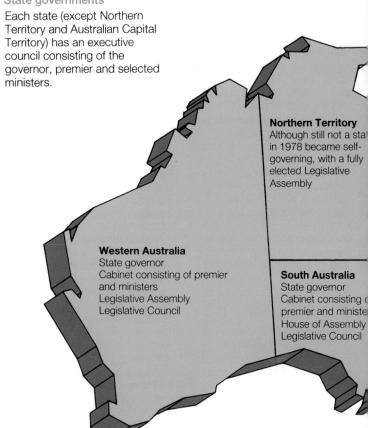

Northern Territory
Although still not a sta
in 1978 became self-
governing, with a fully
elected Legislative
Assembly

Western Australia
State governor
Cabinet consisting of premier
and ministers
Legislative Assembly
Legislative Council

South Australia
State governor
Cabinet consisting c
premier and ministe
House of Assembly
Legislative Council

DID YOU KNOW?
The world's largest electorate (2 255 278 square
kilometres) is Kalgoorlie, Western Australia.

State

State governments are also modelled on the British Westminster system, each having a premier as leader of the cabinet and ministry.

The state parliaments deal with domestic affairs, such as housing, trade, education, industry and law enforcement within the states, as well as sharing mutual responsibilities with the federal parliament.

Local

The *Local Government Act* was passed in 1919. This gave power to areas as small as cities, municipalities and shires, to provide a more satisfactory system of government within the local area with a mayor or president as leader. Australia has 900 bodies at local government level. They have varying responsibilities which may include urban planning, road construction, water, sewerage and drainage, and local community activities.

Queensland
State governor
Cabinet consisting of premier and ministers
Legislative Assembly

New South Wales
State governor
Cabinet consisting of premier and ministers
Legislative Assembly
Legislative Council

Australian Capital Territory
Legislative Assembly

Victoria
State governor
Cabinet consisting of premier and ministers
Legislative Assembly
Legislative Council

Tasmania
State governor
Cabinet consisting of premier and ministers
House of Assembly
Legislative Council

Voting is compulsory in some states

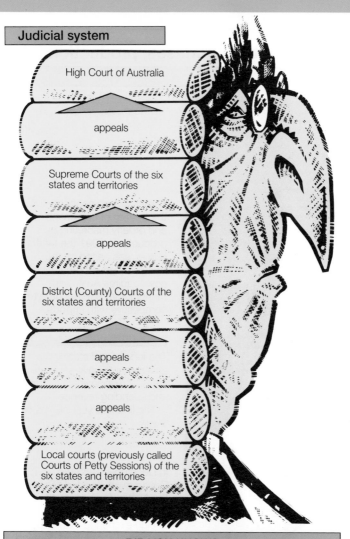

Judicial system

High Court of Australia

appeals

Supreme Courts of the six states and territories

appeals

District (County) Courts of the six states and territories

appeals

appeals

Local courts (previously called Courts of Petty Sessions) of the six states and territories

DID YOU KNOW?

There are approximately 175 local courts in each state which deal with 98 per cent of all cases heard in Australia.

Payments, purchases, production

The Australian economy follows the system of free enterprise and orderly marketing of products. In 1991 the tariff barrier was eased by the Australian government which now requires Australian manufacturers to become more competitive with imports.

Income and expenditure

The federal and state governments have separate areas of responsibility for raising and spending revenue.

The financial year begins on 1 July.

Floating of the Australian dollar

In December 1983 the Government decided to allow the Australian dollar to *float*, that is, to establish its value in the foreign exchange market by the process of supply and demand. Prior to this the Reserve Bank set the value for the Australian dollar against the US dollar, on a daily basis.

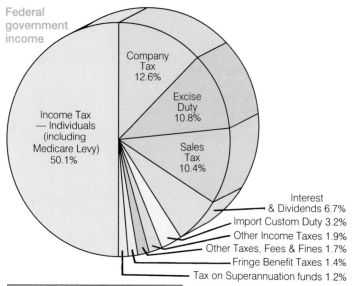

Federal government income

Company Tax 12.6%

Excise Duty 10.8%

Income Tax — Individuals (including Medicare Levy) 50.1%

Sales Tax 10.4%

Interest & Dividends 6.7%
Import Custom Duty 3.2%
Other Income Taxes 1.9%
Other Taxes, Fees & Fines 1.7%
Fringe Benefit Taxes 1.4%
Tax on Superannuation funds 1.2%

Income and expenditure

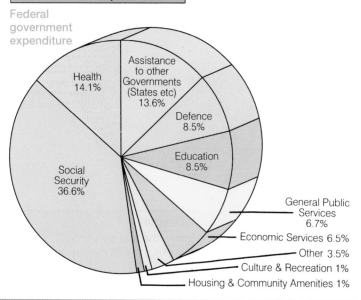

Federal government expenditure

Health 14.1%

Assistance to other Governments (States etc) 13.6%

Defence 8.5%

Social Security 36.6%

Education 8.5%

General Public Services 6.7%
Economic Services 6.5%
Other 3.5%
Culture & Recreation 1%
Housing & Community Amenities 1%

Basket of currencies – Trade Weighted Index

The *Trade Weighted Index* (TWI) is a measure of performance of the value of the Australian dollar against a 'basket' of such currencies as the US dollar, Japanese yen, English pound, Deutsche–mark, New Zealand dollar, etc. These are weighted in percentage terms to approximately the value of each country's trade with Australia.

State government income

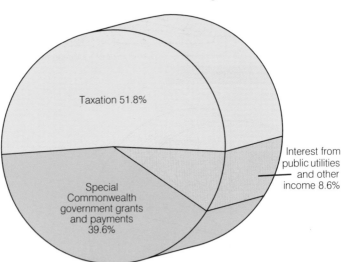

Taxation 51.8%

Interest from public utilities and other income 8.6%

Special Commonwealth government grants and payments 39.6%

DID YOU KNOW?
South Australia, in 1894, became the first colony to extend political equality to women. In 1902 Australian women won the right to vote.

Federal versus State

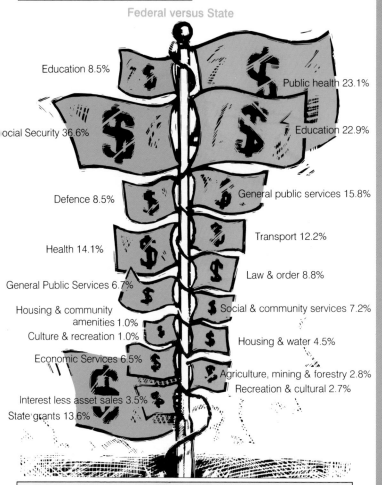

Education 8.5%

Public health 23.1%

ocial Security 36.6%

Education 22.9%

Defence 8.5%

General public services 15.8%

Transport 12.2%

Health 14.1%

Law & order 8.8%

General Public Services 6.7%

Housing & community
amenities 1.0%

Social & community services 7.2%

Culture & recreation 1.0%

Housing & water 4.5%

Economic Services 6.5%

Agriculture, mining & forestry 2.8%

Recreation & cultural 2.7%

Interest less asset sales 3.5%

State grants 13.6%

DID YOU KNOW?

The longest river in Australia is the Darling, which rises in central Queensland and joins the Murray in north-western Victoria, 2736 km away.

Major Australian Exports 1994–95

Total $64 611.0 m

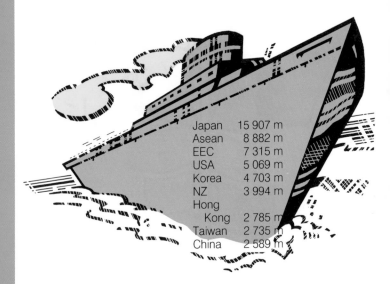

Japan	15 907 m
Asean	8 882 m
EEC	7 315 m
USA	5 069 m
Korea	4 703 m
NZ	3 994 m
Hong Kong	2 785 m
Taiwan	2 735 m
China	2 589 m

Balance of Payments

Australia's Balance of Payments is not just the difference between our Exports and Imports. It is made up of the following segments:
a) The inflow of money in payment for goods exported and the outflow of money in payment for goods imported. (This is called the Trade Account).
b) The inflow of money for 'Services' and the outflow of money for 'Services'. (Services can include travellers' funds, freight and insurance costs, money gifts, royalty payments and payments for 'know-how' and the like – i.e. transactions of a mainly non-trade nature.)
c) The amount of dividends and interest on loans paid to foreigners less the amount of dividends and interest on loans paid by foreigners. (This is called Net income.)

Major Australian Imports 1994–95

Total $64 473 m

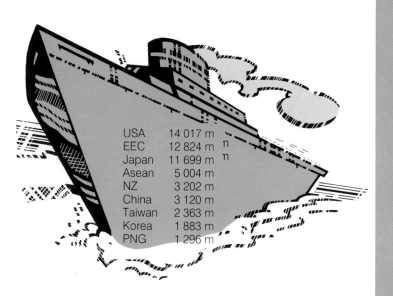

USA	14 017 m
EEC	12 824 m
Japan	11 699 m
Asean	5 004 m
NZ	3 202 m
China	3 120 m
Taiwan	2 363 m
Korea	1 883 m
PNG	1 296 m

For example in 1994–95:

a) Total export of goods $64 611m
   Total import of goods $64 473m
   Surplus on Trade Account +$138m

b) Inflow of money for Services $18 300m
   Outflow of money for Services $19 700m
   Deficiency on Services −$1 400m

c) Dividends/interest paid to foreigners $ n.a.
   Dividends/interest paid by foreigners $ n.a.
   Deficiency on Net income −$14 800m
   Total Deficiency (Adverse Balance of Payments) −$16 062m

(Adverse Balance of Payments sometimes referred to as Current Account Deficit.)

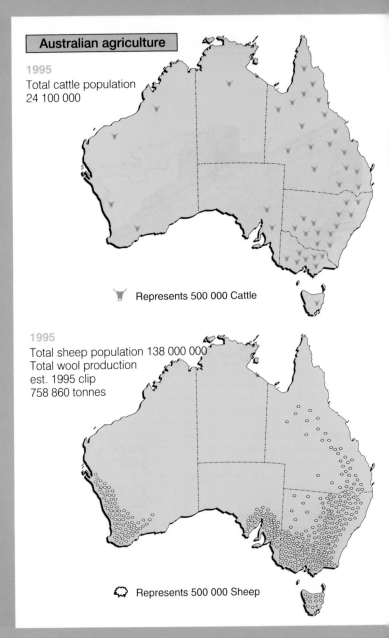

Australian agriculture

1995
Total cattle population
24 100 000

Represents 500 000 Cattle

1995
Total sheep population 138 000 000
Total wool production
est. 1995 clip
758 860 tonnes

Represents 500 000 Sheep

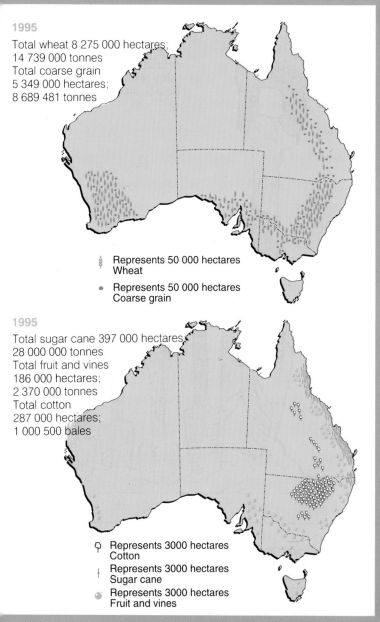

1995

Total wheat 8 275 000 hectares;
14 739 000 tonnes
Total coarse grain
5 349 000 hectares;
8 689 481 tonnes

Represents 50 000 hectares
Wheat

Represents 50 000 hectares
Coarse grain

1995

Total sugar cane 397 000 hectares;
28 000 000 tonnes
Total fruit and vines
186 000 hectares;
2 370 000 tonnes
Total cotton
287 000 hectares;
1 000 500 bales

Represents 3000 hectares
Cotton

Represents 3000 hectares
Sugar cane

Represents 3000 hectares
Fruit and vines

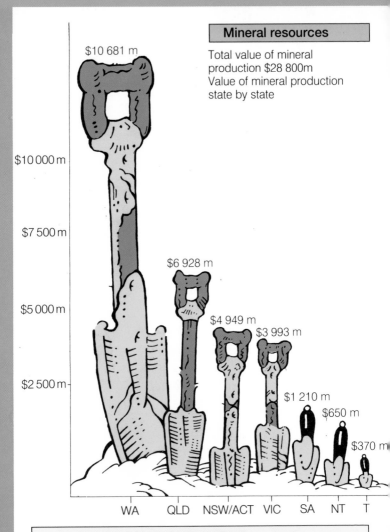

Mineral resources

Total value of mineral production $28 800m
Value of mineral production state by state

$10 681 m

$6 928 m

$4 949 m

$3 993 m

$1 210 m

$650 m

$370 m

$10 000 m

$7 500 m

$5 000 m

$2 500 m

WA · QLD · NSW/ACT · VIC · SA · NT · T

DID YOU KNOW?

The Argyle Diamond Mine, south of Kununurra in Western Australia, is the world's most modern and the main source of rare intense pink diamonds.

Australia's mineral resources

- □ Silver, lead, zinc
- ▲ Oil
- × Gas
- △ Bauxite
- ■ Coal
- ○ Gold
- ▲ Iron ore
- ◆ Uranium
- ● Copper
- ▼ Nickel

Australia's oil and gas fields

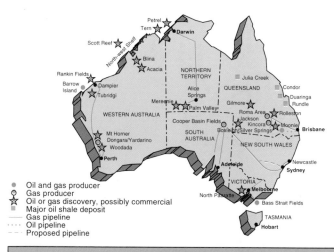

- ● Oil and gas producer
- ⚲ Gas producer
- ☆ Oil or gas discovery, possibly commercial
- ■ Major oil shale deposit
- —— Gas pipeline
- ···· Oil pipeline
- –– Proposed pipeline

DID YOU KNOW?
Australia's three main opal fields are in Quilpie (Queensland), Lightning Ridge (New South Wales), and Coober Pedy (South Australia).

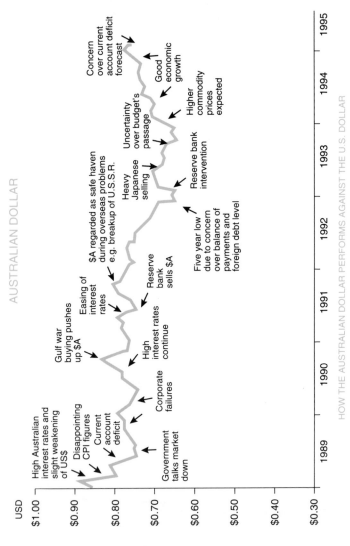

The Australian Economy

How the Australian dollar performs against the U.S dollar

AUSTRALIAN DOLLAR

Concern over current account deficit forecast

Good economic growth

Uncertainty over budget's passage

Higher commodity prices expected

$A regarded as safe haven during overseas problems e.g. breakup of U.S.S.R.

Heavy Japanese selling

Reserve bank intervention

Easing of interest rates

Reserve bank sells $A

Five year low due to concern over balance of payments and foreign debt level

Gulf war buying pushes up $A

High interest rates continue

High Australian interest rates and slight weakening of US$

Disappointing CPI figures

Current account deficit

Corporate failures

Government talks market down

USD	
$1.00	
$0.90	
$0.80	
$0.70	
$0.60	
$0.50	
$0.40	
$0.30	

1989   1990   1991   1992   1993   1994   1995

HOW THE AUSTRALIAN DOLLAR PERFORMS AGAINST THE U.S. DOLLAR

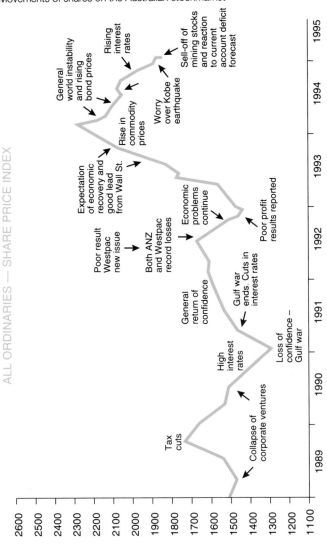

The Australian Stockmarket

Movements of shares on the Australian stockmarket

ALL ORDINARIES — SHARE PRICE INDEX

Tax cuts

Collapse of corporate ventures

High interest rates

Loss of confidence – Gulf war

General return of confidence

Gulf war ends. Cuts in interest rates

Poor result Westpac new issue

Both ANZ and Westpac record losses

Economic problems continue

Poor profit results reported

Expectation of economic recovery and good lead from Wall St.

Rise in commodity prices

General world instability and rising bond prices

Worry over Kobe earthquake

Rising interest rates

Sell-off of mining stocks and reaction to current account deficit forecast

1989 1990 1991 1992 1993 1994 1995

2600 2500 2400 2300 2200 2100 2000 1900 1800 1700 1600 1500 1400 1300 1200 1100

SHARE PRICE MOVEMENTS ON THE AUSTRALIAN STOCK EXCHANGE

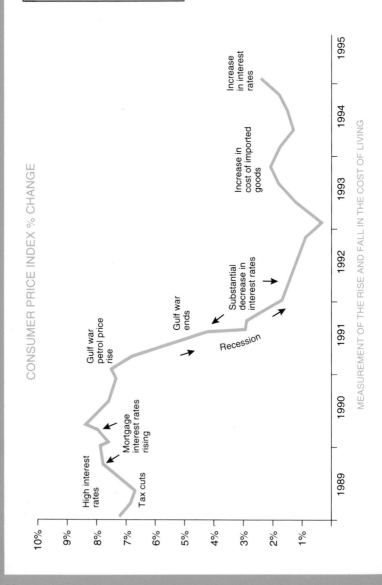

Consumer Price Index

CONSUMER PRICE INDEX % CHANGE

MEASUREMENT OF THE RISE AND FALL IN THE COST OF LIVING

High interest rates

Tax cuts

Mortgage interest rates rising

Gulf war petrol price rise

Gulf war ends

Recession

Substantial decrease in interest rates

Increase in cost of imported goods

Increase in interest rates

10%
9%
8%
7%
6%
5%
4%
3%
2%
1%

1989   1990   1991   1992   1993   1994   1995

The fiscal clock

Top of the boom

Rising real estate values **12.**

Easier money **11.**

1. Rising interest rates

Rising **10.** overseas reserves

2. Falling share prices

Rising **9.** commodity prices

3. Falling commodity prices

Rising **8.** share prices

4. Falling overseas reserves

Falling interest **7.** rates

5. Tighter money

6. Falling real estate values

Depth of the recession

The stock market leads the economy by 6 to 8 months.

The whole clock can take anything up to eight years to complete.

Average Weekly earnings

1919
$6.00

1948
$11.60

1970
$76.00

1975
$148.00

1980
$247.60

1982
$307.00

1986
$418.90

1994–5
$620.40

DID YOU KNOW?

The highest paid jobs for males are in the mining industry; for females, in the mining industry and community services (health, education, etc).

Currency

Until 1966 Australia followed the British system of currency, of pounds, shillings and pence. On 14 February 1966, decimal currency was introduced with the dollar ($A) being the unit of currency consisting of 100 cents (c). The currency has six coins and five notes in circulation as well as periodic commemorative notes and coins.

Coins

On all coins, the obverse side displays an image of Queen Elizabeth II.

The reverse side mostly depicts Australian native fauna.

The 5c coin has the echidna or spiny ant-eater, one of the only two egg-laying mammals in the world.

The 10c coin shows a male lyrebird dancing, its magnificent tail spread and thrown forward over its head.

The 20c coin shows the only other egg-laying mammal, the platypus.

The 50c coin carries the coat of arms of the Commonwealth of Australia.

These coins are cupro-nickel.

The $1 coin portrays five kangaroos and has interrupted milling on the edge to assist the visually impaired.

The $2 coin has the bust of an Aboriginal against the background of the Southern Cross.

These coins are made of aluminium-bronze.

Sometimes the 20c, 50c, and $1 coins are minted with a special design for commemorative purposes and are circulated.

A $5 coin, a $10 coin (made of sterling silver) and a $200 coin (made of 22 carat gold), have been minted but not generally circulated, although are legal tender.

Notes

The currency has five notes, each increasing in size with its value. All depict personalities or themes of Australian historical interest. The $5 note features, in raised print for the visually impaired, the portrait of Queen Elizabeth II and a spray of gum leaves. On the reverse side is Parliament House and landscape plans. A gum flower in a transparent area and a seven pointed star are the anti-counterfeiting devices. A watermark of the Australian Coat of Arms can be seen clearly when the note is held up to the light.

The $10 note features, in raised print, the portrait of A.B. (Banjo) Paterson, and a scene from his famous poem, 'The Man from Snowy River'. An anti-counterfeiting device of a windmill, a symbol of the outback surrounded by a transparent area can be seen.

On the reverse side there is the 19th century poet and champion of the oppressed, Dame Mary Gilmore, with a bullock team in the background.

The $20 dollar note features the portrait of Mary Reibey, who came to the colony as a convict, and later became a respected businesswoman with interests in property and shipping. The reverse side commemorates the work of the Reverend John Flynn, founder of the world acclaimed Flying Doctor Service. An anti-counterfeiting device is a clear window surrounded by a printed image of a compass.

These notes replaced the old notes in 1992, 1993 and 1994 respectively and are the first in a series of polymer notes.

The $50 note portrays Nobel prize winner, Sir Howard Florey, a pathologist whose experiments led to the discovery of the clinical value of penicillin. The reverse side depicts Sir Ian Clunies-Ross, famous scientist renowned for his long association with CSIRO. The $100 note has the famous Antarctic explorer and geologist, Sir Douglas Mawson on the front and on the reverse is John Tebbutt, the astronomer who laid the foundations of astronomy in Australia.

These two notes are soon to be replaced by polymer notes.

Australian Capital Territory

Jervis Bay

Two areas transferred to the Commonwealth of Australia by the state of New South Wales make up the Australian Capital Territory. In 1908 the larger area around Canberra was chosen for the federal capital site, and in 1915 the smaller area of Jervis Bay on the New South Wales coast was transferred to the Commonwealth of Australia. The seat of government was moved from Melbourne to Canberra in 1927.

Location

The greater part of the Australian Capital Territory is in south-eastern New South Wales, west of the Great Dividing Range. The smaller, Jervis Bay area is on the New South Wales southern coast.

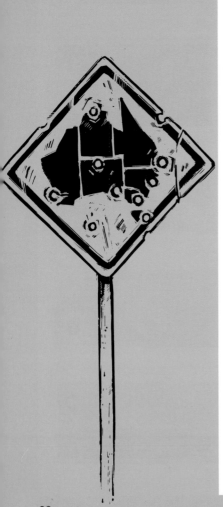

Australian Capital Territory, gross value of production

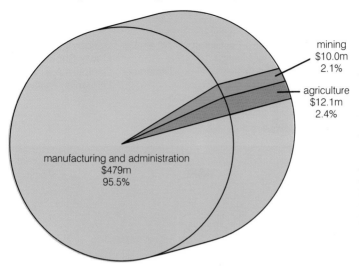

mining
$10.0m
2.1%

agriculture
$12.1m
2.4%

manufacturing and administration
$479m
95.5%

Area

The area around Canberra is 2400 square kilometres; Jervis Bay consists of 73 square kilometres.

Landform

Rolling plains and grasslands. Gentle slopes and coastal plains in Jervis Bay area.

Population

324 600, mostly residents of Canberra.

Climate

Mainly temperate: cold nights and cool to very cold days in winter, warm to hot days and cool nights in summer. Slightly humid in coastal areas.

Administrative centre

Canberra is situated at the northern end of the Australian Capital Territory. It has an area of 805 square kilometres and a population of 298,425, of which 28 per cent are public servants. Average daily hours of sunshine, 7.2.

Main attractions

Parliament House, Lake Burley Griffin, High Courts of Australia, Captain Cook Water Spout, Red Hill, Black Mountain, Telecom Tower, American War Memorial, Australian War Museum, foreign legations, Yarralumla (governor-general's residence). Vietnam war memorial.

Major festivals

February	Royal Canberra Show	September	Floriade Festival
March	Canberra Festival	October	Canberra Oktoberfest
June	Canberra Festival of Drama	November	Canberra Spring Flower Show
	Canberra Embassies' Open Day	December	Canberra Australian Lithuanian Festival

Sister city Versailles (France)

New Parliament House, Canberra

DID YOU KNOW?
Parliament House, Canberra, covers 15% of a 32 hectare site, and is one of the largest buildings in the southern hemisphere. There are 4500 rooms and 250 000 square metres of floor area. The building is made of 300 000 cubic metres of concrete, enough to build twenty-five Sydney Opera Houses.

New South Wales

Location

NSW lies in the south-east of the continent on the Pacific Ocean, with Queensland to the north and Victoria to the south.

Area

It is the fourth-largest state in Australia, and is 801 600 square kilometres (seven times larger than England).

Landform

Coastal slopes, plateaus and river flats are bounded by the Great Dividing Range, which runs north and south. West of the Dividing Range are rolling plains which deteriorate into semi-arid desert.

Population

6 051 400. The majority live in the three main cities – Sydney, Newcastle, and Wollongong. Over half the people of the state live in Sydney.

Climate

Temperate and slightly humid in coastal areas with the deserts of the interior experiencing cold nights and hot days. Irregular floods and droughts occur.

State capital

Sydney is built on Port Jackson, a sea inlet on the Pacific Ocean. The city has an area of 12 407 square kilometres (including Penrith and Gosford), and a population of 3 719 000. Average daily hours of sunshine, 6.7.

NSW animal emblem: platypus

NSW floral emblem: waratah

DID YOU KNOW?

Sydney Harbour Bridge has an arch span of 503 metres. The top arch is 134 metres above sea level. Overall length of arch and approaches is 1149 metres, with a deck width of 49 metres. The bridge weighs approximately 52 800 tonnes and the weight of the steel in the arch is 39 000 tonnes.

New South Wales, gross value of production

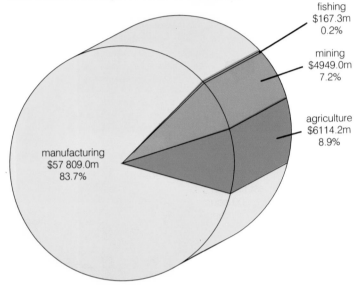

fishing
$167.3m
0.2%

mining
$4949.0m
7.2%

agriculture
$6114.2m
8.9%

manufacturing
$57 809.0m
83.7%

Largest cities

Sydney (3 719 000)
Newcastle (545 500)
Wollongong (360 350)
Wagga Wagga (56 070)
Albury (47 950)
Tamworth (36 380)
Broken Hill (24 140)

Chief products

Agriculture:

Cotton, dairy products, fruit, honey, mutton, poultry, sugar, wheat, wool, timber.

Fishing:

Many varieties of fish and shellfish.

Manufacturing:

Agricultural implements, chemicals, clothing, fertiliser, glassware, iron and steel, machinery, motor cars, paper, textiles.

Mining:

Coal, copper, gold, lead, mineral sands, silver, zinc.

Main attractions

Sydney Harbour Bridge, Opera House, Darling Harbour, Rocks area, Blue Mountains, Murrumbidgee irrigation area, Snowy Mountains, national parks, surfing beaches, fishing, wineries.

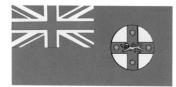

NSW flag

NSW coat of arms

Flag

The New South Wales flag is based on the Blue Ensign, with the state badge superimposed on the right-hand side. The badge consists of a golden lion on a red St George Cross within a white circle. This badge was proclaimed in 1876.

Coat of arms

The present coat of arms was approved in 1906 by King Edward VII. It consists of a shield with the red cross of St George. In the quarters are displayed sheaves of wheat and fleece from the sheep, representing the agricultural and pastoral industries of the state. The shield is supported by a lion and a kangaroo. The crest is a rising sun with rays, each tagged with the flame of fire. The scroll at the base bears the motto, *Orta recens quam pura nites* (Newly arisen, how brightly you shine).

Sydney Opera House

Major festivals

January	Festival of Sydney
	Tamworth Country Music Festival
March	Orange Festival of Arts
April	Bathurst Grand Prix Motor-Bike Races
	Albury Heritage Week
	Tumut Festival of the Fallen Leaf
May	Coonabarabran Chrysanthemum Show
August	Leeton Citrus Festival
	Lightning Ridge Opal Festival
	Newcastle Mattara Festival
	Wagga Wagga School of Arts Drama Festival
September	Bowral Tulip Time
	Gosford Festival of the Waters
	Goulburn Lilac Time Festival
	Tuncurry and Forster Great Lakes Oyster Festival
October	Bathurst 1000 Car Race
	Grafton Jacaranda Festival
	Tamworth Australian Country Music Star Maker Quest
November	Blackheath Rhododendron Festival
	Glen Innes, The Land of the Beardies, Bush Festival
December	Berrima Arts Festival
	Stroud Charity Carnival

Sister cities

Coffs Harbour	Hayama, Sasebo (Japan)
Cooma	Kamoto-cho (Japan), Taupo (New Zealand)
Lismore	Yamato-takada (Japan)
Manly	Avon, Bath (UK), Selma (USA), Taito-ku, Tokyo (Japan)
Newcastle	Arcadia (USA), Ube (Japan)
Orange	Kofu (Japan), Orange (USA), Timaru (New Zealand)
Sydney	Guangzhou (People's Republic of China), Hampshire, Portsmouth (UK), Nagoya (Japan), San Francisco (USA), Wellington (New Zealand)
Wollongong	Kimitsu (Japan), Lae (Papua New Guinea), Ohird (Yugoslavia)

DID YOU KNOW?
Sydney Tower, at Centrepoint, is the highest building in the southern hemisphere, 324.8 metres above sea level.

Victoria

Location

Victoria lies in the south-eastern corner of the continent.

Area

It is the smallest state on the mainland, and is 227 600 square kilometres in area.

Landform

Mountainous areas in the north-east, and semi-desert areas in north-west. Most land is well suited to farming, and as a result Victoria is often referred to as 'The Garden State'.

Population

4 476 100. Victoria is the most densely populated and most highly urbanised of all the states.

Climate

Generally temperate, although the climate is subject to wide variation. High rainfall, extremes of summer heat and irregular floods and droughts occur.

State capital

Melbourne is situated on the Yarra River, on Port Phillip Bay. It has an area of 6109 square kilometres and a population of 3 187 450 (about seven-tenths of the state's population). Melbourne's motto is *Vires acquirit eundo* (We gather strength as we grow). Average daily hours of sunshine, 5.7.

Largest cities

Melbourne (3 187 450)
Geelong and environs (151 820)
Ballarat (81 870)
Bendigo (71 230)
Shepparton (40 430)

Victorian floral emblem: pink heath

Victorian animal emblem: Leadbeater's possum

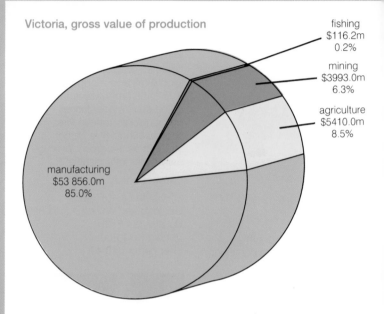

Victoria, gross value of production

fishing
$116.2m
0.2%

mining
$3993.0m
6.3%

agriculture
$5410.0m
8.5%

manufacturing
$53 856.0m
85.0%

Chief products

Agriculture:

Cattle, forest products, fruit, hay and straw, milk and dairy products, poultry and eggs, sheep, vegetables, wheat and wool.

Manufacturing:

Building materials, chemical products, clothing, farm machinery, footwear, light engineering, motor vehicles, textiles.

Mining:

Brown coal, natural gas, oil.

Main attractions

Melbourne Cup (began 1861) Australian Rules Football, National Tennis Centre, Phillip Island (penguins), wineries, prospecting, river boat cruising, surfing, snowfields, national parks, sailing, fishing. Educational system, cultural institutions and communications media are well advanced.

DID YOU KNOW?
The secret ballot box, the most prized symbol of democracy, was pioneered in Victoria in 1856.

Flag

Victoria was the first state to have its own flag. The flag is made up of the Blue Ensign with the badge of the state. This consists of five white stars of the Southern Cross in the fly, above which is a crown. It was used as early as 1870.

Victorian flag

Coat of arms

The present coat of arms was granted by Queen Elizabeth II in 1972. It incorporates a shield with five stars representing the constellation of the Southern Cross. On either side stands a female figure, one representing peace and the other representing prosperity. The figure of peace is holding an olive branch and the figure of prosperity is holding a cornucopia, or horn of plenty.

Victorian coat of arms

The crest consists of a kangaroo, bearing in its paws an Imperial Crown. Below the shields is the motto, 'Peace and prosperity'.

Paddle steamer on the Murray River

Major festivals

January/ February	Cobram Peaches and Cream Festival (bi-annual)
March	Ballarat Begonia Festival Melbourne Moomba Festival
Easter	Beechworth Golden Horseshoes Easter Festival Bendigo Easter Fair Stawell Gift (Easter Monday)
April/May	Bright's Autumn Festival
June	Echuca Steam Rally
September/ October	Halls Gap Wildflower Exhibition Melbourne Writers' Festival
October	Benalla Rose Festival Dandenong Tulip Festival Euroa Wool Week Hamilton Heritage Festival Mildura Bottlebrush Festival
November	Mansfield Mountain Country Festival Melbourne Cup Melbourne Lygon Street Festa Melbourne Oktoberfest

Sister cities

Altona	Anjo (Japan)
Bendigo	Los Altos (USA)
Box Hill	Matsudo (Japan)
Frankston	Suson (Japan)
Melbourne	Boston (USA), Florence (Italy), Osaka (Japan), Thessalonika (Greece), Tianjin (China)
Portland	Uchiura-cho (Japan)
Shepparton	Esashi (Japan), Florina (Greece), Resen (Yugoslavia)
Swan Hill	Grand Junction (USA), Yamagata (Japan)
Warrnambool	Miura (Japan), Palmerston (New Zealand)
Yarrawonga	Katsuyama-mura (Japan)

DID YOU KNOW?

In 1854 a large meteorite weighing more than 5 tonnes
was found at Cranbourne, Victoria.

Queensland

Location

Queensland lies on the north-east of the continent, bordering the Pacific Ocean to the east, and Torres Strait to the north.

Area

Second-largest state in Australia; 1 727 200 square kilometres.

Landform

The north coast is sheltered by islands and the Great Barrier Reef system. Behind the coastal slopes of the Great Dividing Range and river flats, are rolling plains. Then the land becomes semi-arid desert.

Population

3 196 900, mostly in four coastal areas.

Climate

The climate is mostly tropical, with two main seasons – wet and dry. Queensland is known as 'The Sunshine State' because of pleasantly warm winters and long hours of sunshine.

State capital

Brisbane, situated on the Brisbane River on the east coast. It has an area of 3080 square kilometres, and a population of 1 420 062. Average daily hours of sunshine, 7.5.

Largest cities

Brisbane (1 420 062)
Gold Coast (141 662)
Townsville (87 584)
Cairns (92 830)
Rockhampton (65 868)
Mackay (55 772)
Mt Isa (24 251)

Queensland animal emblem: koala

Queensland floral emblem: Cooktown orchid

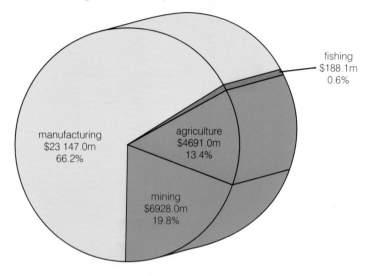

Queensland, gross value of production

fishing
$188.1m
0.6%

manufacturing
$23 147.0m
66.2%

agriculture
$4691.0m
13.4%

mining
$6928.0m
19.8%

Chief products

Agriculture:

Barley, cattle, cotton, fruit, maize, peanuts, pigs, sheep, sugar, tobacco, wheat.

Manufacturing:

Aerated waters, basic metal products, brick making, dairy products, electricity generation, meat products, ready mixed concrete, timber and log processing.

Mining:

Bauxite, coal, copper, gold, lead, mineral sands, nickel, salt, tin, uranium, zinc.

Main attractions

The Great Barrier Reef (a complex organic system and one of the greatest biological wonders of the world). Gold Coast, Sunshine Coast, Cape York Peninsula, Indianapolis car race, surfing beaches, fishing, palm-fringed coastline, tropical islands, prospecting, national parks, tropical rainforests.

DID YOU KNOW?
The Great Barrier Reef is the longest coral reef in the world, extending over 2012.5 kilometres.

Flag

The flag of Queensland is based on the Blue Ensign, with the state badge superimposed on the right-hand side. It has a blue Maltese Cross with the Imperial Crown in the centre. This badge was proclaimed in 1876.

Queensland flag

Coat of arms

The present coat of arms was granted by Queen Elizabeth II in 1977. Within the shield is a bull's head and a ram's head, in profile, representing the pastoral industry. There is also a mound of quartz emerging from a golden pyramid, in front of which is a spade and pick representing the mining industry. In the other quarter is a sheaf of wheat representing the agricultural industry. The shield is supported by a red deer and a brolga. The crest comprises the Maltese Cross super-imposed by the Imperial Crown. These are held between two stalks of sugar cane. At the base is the motto, *Audax at fidelis* (Bold, aye, but faithful too.)

Queensland coat of arms

Elliott Falls: Cape York

DID YOU KNOW?
Tully in Queensland is the wettest town in Australia with an average annual rainfall of 355.6 centimetres.

Major festivals

January	Clermont Beef 'n' Beer Festival
May	Dimbulah Tobacco Festival
June	Brisbane Festival of Creative Arts
July	Thursday Island Coming of the Light Festival
September	Mackay Sugartime Festival
	Maryborough Spring Festival
	Stradbroke Island Wildflower Festival
	Toowoomba Carnival of Flowers
October	Bundaberg Harvest Festival
	Cairns Fun in the Sun Festival
	Coolangatta Tropicarnival
	Gympie Gold Rush Festival
	Ipswich Country Music Festival
	Rockhampton Rocktoberfest
	Warana Festival
November	Yeppoon Pineapple Festival
December	Beaudesert Lions' Christmas Carnival

Sister cities

Brisbane	Brisbane, California (USA), Kobe (Japan), Nice (France)
Cairns	Hiwasa-cho (Japan), Lae (Papua New Guinea), Scottsdale (USA), Sidney (Canada)
Rockhampton	Ibusuki (Japan)

Boom netting, Great Barrier Reef, Qld.

South Australia

Location
South Australia occupies a central position on the southern coastline. Seaward is the Great Australian Bight.

Area
It is the third-largest state, and covers one-eighth of the total area of Australia. It is 984 000 square kilometres in area, with a coastline of 3700 kilometres.

Landform
Undulating hills, grasslands and valleys. Semi-arid to arid deserts to the north.

Population
Sparsely populated, with 1 496 800 people, mainly concentrated in the south-east corner of the state.

Climate
Mostly a mediterranean climate, warm to hot in summer and cool in winter. It is the driest state, with four-fifths of its total area receiving less than 254 millimetres of rainfall a year.

State capital
Adelaide, situated on the Torrens River in St Vincent Gulf, is sheltered by the Mount Lofty Range. The population is 1 070 240, and its area is 1870 square kilometres. Average daily hours of sunshine, 6.9.

Largest cities and towns
Adelaide (1 070 240)
Elizabeth (28 578)
Whyalla (25 416)
Mt Gambier (22 439)
Port Augusta (14 747)
Port Pirie (14 817)

South Australian animal emblem: hairy-nosed wombat

South Australian floral emblem: Sturt's desert pea

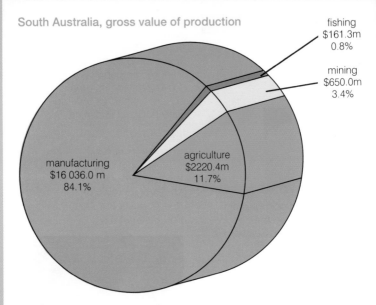

South Australia, gross value of production

fishing
$161.3m
0.8%

mining
$650.0m
3.4%

manufacturing
$16 036.0 m
84.1%

agriculture
$2220.4m
11.7%

Chief products

Agriculture:

Almonds, barley, beef, dairy products, fruits, vegetables, wheat, wine, wool.

Manufacturing:

Carriages and wagons, chemicals, cotton, electrical goods, iron and steel, machinery, motor cars, pipes.

Mining:

Barytes, coal, copper, dolomite, gypsum, iron ore, natural gas, opals, salt, talc.

Main attractions

Vineyards in Barossa Valley, Flinders Ranges, opal fields, Blue Lake–Mt Gambier, Kangaroo Island, Moonta and Burra Burra copper mine sites, The Barrages at Goolwa, Victor Harbor, Grand Prix motor car race, Nullarbor Plain, whale watching.

DID YOU KNOW?

The Murray River flows with its own current through Lake Alexandrina, South Australia, on its course to its mouth at the Southern Ocean.

Flag

The flag of South Australia is based on the Blue Ensign and has the badge of the state superimposed on the right-hand side. It consists of a piping shrike with wings outstretched, on a yellow background. This was adopted in 1904.

South Australian flag

Coat of arms

The present coat of arms was conferred by Queen Elizabeth II in 1984. It incorporates a shield with a piping shrike displayed standing on the branch of a gum tree. The shield is supported on a grassy mound from which two vines grow, entwining the stakes of the shield; on either side, stalks of wheat and barley appear; lying on the mound are two cog wheels and a miner's pick. All these represent aspects of industry in South Australia. Above the shield is a crest of four sprigs of Sturt's desert pe and at the base is a scroll with the words 'South Australia'.

South Australian coat of arms

Flinders Ranges, South Australia

DID YOU KNOW?

The Great Artesian Basin is the largest in the world, with an area of 1 716 200 square kilometres. It stretches from south-west Queensland and north-west New South Wales into the Northern Territory and South Australia. Artesian water occurs over 60 per cent of the continent.

Major festivals

January	Hahndorf German Shooting Festival
	Tanunda Oom-pah Festival
February	Mt Gambier Italian Festival
	Adelaide Festival of Arts (in even-numbered years)
March	Adelaide Glendi Festival
	Tanunda Essenfest
April	Barossa Valley Vintage Festival
	(in odd-numbered years)
Easter	Clare Valley Wine Festival (in even-numbered years)
	Kapunda Celtic Music Festival
May	Adelaide Creative Arts Festival for the Young
	Melrose Mountain Fun Festival
	Moonta Cornish Festival
July	Willunga Almond Blossom Festival
October	Coober Pedy Outback Festival
	Grand Prix
	Murray Bridge Sagra Festival
	Victor Harbor Heritage Festival
November	Adelaide Christmas Pageant
December	Adelaide Christmas Earth Fair

Sister cities

Adelaide	Austin (Texas, USA), Christchurch (New Zealand), Georgetown (Penang, Malaysia), Himeji (Japan)

Isolated Cape Adieu, S.A.

Western Australia

Location

Western Australia occupies the western third of the continent, bordered by the Indian Ocean in the west and the Southern Ocean in the south.

Area

It is the largest state in Australia, and is 2 525 500 square kilometres in area.

Landform

The state extends from vast arable southern areas to interior semi-desert to desert landscapes and the mineral-rich Great Sandy and Gibson deserts to the north. The mountain ranges are Stirling, Kimberley and Hamersley ranges.

Population

1 701 900 (concentrated on south-west coast), representing only 9 per cent of the total Australian population. The large desert and semi-desert areas are unsuitable for cultivation or close settlement.

Climate

Western Australia has three broad climate divisions. The northern part is dry tropical, receiving summer rainfall. The south-west corner has a mediterranean climate, with long hot summers and wet winters. The remainder is mostly arid land or desert climates.

State capital

Perth, situated on the Swan River on the seaboard of the Indian Ocean. It is 5306 square kilometres in area and has a population of 1 222 139. Average daily hours of sunshine, 7.9.

Largest cities

Perth (1 222 139)
Bunbury (27 833)
Fremantle (23 845)
Geraldton (21 335)
Albany (15 629)
Port Hedland (11 980)
Boulder-Kalgoorlie (27 142)

Western Australian animal emblem: numbat

Western Australian floral emblem: red and green kangaroo paw

Western Australia, gross value of production

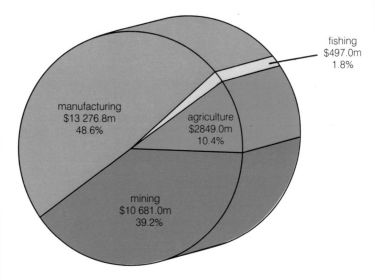

fishing
$497.0m
1.8%

manufacturing
$13 276.8m
48.6%

agriculture
$2849.0m
10.4%

mining
$10 681.0m
39.2%

Chief products

Agriculture:

Cattle, fruit, hardwoods, rock
lobsters, wheat, wool.

Manufacturing:

Building materials, food and
drink, metal, machinery, other
mineral products, petroleum
products, wood products.

Mining:

Bauxite, gold, ilmenite, iron ore,
nickel, oil, salt.

Main attractions

Margaret River, Kalgoorlie
goldfields, Esperance, Mt Tom
Price, Mt Newman, Ord River,
Kimberley and Hamersley
ranges, Broome, surfing, fishing,
sailing, wildflowers, Monkey Mia
(dolphins), Pinnacle Desert,
Bungle Bungles.

DID YOU KNOW?
**Western Australia is three and a half times bigger than
Texas.**

Flag

The flag of Western Australia is based on the Blue Ensign, with the badge of the state superimposed on the right-hand side. It has a black swan within a yellow circle. This badge was granted in 1875.

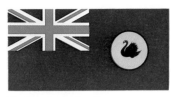

Western Australian flag

Coat of arms

The present coat of arms was granted by Queen Elizabeth II in 1969. It incorporates a shield depicting a black swan, the bird emblem of the state. It is supported by two kangaroos, each holding a boomerang. The crest features an Imperial Crown surrounded by branches of kangaroo-paw, the state's floral emblem.

Western Australian coat of arms

Bungle Bungles, W.A.

Major festivals

January	Mandurah Kanyana Festival
	Perth Hyde Park Festival
February	Festival of Perth
March	Albany Mardi Gras
	Perth Swan Valley Wine Festival
	Swan River Festival
August	Broome Shinju Matsuri Festival
	Carnarvon Tropical Festival
	Derby Boat Festival
	Exmouth Gala Festival
	Geraldton Sunshine Festival
	Karratha–Dampier Fenacl Festival
	Kununurra–Ord Festival
	Newman Fortescue Festival
	Paraburdoo Paragala Festival
	Tom Price Nameless Festival
	Wyndham Top of the West Festival
September	Perth Italian Spring Festival
October	Perth Oktoberfest
November	Fremantle Week
December	Perth – Australian Latvian Arts Festival

Sister cities

Albany	Albany (USA), Fielding (New Zealand), Kessennuma (Japan)
Broome	Taichi-Cho (Japan)
Fremantle	Capo D'Orlando (Sicily), Molfetta (Italy), Wellesley (Malaysia), Yokosuka (Japan)
Perth	Houston (Texas, USA), Island of Megisti (Greece), Kagoshima (Japan), Rhodes (Greece), San Diego (USA)

DID YOU KNOW?
Wolf Creek, Western Australia, has the largest meteorite crater in Australia, 853.44 metres in diameter and 61 metres deep.

Tasmania

State capital

Hobart, the second oldest city in Australia, is situated on the Derwent River on the Tasman Peninsula. It has an area of 936 square kilometres, and a population of 193 249. Average daily hours of sunshine, 5.8.

Largest cities

Hobart (193 249)
Launceston (97 463)
Burnie and Devonport (79 031)

Tasmanian floral emblem: southern blue gum

Location

The island state lies 240 kilometres off the south-eastern corner of the Australian continent, and is separated from the mainland by Bass Strait.

Area

It is the smallest state in Australia, with an area of 67 800 square kilometres.

Landform

Mountainous, with lakes, cascades and steeply falling rivers.

Population

472 405, mostly on the north and east coasts.

Climate

Generally temperate, but the temperature often falls below 0°C. There is high rainfall, very cold winters and cool summers.

Cradle Mountain, Lake St Clair National Park

Tasmania, gross value of production

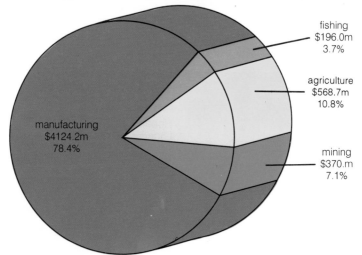

fishing
$196.0m
3.7%

agriculture
$568.7m
10.8%

manufacturing
$4124.2m
78.4%

mining
$370.m
7.1%

Chief products

Agriculture:
Beef, canned fruit, dairy products, hops, lavender, mutton, potatoes, timber, wool.

Fishing:
Barracouta, crayfish, salmon, scallops.

Manufacturing:
Alginate, aluminium, frozen food, paper, pulp.

Mining:
Coal, copper, gold, iron, lead, tin, zinc.

Main attractions

Snowfields, unspoiled mountain landscapes, historical places, Launceston and Hobart casinos, national parks, fishing, Franklin River, magnificent seascapes, thermal pools, Tasmanian devil, Gordon River. Tasmania is known as 'The Holiday Isle', and tourism is an important industry.

DID YOU KNOW?
The tranquil Lake St Clair, Tasmania, is over 200 metres deep, and occupies a basin gouged out by two glaciers more than 20 000 years ago.

Flag

The flag of Tasmania is based on the Blue Ensign, with the badge of the state superimposed on the right-hand side. It consists of a red lion in a white circle. This badge was chosen in 1876.

Tasmanian flag

Coat of arms

The present coat of arms was granted by King George V in 1917. It incorporates a shield on which is depicted a ram, a sheaf of wheat and apples, representing the pastoral and agricultural industries. Also included is a thunderbolt, which represents the hydro-electric schemes. The crest consists of a red lion standing with one paw resting on a spade and pickaxe which represents the mining industry. The shield is supported by two Tasmanian tigers. These are standing on ornamental supports above the motto, *Ubertas et fidelitas* (Productiveness and faithfulness).

Tasmanian coat of arms

Colourful Salamanca Place, Hobart

DID YOU KNOW?

To prevent convicts escaping from the penal settlement at Port Arthur, a pack of ferocious dogs guarded the Eaglehawk Neck isthmus leading to Forestier Peninsula, which was the convicts' only avenue of escape by land.

Major festivals

January	Devonport to Melbourne Yacht Race
	Huon Open Market
	Sydney to Hobart Yacht Race (arrival)
March	Devonport Mersey Valley Festival of Music
	Launceston Batman Festival
April	State-wide National Heritage Week
September	Stanley Circular Head Arts Festival
October	Devonport Rhododendron Festival
November	Deloraine Tasmania Cottage Industry Exhibition and Trade Fair
December	Hobart Salamanca Arts Festival

Sister cities

Hobart	Invercargill (New Zealand), Yaizu (Japan)
Launceston	Ikeda (Japan), Launceston (UK), Livingston (Zambia), Seremban (Malaysia)

Port Arthur, with ruins of prison cells four storeys high in background

Northern Territory

Location

The Northern Territory occupies a huge area of the continent's north and centre. It is bordered by the Timor Sea to the north, Queensland to the east, Western Australia to the west and South Australia to the south. Usually known as 'Outback Australia'.

Area

The Northern Territory comprises one-sixth of Australia's land mass, and is 1 346 200 square kilometres in area.

Landform

Mostly desert and tablelands.

Population

171 100. Few people live in the huge dry areas, and almost half the population are residents of Darwin. More than one-quarter of the people are Aboriginals.

Climate

The Northern Territory lies in the torrid zone. There are two broad climatic divisions: the northern part, known as 'The Top End', receives heavy rainfall for three to five months of the year, and the southern area, known as 'The Centre', has a low rainfall and no permanent rivers.

Administrative centre

Darwin is situated in Beagle Gulf on the Timor Sea, and is 1660 square kilometres in area. It has a population of 77 366. Average daily hours of sunshine, 8.5.

Chief towns

Darwin (77 366)
Alice Springs (24 678)
Katherine (8 492)
Nhulunbuy (3 923)
Tennant Creek (3 140)

Northern Territory animal emblem: red kangaroo

Northern Territory floral emblem: Sturt's desert rose

Northern Territory, gross value of production

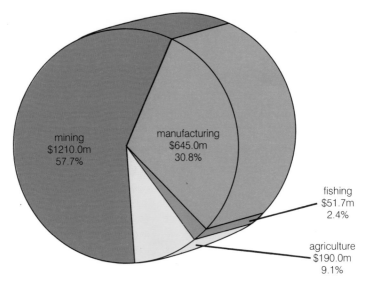

mining
$1210.0m
57.7%

manufacturing
$645.0m
30.8%

fishing
$51.7m
2.4%

agriculture
$190.0m
9.1%

Chief products

Agriculture:

Beef cattle, citrus fruits, lucerne, peanuts, pineapples, timber, tomatoes.

Fishing:

Fish and prawns.

Mining:

Aluminium, bauxite, copper, gold, iron, manganese, tin, uranium.

Main attractions

Mt Olga National Park, Kings Canyon, Standley Chasm, The Ghan (the train from Adelaide to Alice Springs), Katherine Gorge, Bathurst and Melville Islands, Kakadu National Park, Uluru National Park (Ayers Rock), Devil's Marbles, Mataranka thermal pools, Litchfield National Park.

DID YOU KNOW?

Uluru (Ayers Rock) is a monolith of greyish-red arkose, standing 159.53 metres above sea level. It is 8.85 kilometres in circumference, and is 347.3 metres above the plain.

Flag

The flag of the Northern Territory is very different from the other states' flags. Traditional Territory colours are used: black, white, and red ochre. The stars on the black panel represent the Southern Cross. On the red ochre panel appears Sturt's desert rose. This flag was proclaimed in 1978.

Northern Territory flag

Coat of arms

The present coat of arms was granted by Queen Elizabeth II in 1978. It incorporates a shield depicting an Arnhem Land rock painting of an Aboriginal woman. On either side there are stylised journey or path markings of the Aboriginals. The shield is supported by two red kangaroos. In the fore-paw of one is a true heart cockle and in the fore-paw of the other is a spider conch. This all rests on a grassy mound from which grow Sturt's desert roses. The crest consists of a wedge-tailed eagle with wings splayed and its talons grasping an Aboriginal ritual stone or *Tjurunga*.

Northern Territory coat of arms

Katherine Gorge

DID YOU KNOW?

Lake Eyre, 16 metres below sea level, is the lowest elevation in Australia. It is the driest area, receiving only 8–12 mm annual rainfall. Alice Springs is 609.6 metres above sea level.

Major festivals

January	Katherine Australia Day Bush Picnic
May	Alice Springs Bangtail Muster
	Alice Springs Lions' Camel Cup Carnival
	Tennant Creek Lions' Gold Rush Festival
June	Katherine Carnival
July	Darwin Beer Can Regatta
August	Alice Springs Henley-on-Todd Regatta
	Mataranka Bushman's Carnival
	Tennant Creek Folk Festival

Sister cities

Darwin	Ambon (Indonesia), Anchorage (Alaska, USA), Kalymnos (Greece), Xiamen (China)

Devil's Marbles

DID YOU KNOW?

Uluru (Ayers Rock) is almost at the centre of the Australian continent. As the crow flies, it is 2300 kilometres from Brisbane, 2100 kilometres from Sydney, 1900 kilometres from Melbourne, 1300 kilometres from Adelaide, 1600 kilometres from Perth, and 1450 kilometres from Darwin.

People and performances

Prime ministers

Sir Edmund Barton
(1 Jan 1901 – 24 Sept 1903)

Alfred Deakin
(24 Sept 1903 – 27 Apr 1904)

John Christian Watson
(27 Apr 1904 – 18 Aug 1904)

George Reid
(18 Aug 1904 – 5 July 1905)

Alfred Deakin
(5 July 1905 – 13 Nov 1908)

Andrew Fisher
(13 Nov 1908 – 2 June 1909)

Alfred Deakin
(2 June 1909 – 29 Apr 1910)

Andrew Fisher
(29 Apr 1910 – 24 June 1913)

Sir Joseph Cook
(24 June 1913 – 17 Sept 1914)

Andrew Fisher
(17 Sept 1914 – 27 Oct 1915)

William Morris Hughes
(27 Oct 1915 – 9 Feb 1922)

Stanley Melbourne Bruce
(9 Feb 1922 – 22 Oct 1929)

James Henry Scullin
(22 Oct 1929 – 6 Jan 1932)

Joseph Aloysius Lyons
(6 Jan 1932 – 7 Apr 1939)

Sir Earle Page
(7 Apr 1939 – 26 Apr 1939)

Sir Robert Gordon Menzies
(26 Apr 1939 – 29 Aug 1941)

Sir Arthur W Fadden
(29 Aug 1941 – 7 Oct 1941)

John Curtin
(7 Oct 1941 – 5 July 1945)

Francis Michael Forde
(6 July 1945 – 13 July 1945)

Joseph Benedict Chifley
(13 July 1945 – 19 Dec 1949)

Sir Robert Gordon Menzies
(19 Dec 1949 – 26 Jan 1966)

Harold Edward Holt
(26 Jan 1966 – 19 Dec 1967)

Sir John McEwen
(19 Dec 1967 – 10 Jan 1968)

Sir John Grey Gorton
(10 Jan 1968 – 10 Mar 1971)

Sir William McMahon
(10 Mar 1971 – 8 Dec 1972)

Edward Gough Whitlam
(8 Dec 1972 – 11 Nov 1975)

John Malcolm Fraser
(11 Nov 1975 – 5 Mar 1983)
(caretaker prime minister from
11 Nov – 13 Dec 1975)

Robert James Lee Hawke
(5 Mar 1983 – 19 December
1991)

Paul John Keating
(19 December 1991 –)

Architects

*Australian architecture reflected
many styles and influences,
particularly British and
American. Lately, however, a
warmer, more textured style has
evolved, which is not only more
suitable to our environment but
more aesthetically pleasing and
thoroughly Australian.*

Walter Burley Griffin
1876–1937

An American, whose brilliant
plan won first prize in a worldwide competition for the design
of Australia's national capital,
Canberra, in 1913. Later he and
his wife designed the highly
innovative Capitol Theatre,
Melbourne, and in 1924 they
designed the harbourside
suburb of Castlecrag, Sydney.

Edmund Blacket 1817–83

One of our great colonial
architects of churches and
public buildings. His most
famous building is the Great Hall
of the University of Sydney, built
in 1857, considered to be the
finest example of Gothic Revival
style in Australia.

James Blackburn 1803–54

He was one of Tasmania's
advanced architects, and was

responsible for many beautiful Gothic style buildings of the 1930s. He designed the Yan Yean Reservoir in Victoria in 1849, and was considered to be one of the greatest engineers of that time.

Robin Boyd 1919–71

He was a writer as well as an architect. An influential critic of Australian aesthetics, he wrote *The Australian Ugliness* in 1960.

Francis Greenway 1777–1837

In 1816 Greenway, a convict, became the colony's official architect, under the guidance of Governor Macquarie. In his time he designed more than 40 buildings including Macquarie Light House at South Head, for which he obtained his pardon.

Sir Roy Grounds 1905–81

Exponent of the new 'international' style of architecture of the 1950s. He is best known for his Academy of Sciences building in Canberra and the Victorian Arts Centre in Melbourne.

Harry Seidler 1923–

Contemporary Australian architect. Designed Australia Square Tower and the MLC Building in Sydney, the Hong Kong Club, and the Australian embassy in Paris.

Joern Utzon 1918–

The Danish architect and designer of the Sydney Opera House. He broke new ground in design and use of building materials. Construction began in 1959, and the Opera House was officially opened in 1973 by Queen Elizabeth II. Three Australian architects, David Littlemore, Lionel Todd and Peter Hall, took over from Utzon in 1966.

Victorian Arts Centre

Aviators

Many contributed to the race to be airborne, and when it was possible many joined another race – the race to conquer Australia's distance and isolation from the rest of the world.

Sir Reginald Ansett 1909–81

A businessman and outspoken champion of private enterprise. His companies were involved in aviation, transport, tourism and television.

Maude (Lores) Bonney 1897–1994

In the 'golden age' of aviation between 1934 and 1937 she was the first woman to circumnavigate Australia by air, the first woman to fly from Australia to England, and the first person to link Australia with South Africa by air.

John Duigan 1882–1951

In 1910 he constructed the first Australian-built aeroplane to fly.

Sir Hudson Fysh 1895–1974

Together with P. J. McGinness he founded the airline Queensland and Northern Territory Air Services (QANTAS) in 1920.

Lawrence Hargrave 1850–1915 and George A. Taylor 1872–1928

In the 1890s these two men experimented with box kites. Taylor in 1909 achieved a flight of 100 metres at Narrabeen Heads, New South Wales.

Harry George Hawker 1889–1921

Hawker became internationally famous in 1913 for the most successful attempt to circumnavigate the British Isles in 72 hours.

Bert Hinkler 1892–1933

Known as 'The Lone Eagle', in 1928 he flew the longest solo flight from London to Darwin, in a record 16 days.

Amy Johnson 1903–41

She was the first woman to fly from England to Australia. Her 1930 epic solo flight, in a DH Moth, took 19 days.

Sir Charles Kingsford Smith 1897–1935

Pioneer aviator. In 1928, flying the famous monoplane *Southern Cross*, he, Charles Ulm (1897–1934) and two Americans were the first men to fly across the Pacific from America to Australia. This venture included one of the longest non-stop flights ever attempted between Honolulu and Suva (35 hours). Total flying time, 83 hours 38 minutes.

Keith Smith 1890–1955 and Ross Smith 1892–1922

They pioneered the London to Sydney air route in 1919, taking 27 days 27 minutes – total flying time for the 18 500 kilometres was 135 hours 50 minutes.

DID YOU KNOW?

John Pascoe Fawkner, an early settler in Port Phillip, built the first hotel in Victoria in 1835. It offered 'mental and bodily refreshments unrivalled in this quarter of the globe'.

People in business

Corporate failures, Royal Commissions, beleaguered businessmen and high interest rates have been the scenario since the turbulent collapse of the stock market in October 1987. Shareholders have suffered, some entrepreneurs face possible court action, and some have faded from the scene. Even so, Australia has been fortunate in having many well-known and respected businessmen and women. Here are but a few.

Sir Peter Abeles 1924–

His astute management from 1967 to 1992 enabled TNT to expand worldwide.

Herbert Cole (Nugget) Coombs 1906–

An economist, he was Governor of the Reserve Bank until 1968, and advised prime ministers as well as governments in the post-war years. In 1954 he was a key figure in establishing the Elizabethan Trust. He was chairman of the Australian National University, the Aboriginal Council, and the Council for the Arts.

Sir Warwick Fairfax 1901–87

Former chairman of John Fairfax Ltd, with interests in newspapers, magazines, television and radio. His influence on the editorial policy of the *Sydney Morning Herald* had a great impact on Australian society.

Lang Hancock 1909–92

Discovered massive iron-ore deposits in the Pilbara region, WA, where he began the Australian iron-ore mining industry, 1952–62.

Robert Holmes à Court 1937–90

Renowned for his astute business acumen in assessing takeover opportunities. Former Chairman of Bell Group of companies (taken over by Bond Corporation). His abortive attempts to take over BHP forced it to re-assess its vulnerability. His widow Janet, continues to run the family company, Heytesbury Holdings.

Sir Sidney Kidman 1857–1935

He left home at 13 with a one-eyed horse called Cyclops, and five shillings (50 cents) in his pocket. He became one of the largest landowners in Australian history. Some estimates are that he owned nearly 495 000 square kilometres of land in the interior.

John Macarthur 1767–1834

A pioneer pastoralist entrepreneur and exporter of wool to England in the early days of the colony. He and his wife Elizabeth made a great contribution to the wool industry by successfully breeding fine wool merino sheep.

Rupert Murdoch 1931–

An international newspaper magnate. He became an American citizen in 1985. He owns newspaper and television stations, as well as interests in energy resources, around the world.

Kerry Packer 1937–

He is Chairman of Consolidated Press Holdings Ltd and Publishing and Broadcasting Ltd. He remains Australia's richest man with vast commercial and rural holdings.

Sir Leslie Thiess 1909–92

A country boy cum earth-mover who fathered Queensland's huge coal export industry.

Cartoonists

There has always been a recognisable Australian style of cartoon which is an ever-popular part of the printed page.

J. C. Banks 1880–1952

Created the much-loved character, Ginger Meggs. He worked for the *Sydney Sun*, and drew this character for 21 years.

Frank Benier c. 1923–

A highly talented, traditional cartoonist whose humour has spanned several decades. His cartoons of Henry Bolte, the premier of Victoria 1955–72, are legendary.

Stan Cross 1888–1977

An American, he created the long-running comic strip, 'The Potts', in 1919. He became the highest-paid black-and-white artist ever when he drew for *Smith's Weekly* in 1933. He is responsible for what is thought to be Australia's funniest cartoon.

"For gorsake, stop laughing: this is serious!"

DID YOU KNOW?

In 1991 Kerry Packer was listed as Australia's only billionaire, the wealthiest person in Australia. Janet Holmes à Court heads the millionaires, followed by the Smorgon family, then the Murdoch family, the Liebermans, David Hains, and the Myer family, all with wealth exceeding $600 million.

Eric Jolliffe c. 1907–

A post-war comic artist whose series *Witchetty's Tribe*, with its contrasts of Aboriginal and Western values, has been popular for decades.

Lennie Lower 1903–47

He was a prolific newspaper columnist of the 1930s and 40s, and one of Australia's greatest humorists. *Here's Another*, published in 1932, was a collection of humorous sketches.

Emile Mercier c. 1909–81

A vigorous comic artist of the 1950s and 60s, whose zany humour is forever remembered for its incidental details, particularly about gravy cans.

Syd Nicholls 1897–1977

His cartoon character, Fatty Finn, was second only to Ginger Meggs in popularity and longevity.

Bruce Petty 1929–

He is widely regarded as one of the world's finest political cartoonists and as the most committed and intellectual of contemporary Australian cartoonists. His cartoons began to appear in the *Australian* in 1965.

Ron Tandberg 1943–

A political cartoonist with major newspapers. His simple line drawings make terse comments on current news stories.

Engineers and inventors

Most original ideas which succeed are usually developed from a great need to make life easier. The following are a few noteworthy Australians who have proved the old adage that 'necessity is the mother of invention'.

Sir John (Jack) Brabham 1926–

Racing-car driver. He went from winning the 1948 Australian Speedway Championship in a home-made car, to winning three World Grand Prix.

John Bradfield 1867–1943

He designed the Sydney Harbour Bridge, which was begun in 1923 and completed in 1932, at a cost of £9 577 507 (equivalent to about $200 million in current terms).

William James Farrer 1845–1906

An agricultural scientist, whose pioneering development in the late 1800s of early strains of wheat (particularly the 'Federation' variety) laid the foundation for the Australian wheat industry.

Sir Edward Hallstrom 1886–1970

A philanthropist, zoologist and inventor who helped develop refrigeration in Australia. His 1940s plan was for every

Australian household to have a Silent Knight refrigerator.

Sir William Hudson 1896–1978

Commissioner in charge of the Snowy Mountains Hydro-Electric Scheme which diverts the waters of the Snowy and Eucumbene Rivers through two tunnel systems, westwards under the Great Dividing Range, to feed two inland rivers, the Murray and Murrumbidgee. The scheme provides water for irrigation and also produces electricity from seven power stations for NSW, Victoria, and the ACT.

Walter Hume 1873–1943

An inventor who disregarded conventional theories. His centrifugal painting machine led to his inventing the Hume-spun cement pipes. It was an innovation of international significance; factories all over the world now make pipes by the Hume-spun method.

George Julius 1873–1946

An engineer, whose totalizator machine of 1913 and the fully automatic totalizator of 1932 sold worldwide.

Essington Lewis 1881–1961

Industrialist responsible for the Broken Hill Proprietary Company shifting its emphasis from mining to steel. BHP is Australia's largest company.

Ben Lexcen 1936–88

One of Australia's great marine engineers. He designed the famed *Australia II*, a 12-metre yacht with an incredible 'winged keel', which in 1983 won for Australia the America's Cup. It was the first time in 132 years that America had lost the cup.

Hugh Victor McKay 1865–1926

His 1884 invention, the stripper harvester, not only stripped but also thrashed and cleaned grain. He established many factories for producing the McKay Harvester, and revolutionised the wheat industry.

Evelyn Ernest Owen 1915–49

In the 1930s he invented the revolutionary Owen sub-machine-gun.

Mervyn Victor Richardson 1894–1972

He invented the Victa rotary mower in 1952–53, which revolutionised mowing for future generations of handymen and gardeners.

John Ridley 1806–87

A pioneer miller and inventor, who in 1842 developed the Ridley Stripper, a machine which proved so popular that, by 1855, 30 000 had been sold.

Ralph Sarich 1938–

An inventor with many innovative projects to his credit. These are in the field of fuel injection and irrigation systems. He is more widely known for his research in the development of the orbital combustion process engine and associated technologies.

Headlie Taylor 1883–1957

He was the most prolific inventor of farm machinery in Australia, the most famous of which was his Sunshine Header Harvester in 1915. By 1965 the Sunshine Harvester had been redesigned to be self-propelled.

John Paul Wild 1923–

A radio astronomer, whose interests and subsequent experiments on the effects of the sun's rays on the earth's surface led to the development of Interscan, a new type of radio landing-gear for aircraft. He was chairman of the CSIRO from 1978 to 1991.

Scientists and medicos

There has been progress of great significance in the field of science and medicine and here are a few who have made outstanding contributions.

Sir Macfarlane Burnet 1899–1985

Researcher and biologist. Winner of Nobel Prize for medicine, noted for his research into control of disease, particularly poliomyelitis.

Dr Victor Chang c. 1940–91

He re-established the heart transplant program at St Vincent's Hospital, Sydney, in 1984 after a lapse of ten years. Since then 300 transplants have been performed with an 85% success rate. In 1986 he and his team performed the first heart/lung transplant in Australia, and in 1990 the first lung transplant. He was murdered in 1991, a tragedy for Australia.

Professor Graeme Clarke 1935–

A researcher and professor of Otolaryngology at Melbourne University. In the late 1970s he was responsible for the development of the bionic ear, a cochlea implant designed to provide electrical stimulation to the inner ear to overcome profound deafness.

Sir Ian Clunies-Ross 1899–1959

A scientist and administrator and the first director of the CSIRO.

Sir Edward 'Weary' Dunlop 1907–93

In World War II he was appointed commander of the Allied General Hospital in Java, in 1942. He became a Japanese prisoner of war. Through the testimony of hundreds of returning prisoners it was clear that he became their inspiration in the fight for physical and spiritual survival against the horrors of the

Burma–Thailand railway prison camps.

Sir John Eccles 1903–

A scientist who contributed greatly to the knowledge of the way nerves interact with the spinal cord.

Lord (Howard) Florey 1898–1968

A scientist and Nobel Prize winner. He carried out the crucial experiments in the 1930s that demonstrated the great therapeutic value of penicillin.

Reverend John Flynn 1880–1951

The founder of the world-acclaimed Flying Doctor Service. In 1928, with the help of Alf Fraegar's pedal radio, he began a medical service for the people of the outback. (Now the Royal Flying Doctor Service of Australia.)

Professor Fred Hollows 1929–1993

Chairman of ophthalmology at the University of New South Wales, he was also co-founder of the Aboriginal Medical Service. He was director of the National Trachoma and Eye Health program, and worked extensively in Eritrea and Nepal establishing eye health programs.

Sister Kenny 1886–1952

A world-recognised nurse/innovator. In the 1930s, with the royalties from a revolutionary stretcher she invented, she opened one of many world-wide clinics, where she achieved remarkable success in the treatment of the life-threatening disease, poliomyelitis.

Dr Priscilla Kincaid-Smith 1926–

The director of nephrology at Royal Melbourne Hospital. In 1968 she was the first person to link long-term dosing with analgesics to renal disease.

Sir Marcus Oliphant 1901–

Nuclear physicist and first president of Australian Academy of Science. Assistant director of research at the Cavendish Laboratory in Cambridge in 1935. He is a strong opponent to nuclear weapons.

William Redfern c. 1774–1833

A pardoned convict, this pioneer surgeon was assistant surgeon at Norfolk Island prison hospital before he was placed in charge of Sydney Hospital in 1816. In 1814 he assisted in what was said to be the first public health report in Australian history, which exposed the horrifying conditions aboard convict ships.

Dr Harry Windsor 1915–87

He pioneered and performed the first mitral valvotomy in Australia (1950), and the first aortic valve replacement in 1963 which led to the first heart transplant in Australia in 1968.

The international acceptance of Australian literature over the past four decades has resulted in an exciting period of extraordinary diversity among Australian writers, who have made a great contribution to the way Australians perceive themselves. This modest list is just a cursory view of some past and present authors who are noted for their craftsmanship and originality.

Novelists and writers

Blanche d'Alpuget 1944–

Her thumbnail descriptions of characters and atmosphere, together with her quick wit and competence, have produced engaging novels such as *Monkeys in the Dark* (1980), *Turtle Beach* (1981) and *Winter in Jerusalem* (1986).

Thea Astley 1925–

A novelist, three-time winner of the Miles Franklin Award. Her books include *An Item from the Late News* (1982), *Beachmasters* (1985) and *It's Raining in Mango* (1987).

Murray Bail 1941–

He experimented with a new form of short-story writing in the 1970s. *Contemporary Portraits and Other Stories* (1975), *Homesickness* (1980) and *Holden's Performance* (1987) show his preoccupation with the way environment shapes identity.

Peter Carey 1943–

Considered to be one of our finest novelists. He won the prestigious Booker Prize in 1988 and the coveted Miles Franklin Award for his novel, *Oscar and Lucinda*. In 1981 he wrote the movie script for *Bliss*. Then came *Illywacker* (1985), *The Tax Inspector* (1992) and *The Unusual Life of Tristan Smith* (1994).

Professor Manning Clark 1915–91

Australia's most celebrated historian. His six-volume *History of Australia* is an invaluable reference point for gaining an understanding of the forces, struggles and events which shaped Australia.

Jon Cleary 1917–

Acclaimed novelist and script writer whose 1946 novel, *You Can't See Round Corners* launched his career which spanned from stories of inner-city poverty to film scripts for Hollywood. *The Sundowners* (1959), *The High Commissioner* (1956) and *Dark Summer* (1956) were his well-known works.

Peter Corris 1942–

A skilful and sophisticated writer of detective yarns, which are pithy and episodic. He wrote one book after another with rapid fire. *White Meat* (1981) and *The Empty Beach* (1983) are a few in the series of stories about Cliff Hardy, champion-of-the-underdog investigator.

Robert Drewe 1943–

He draws ironic parallels in his short stories which, on the surface seem simple, but are full of inner disturbances and insecurities. *A Cry in the Jungle Bar* (1979), *The Body Surfers* (1983) and *The Bay of Contented Men* (1989) confirm his skill as a storyteller.

Miles Franklin 1879–1954

She wrote the satirical novel *My Brilliant Career* about 1899, *All That Swagger* in 1936, and *My Career Goes Bung* in 1946. The Miles Franklin Award, a bequest from her estate, is awarded annually for a novel portraying some aspect of Australian life.

Kate Grenville 1950–

Lilian's Story (1985), *Dreamhouse* (1986) and *Joan Makes History* (1988) are examples of her ingeniously conceived stories, which have a strong feminist theme, containing a touch of black comedy.

Frank Hardy 1917–1994

A hard-hitting and unrelenting novelist and writer of short stories. His remarkable fact-fiction account of crime in *Power Without Glory* (1950), resulted in an unsuccessful libel suit against him. *But the Dead Are Many* (1975) is considered to be his masterpiece.

Xavier Herbert 1901–84

His novel, *Capricornia* (1938), is one of the classics of Australian literature. His later work, *Poor Fellow My Country* (1975), is considered to be his final judgement on Australian society and history.

Donald Horne 1921–

A political and social commentator, he wrote *A Lucky Country* (1967) and *The Story of the Australian People* (1972).

David Ireland 1927–

One of Australia's foremost novelists, his works include *The Unknown Industrial Prisoner* (1971), *The Glass Canoe* (1976), *Woman of the Future* (1979) and *Bloodfather* (1988).

Elizabeth Jolley 1923–

Her novels deal not so much about the characters but the implied relationships between the characters. These include *Miss Peabody's Inheritance* (1983), *The Sugar Mother* (1989), *My Father's Moon* (1989), and *Cabin Fever* (1991).

Thomas Keneally 1935–

Won the Miles Franklin Award in 1967 for the novel *Bring Larks and Heroes*. He wrote *A Dutiful Daughter* in 1972 and *The Chant of Jimmie Blacksmith* (1973). *Family Madness* (1985) and *Schindler's Ark* (1992).

Christopher Koch 1932–

One of Australia's finest writers, he pursues related themes through symbolism and imagery with care and sensitivity.

Included in his works are *The Boys in the Island* (1958), *The Year of Living Dangerously* (1978) and *Doubleman* (1985).

Morris Lurie 1938–

Writes in a variety of genres from autobiographical to children's literature but is best known for his short stories, such as *Rappaport* (1966) and *Flying Home* (1978). The novel *Two Brothers Running* (1990) shows his deft and economical use of words.

David Malouf 1934–

A poet and novelist, his works include *Bicycles* (1970), *First Things Last*, his prose narrative *An Imaginary Life* (1980), and *Antipodes* (1986) a collection of sensitive short stories.

Sally Morgan 1951–

An Aboriginal author and artist, her sensitive novels include her autobiographical *My Place* (1988) and *Wanamurraganya* (1989).

Ruth Park 1926–

A skilful storyteller, success was assured in 1947 when *Harp in the South* won critical acclaim. Her stories deal with hard times and how ordinary people struggle to survive. Other novels include *Poor Man's Orange* (1949) and *Swords and Crowns and Rings* (1977).

Henry Handel Richardson 1870–1946

This was the pen-name of Ethel Robertson. In 1917 she began work on her masterpiece trilogy *The Fortunes of Richard Mahony*, fully published in 1929, to great acclaim.

Kylie Tennant 1912–88

Her novels involve her first-hand knowledge of the fringe-dwelling element in Australian society. *Tiburon* (1935), *The Battlers* (1941), and *Tell Morning This* (1967) deal with the brutality and corruption of any large city.

Morris West 1916–

He deliberately sought experiences to enrich his writing. His novels include *Children of the Sun* (1957), *The Shoes of the Fishermen* (1963) and *Cassidy* (1986).

Patrick White 1912–90

Considered to be Australia's greatest novelist, he was the first Australian writer to be awarded the Nobel Prize for literature (1973). He wrote *The Tree of Man* (1955), *Voss* (1957), *The Vivisector* (1973), *A Fringe of Leaves* (1977), *The Twyborn Affair* (1981) and *Three Uneasy Pieces* (1987).

Tim Winton 1960–

A prolific writer, he wrote five novels in six years. *Cloudstreet* won the Miles Franklin Award in 1992 and shows his preoccupation with place.

Other novelists include: Dora Birtles, Judy Brett, Bryce Courtenay, Eleanor Dark, Helen

Garner, Germaine Greer, Rodney Hall, George Johnston, Drusilla Modjeska, Frank Moorhouse, Brenda Niall, Katharine Susannah Prichard, Steele Rudd, Christina Stead and Randolph Stow.

Playwrights

Richard Beynon 1925–

An actor and TV writer as well as playwright, he draws on his memories of working-class Melbourne. In 1957 he wrote *The Shifting Heart*, a play concerned with racial prejudice of that time, and *Epitaph for Two Faces* in 1964.

Alexander Buzo 1944–

A satirist of Australian morals and manners, he wrote the plays *Martello Towers* (1976), *Norm and Ahmed* (1967), and the novel, *The Search for Harry Allway* (1985).

Peter Kenna 1930–

An established radio actor, his plays explore the themes of corruption and absence of intimacy in modern life. *A Hard God* (1974), *Furtive Love* (1978) and *An Eager Hope* (1978) complete a trilogy of plays agonising over inadequate relationships.

Ray Lawler 1922–

Playwright and actor. His play *The Summer of the Seventeenth Doll*, challenging mateship and toughness, broke new ground in Australian theatre in 1955.

Sumner Locke Elliott 1917–91

An actor and writer for radio. There was a public storm over censorship of language when his play *Rusty Bugles* was produced in 1949. His novel, *Careful, He Might Hear You* (1963), was made into a film in 1983.

Hal Porter 1911–84

Acute awareness of the sense of time and the unique phenemona of memory and self-analysis is reflected in all that he wrote. His works include *The Watcher on the Cast-Iron Balcony* (1964) and the play *Eden House* (1969).

Alan Seymour 1927–

A theatre critic, he wrote for the stage and TV, drawing frequently from life in the 1940s. His *One Day of the Year* (1961) questioned the traditional veneration of Anzac Day. Other plays include *Swamp Creatures* (1955–56) and *A Break in the Music* (1966).

David Williamson 1942–

Internationally acclaimed playwright. His raucous, fast-moving plots are witty and recognisable, and his plays include *The Removalist* (1971), *The Club* (1978) and *Emerald City* (1986). He wrote the film scripts for *Gallipoli* (1982) and *Phar Lap* (1983).

Poets

Bruce Dawe 1930–

A poet and novelist, his works include *No Fixed Address* (1962), *Condolences of the Season* (1971) and *Over Here, Harv! and Other Stories* (1983).

C. J. Dennis 1876–1938

He was known as 'the laureate of the larrikin' because he wrote a series of verse stories told in slang. One of these was the best-seller of World War 1, *The Song of the Sentimental Bloke.*

Dame Mary Gilmore 1865–1962

A poet, writer and social worker who championed the underdog. Among her published works were *The Passionate Heart* (1918), *Old Days, Old Ways* (1934) and *Battlefields* (1939).

Alec Derwent Hope 1907–

He is noted for his sarcastic wit and precise expression. His poetry deals with disillusionment with human nature, blended with compassion. His many books include *The Wandering Islands* (1955), *The Drifting Continent* (1979) and *Antechinus* (1981).

Max Harris 1921–1995

A poet, critic and journalist. He was the central figure in the modern verse movement in Adelaide in the 1940s. He published the *Angry Penguins* journal from 1941 to 1964.

Gwen Harwood 1920–

A prolific writer of poetry of an immensely personal nature, she also writes librettos for musicals.

Henry Lawson 1867–1922

One of the most widely acclaimed Australian writers. His ballads and stories depict the nobility and humour found in the ordinary man facing hardship. Most famous are the selection of poems *In the Days When the World Was Wide* (1896), and the short-story collection *Joe Wilson and his Mates* (1901) (see p. 206).

Les Murray 1938–

A successful poet and verse-novelist, whose subjects are compelling and convincing. His works include *The Vernacular Republic* (1976) and *The Boys Who Stole the Funeral* (1980).

Oodgeroo of the Tribe Noonuccal (formerly Kath Walker) 1920–1993

An Aboriginal poet, who expressed her feelings powerfully and with passion. Her poetry collections include *My People* (1970), *Father Sky and Mother Earth* (1981) and *Stradbroke Dreamtime* (1982) (see p. 5).

Andrew Barton ('Banjo') Paterson 1864–1941

A qualified solicitor, war correspondent in the Boer War, and a remount officer in World War 1. This much-loved poet concentrated on the humorous and exciting side of life in the early part of the century. His works include *The Old Bush Songs* (1905) and his bush ballads *The Man from Snowy River* (1895) and *Clancy of the Overflow* (1895), which are perhaps the best-known poems in Australian literature (see pp. 203 and 208).

Kenneth Slessor 1901–71

Considered one of our finest poets. His writings, and in particular his war poems, are powerful and thought-provoking. They include 'Five Bells' (1939) and 'Beach Burial' (1942).

Douglas Stewart 1913–85

A New Zealander, he was a journalist, poet and literary critic, who for thirty years influenced Australian literature. His works include the radio verse-plays *Fire on the Snow* (1941) and *Ned Kelly* (1943).

John Tranter 1943–

One of Australia's most significant contemporary poets, his poetry is abstract, obscure and experimental, displaying wit and skill. His works include *Parallax* (1970), *Crying in Early Infancy* (1977) and *Dazed in the Ladies Lounge* (1979).

Judith Wright 1915–

A leading poet and author, whose sensitive and powerful works include *Woman to Man*

(1949), *Collected Poems* (1971) and *Cry for the Dead* (1981).

Theatre

For many years, theatre in Australia seemed to be a pale reflection of its British counterpart. All this changed in 1954 when the Elizabethan Trust was established to promote and subsidise the profession in Australia. It created an exciting and flourishing national theatre.

Great personalities of early Australian theatre were:

Dame Judith Anderson 1898–91

An Adelaide actress. She won the prestigious Donaldson Award in 1948 for most distinguished actress in the American theatre. She performed overseas for most of her career, and in later years made guest appearances in soap operas in the USA.

Oscar Asche 1871–1936

Actor and playwright. Author of the Orient-inspired musical, *Chu-Chin-Chow* (1916).

Bert Bailey 1872–1953

He formed the Bert Bailey Dramatic Company in 1912, and was the most successful exponent of the hayseed comedies *On Our Selection* and *Golden Shanty*. (See also Films.)

Dame Doris Fitton 1897–1985

An actress and director, she opened the Sydney Independent Theatre Company in 1930. In 1948 she produced the play *Rusty Bugles*, breaking new ground in the theatre by placing greater emphasis on realism and social criticism.

Joseph Bland Holt c. 1863–1942

Australia's greatest actor/manager. He was hailed as the 'Monarch of the Melodrama' after his spectacular production of *Riding to Win* (1901), featuring a cycle race and a lake on stage.

Nat Phillips 1883–1923 and Roy Rene 1892–1954 ('Stiffy' and 'Mo')

A vaudeville team of the 1920s and 30s, they scandalised and delighted audiences with their bawdy humour. Many of Mo's sayings are still quoted: 'Strike me lucky!' and 'You little trimmer!'

Nellie Stewart 1858–1931

An evergreen musical comedy star and favourite pin-up of the 1890s. She sang the ode 'Australia' at the grand ball after the opening of Federal Parliament in Melbourne on 9 May 1901. Her career spanned 67 years.

J. C. Williamson 1835–1913

Theatrical entrepreneur. His theatrical company dominated Australian theatre for almost a century. He imported many famous performers, such as Anna Pavlova and Sarah Bernhardt. The original company folded in 1982.

When the Elizabethan Theatre Trust produced the controversial plays, The Summer of the Seventeenth Doll (*1955*), The Shifting Heart (*1957*) and The One Day of the Year (*1961*), *significant milestones were reached. These 'new wave' plays not only promoted Australian playwrights, but also local Australian actors. Some of the notable actors are:*

John Bell 1940–

The foremost Australian Shakespearian actor and director, he was co-artistic founder of the Nimrod Theatre, Sydney, where he directed many Shakespearian plays, as well as introducing David Williamson's plays to Australia. He is presently director of the newly formed Bell's Permanent Touring Shakespearian Company.

Gordon Chater 1922–

A versatile character actor, famous for his role in *My Name's McGooley*. In 1984 he starred in the Australian play *The Elocution of Benjamin Franklin*, in the USA.

Colleen Clifford 1898–

This grand lady of theatre is

believed to be the world's oldest working actress. Over her long and incredible career she has worked in radio, stage, film and television. She has been an inspiration to her peers, and much loved by her many students.

Ruth Cracknell 1926–

The doyen of stage and screen, her unique ability to re-create dramatic characters, as well as her perfect timing in comedy roles, brings accolades from far and wide. Outstanding roles are Mrs Beard in 'Mother and Son' (TV) and Rose in *Spider and Rose* (Film–1994).

Ron Hadrick 1929–

A distinguished actor, he trained and performed with the Royal Shakespearian Company. Notable performances were as Jack in *The Club* (1977) and James Tyrone in *Long Day's Journey into Night* (1987).

Barry Humphries 1934–

An international star, he created the character of Dame Edna Everage, housewife from Moonee Ponds, in 1958. Through his many characters he satirises suburban life and values.

Leo McKern 1921–

He joined the Old Vic Company, London, in 1946, and has many fine acting roles to his credit, the most notable being the crusty barrister Rumpole, of the BBC television series 'Rumpole of the Bailey'.

John McCallum 1917– and Googie Withers 1917–

A long-standing husband-and-wife team of superstar proportions. They epitomised the 'golden age' of drawing-room comedy of the 1950s and 60s.

John Meillon 1934–90

He was one of the best-loved and greatest actors of Australian film, television, stage and radio. He appeared in *The Rattle of a Simple Man, The Fourth Wish* and *The Picture Show Man.* His last film appearance was in *Crocodile Dundee II.*

Keith Michell 1928–

An actor of outstanding ability. He has won many international awards for his stage and screen performances, his most notable being for his starring roles in *Man of la Mancha, Cyrano de Bergerac* and *The Six Wives of Henry VIII.*

Jill Perryman 1933–

A leading musical-comedy star who rose to fame in J. C. Williamson's *Call Me Madam* in 1953. Her talents and versatility have shone in musicals such as *Funny Girl* and *Hello Dolly.*

Gwen Plumb 1928–

A grand old trooper who began her career in 1940, she is still constantly in demand. She has played a range of parts from Emma in the radio play *Blue Hills* in the 1950s to Ada in the TV series 'The Young Doctors' in the 1970s.

June Salter 1932–

She began her career in radio theatre in the 1940s. She has gained the respect of her peers and audiences for her performances in theatre and television. These include the television series 'The Mavis Bramston Show', and the plays *Crown Matrimonial* (1980) and *Lettice and Lovage* (1990).

Bryon Syron 1939–

A tough but sensitive actor/director, whose brilliant and dynamic performances in off-Broadway plays have been lauded by critics. His 1994 *Jindalee Lady* is the first feature film to be directed by an Australian Aboriginal.

Geraldine Turner 1951–

This versatile artist has sung and danced across the stage of many popular musicals. Her performances include Nancy in *Oliver* and Mrs Lovett in *Sweeny Todd*.

John Waters 1945–

An actor of stage and screen, he is memorable for his roles in the productions of *They're*

Playing Our Song (1980), *Children of a Lesser God* (1984), and the musical, based on the life and times of John Lennon, *Looking Through a Glass Onion*. (1992)

Jackie Weaver 1947–

This bubbly multi-talented actress has throughout her career graced the stages of theatre, film and television.

Radio

In 1918 Ernest Fisk of Wahroonga, NSW, picked up the first historic wireless broadcast from the Marconi station in Wales. It wasn't until the early 1920s that radio became not only a practical proposition but also an important means of mass communication. In 1932 the Commonwealth government combined all licence-funded A class stations to form the ABC (Australian Broadcasting Commission, now Corporation). B class stations were commercial stations. Pioneers of radio included the following.

George Edwards c. 1886–1953

An actor/producer, top radio pioneer and personality of the 1930s. His best-known radio

---

DID YOU KNOW?
Hobart is the home of Australia's oldest surviving theatre – The Royal in Campbell Street.

---

serial, about the farmers of Snake Gully, was 'Dad and Dave'. Other serials were 'Search for the Golden Boomerang' and 'Courtship and Marriage'.

Ted Howell 1902–86 and Therese Desmond c. 1909–c. 1959

A husband-and-wife team, who in the 1930s popularised Fred and Maggie Everybody, characters in the first Australian radio program to be recorded.

Sir Charles Moses 1900–88

His famous 'synthetic' cricket broadcasts of the Australian/English Test Series of 1934, and his pioneering commentary of the historic landing of the aviatrix Jean Batten on her arrival at Mascot airfield, Sydney from Britain in 1934, are legendary. He later became general manager of the ABC.

Then came 'The Golden Age of Radio'. In the 1940s and 50s radio captivated a vast audience, and was the medium of the imagination. It was the era of quiz shows and high drama sprinkled with a large helping of variety programs. Popular shows were the Lux Radio Theatre, the Amateur Hour, and the Dulux Show.

'Andrea' (Dorothy Gordon Jenner) 1890–1985

Considered the grand duchess of broadcasting, in the 1950s she became the top-rating, irascible and indomitable commentator of daytime radio. Her call sign was 'Hullo, mums and dads'.

Queenie Ashton 1903–

One of the most-loved actresses in Australian show-business history, and together with Alastair Duncan, Muriel Steinbeck, Owen Weingott, Lynn Murphy and others, were popular personalities from long-running serials such as 'Blue Hills', 'Doctor Paul', 'When a Girl Marries' and 'Portia Faces Life'.

Jack Davey 1910–59

A popular and jovial personality of talk and quiz shows of the 1940s and 50s. His famous greeting, 'Hi ho everybody', was known Australia-wide. In his last year of work he completed 682 shows.

Bob Dyer 1907–84

An early radio personality from 'The Last of the Hillbillies' show who made the transition to television without difficulty. (See also under Television.)

Bobby Limb 1924–

A variety performer and band leader who, at times, performed in seven different shows a week. When Jack Davey died, he was invited to host the Dulux Show and the Mobil Show, which involved performing before live

audiences throughout
Australia.

*In the early 1960s radio was
dramatically left behind by the
new medium, television.
However, with the explosion of
the Beatles' music it suddenly
became a young person's
medium for rock and pop
music. Charts of the 'Top Ten'
became essential and DJs, such
as Ward (Pally) Austin, John
Brennan, Phil Hunter, Mike
Walsh, Tony Murphy, John
Laws, Bob Rogers, Ken
Sparkes, Bill Gates, Bob
Francis, Tommy Hannan and
the 'Good Guys' (Phil
Haldeman, John Mahon, John
Fryer, Ian McRae, Guy Burgess)
became the new stars.*

Bob Francis 1938–

A popular personality who in his
30-year association with Station
5AD, contributed greatly to
Adelaide radio.

Bill Gates c. 1945–

In the 1960s he recognised the
unique harmony of the group
which now bears his initials –
the Bee Gees. He also devised
a complete sound selection
system which is used
throughout ABC radio.

Caroline Jones 1938–

One of Australia's most
respected broadcasters, she is
well remembered for her
programme 'City Extra' and 'The
Search for Meaning' on the ABC.

John Laws 1936–

He began his career in country
radio in Victoria in 1955. One of
the first rock DJs, in later years,
with emerging irreverence, he
has presented top-rating, more
sophisticated talk-back shows,
syndicated nationwide.

John Laws

Ian MacNamara 1947–

Affectionately known as
'Macca', is the host of the highly
successful ABC 'Australia All
Over' radio programme. He is
the epitome of the dinkum
Aussie.

Ron Moss 1959– and Marius Webb 1943–

Two innovative presenters of the
progressive ABC 2JJ AM radio
(which later became 2JJJ FM)
playing rock 'n' roll music
pitched solely at huge teenage
audiences.

Rod Muir 1941–

He returned from America in the early 1970s with the tight-format approach to rock music programs with which he rejuvenated flagging radio stations. His 'Room to Move' developed a fanatical audience. He commenced innovative FM radio, and in 1979 he was awarded one of the first two commercial licences in New South Wales.

Bob Rogers 1927–

Phenomenally popular in the 60s, he and John Laws were 'famous enemies' vying for top radio ratings.

The introduction of FM radio in 1974 gave high quality reproduction, and in the 1980s challenged the ratings of conventional AM radio. Listeners were enticed back to new AM talk-back formats with personalities such as Bob Francis, Margaret Throsby, Bob Maumill, Jeremy Cordeaux, Mike Carlton, John Laws, Alan Jones, Ron Casey, John Tingle, Sue Becker and John Raedler.

Jeremy Cordeaux 1945–

He has had over 30 years in Sydney and Adelaide radio. In 1987 he was awarded the Gold Medal by the International Radio Festival of New York as 'The Best Talk/Interview Programme Host' in the world.

Bob Maumill 1938–

Affectionately known as 'old puddin' face'. He was the 'urban larrikin' in the ocker boom·of the 1970s, and his catch-cry was ' 'Ave we got a year fa yew!' He is presently a popular figure in Perth radio.

Clive Robertson (Robbo) 1945–

A radio host, his natural and outrageous humour has made him a household name. He began his chequered career in WA in 1967, where he claimed to have been 'a general announcing dogsbody'.

Clive Robertson

DID YOU KNOW?
The first radio transmitting and receiving station in Australia was built near Pennant Hills, Sydney, in 1912.

Margaret Throsby 1942–

She joined ABC in 1967, and was the first woman announcer to read a news bulletin on ABC radio. She was also the first woman to present a national news bulletin on ABC television. She has a reputation for making fearless statements on a wide range of controversial subjects.

Television

In 1956, on the eve of the Olympic Games in Melbourne, movie and radio were cast aside for the Australian public's first exciting experience of television.
Here are some of the pioneer personalities of the small screen.

Hector Crawford 1914–91

Affectionately known as 'the Silver Fox', he was the pioneer of television drama in Australia. As head of Crawford Productions he produced more than 2000 hours of shows, extending over a period of twenty-five years. He gave the public what they wanted, hence the popularity of shows such as 'Matlock Police', 'Homicide' and 'The Sullivans'.

Max Cullen 1941–

Well-known character actor, whose 'lived in' look has graced a thousand Aussie mini-series. He believes that good acting should always look like an accident!

Bob Dyer 1907–84

An early radio and television personality. With his wife Dolly, he set a record for the longest running television show, 'Pick a Box', 1957–71. His 'Howdy customers', 'Tell them Bob sent you' and 'The money or the box' became household sayings. (See also Radio.)

Graham Kennedy 1934–

Generally referred to as 'The King'. In 1957 he became the outrageous compere of the extremely popular variety show, 'In Melbourne Tonight', which ran until 1970.

Leonard Teale 1922–94

His career in film, television, theatre, cabaret, recording and radio, including over 15 000 radio serial episodes, spanned over forty years. He starred in the television dramas 'Homicide' and 'Seven Little Australians'. His wonderfully modulated voice continues to keep him in great demand.

By the early 1970s, black-and-white television was viewed by 98 per cent of the population. In 1975 colour television began.
Some television stars of the 1970s were the following.

Lorraine Bayly 1939–

A dedicated actress, who has starred in both stage and television screen roles.

Bert Newton 1938–

A winner of thirteen Logies, 'Old

Moon Face', with his twin talents as a natural comedian and sophisticated compere is a favourite with celebrities, viewers and critics alike.

Ernie Sigley 1938–

One of Australia's best variety performers, he was Australia's youngest disc jockey and at the age of sixteen he compered Melbourne's first live television show, 'Teenage Mail-bag'. Other successful shows have been 'The Ernie Sigley Show' and 'Wheel of Fortune'.

Mike Walsh 1938–

From being a country radio announcer in the 1960s he became the host of one of the most popular daytime shows, 'The Mike Walsh Show' (1973–84). He now is involved with cinema and theatre.

Mike Willesee 1942–

At twenty-two he was the youngest-ever fully accredited political correspondent in Canberra. He hosted many current affair programs in the 1970s and 80s. He is now a racing identity.

John Young 1945–

He delighted thousands of children and parents around Australia in the 1970s and 80s with the long-running children's talent show 'Young Talent Time'. In 1990 he was admitted to the Golden Logies Hall of Fame.

In 1980 ethnic television began broadcasting on a permanent basis through SBS.

By 1983 there were 50 commercial channels and the ABC services were available through more than 80 transmitters.

Personalities of the 1980s and 90s include:

Tony Barber 1940–

He was the smiling, genial host of the long-running and popular top-rating quiz show 'Sale of the Century'. He began his career as the 'Cambridge Whistler' in a television cigarette commercial in 1969.

Don Burke 1948–

A horticulturist. His very popular and informative program 'Burke's Backyard', with its theme 'Give me a home amongst the gum trees', has revitalised thousands of amateur gardeners.

Bill Collins 1935–

Australia's amiable 'Mr Movies' is a journalist and cinema historian. He is an authority on motion pictures, particularly those produced during Hollywood's 'Golden Years'.

James Dibble 1923–

A much-respected news reader on ABC radio and television. For over twenty-five years his voice was a familiar one in most Australian homes.

Brian Henderson 1931–

He began his career in radio, but soon made his name in television as host of the popular show 'Bandstand'. His most noteworthy position in latter years is as newsreader for the Nine Network.

Derryn Hinch 1944–

A controversial journalist and broadcaster, and host of a long-running current affairs show. He is noted for his forthright approach to situations, regardless of the consequences.

Clive James 1939–

A journalist and author, he currently appears on BBC television in his own show 'Saturday Night Clive' and 'Postcard' and 'Fame' series.

Garry McDonald 1950–

An actor in comedy and satire, he created the character of 'the little Aussie bleeder', Norman Gunston, the naive interviewer who bewildered many celebrities worldwide. In recent years, he teamed with Ruth Cracknell to make the popular television series 'Mother and Son'.

Ray Martin 1944–

As a journalist he clocked up more than a million miles when he was a reporter for '60 Minutes'. From 1985 to 1993 he was the genial host of the popular 'Midday Show'. He presently hosts 'A Current Affair'.

Doug Mulray 1945–

A radio and TV outrageous non-conformist. He sets his own agenda of black comedy, stretching convention to the limit.

Laurie Oakes 1943–

A leading political commentator. His career spans over thirty years, and he appears regularly on the 'Sunday' program for the Nine Network.

Daryl Somers 1952–

Born into a show-business family, his break came when he appeared on 'New Faces', attracting the attention of the Nine Network. He is the host of the very popular 'Hey, Hey, It's Saturday' show which goes from strength to strength. The unique team of Daryl and Ossie, 'born' 1971, lasted until 1994.

Gary Sweet 1957–

This good-looking action hero, has become the archetypal Australian male. He is universally admired for his film and television roles and is a

---

DID YOU KNOW?
The first television station in Australia opened in 1956 as TCN Channel 9, Sydney.

triple Logie winner. He plays dare-devil Mickey McClintock in the TV adventure drama 'Police Rescue'.

Maximilian Walsh 1938–

A political and economics journalist, he has covered most of the major political stories of the past three decades.

Jana Wendt 1957–

A journalist who joined the '60 Minutes' team in 1982, she quickly established herself as an impressive reporter with a particular talent for interviewing. A leading TV host/reporter, whose honey-sweet voice belies the relentless tenacity with which she conducts her interviews.

Films

Since 1908, when the pioneer film-producer Raymond Longford decided that there was a future for films in Australia, many aspiring actors and actresses have wanted to see their name up in lights. Here are a few of the successful ones.

Take I   Silent films and early talkies 1898–1935

Bert Bailey 1872–1953

Famous for his role as Dad, the genial patriarch, in *On Our Selection* (1931), a feature film comedy based on Steele Rudd's characters.

Lottie Lyall 1891–1925

She was Australia's first film-star, and appeared in many of Longford's films. She starred in *The Silence of Dean Maitland* (1914), and played Doreen in *The Sentimental Bloke* (1919).

Arthur Tauchert 1877–1933

C. J. Dennis chose this former vaudeville actor to play the title-role in *The Sentimental Bloke* (1919). He was the most popular screen actor of the 1920s.

George Wallace 1894–1960

A very popular comedian of the Depression era. His most famous film was *Gone to the Dogs* (c. 1930).

Take II   The talkies 1935–1970

Peter Finch 1915–77

Film and theatre actor of West End fame. He appeared in Charles Chauvel's *The Rats of Tobruk* (1949), *Robbery Under Arms* (1957), *Network* ((1976) and *Raid on Entebbe* (1976), and had fifty-one films to his credit.

Errol Flynn 1909–59

A swashbuckling Hobart-born actor, notorious on and off the screen. His debut in films was in the role of Fletcher Christian in Charles Chauvel's *In the Wake of the Bounty.* He moved to Hollywood, and starred in the film *Captain Blood* (1935).

Chips Rafferty 1909–71

An actor and producer, he was famous for his portrayal of the typical Australian bushman. He appeared in Charles Chauvel's *The Rats of Tobruk* (1949).

Take III   The talkies 1970–91

Ray Barrett 1927–

In 1958 his successful tour with Margaret Rutherford in *The Happiest Days of Our Lives* was the turning-point of his career. Performances to his credit include the television series *Trouble Shooters*, and the films *Don's Party* (1976) and *Goodbye Paradise* (1982).

Bryan Brown 1948–

This very popular, devil-may-care actor is noted for his roles in the films *Breaker Morant* (1979), *Cocktail* (1987), *Gorillas in the Mist* (1989), *Blood Oath* (1990) and *Confidence* (1990) and many more.

Judy Davis 1955–

A sensitive and compelling actress, she played the starring role in the film *My Brilliant Career* (1978). She won AFI Best Actress Award for *Kangaroo* in 1987, and *On My Own* (1988).

Ed Devereaux 1925–

He began his varied career as a child performer in 1930. His countless successes include his performance as Max Hammond in the television series 'Skippy', his lead role in 'My Brother Jack', in the play *The Removalist*, and his portrayal of Ben Chifley in the television drama, 'The True Believers'.

Ernie Dingo 1957–

He began his career with the Middar Aboriginal Dance Theatre but is best known for his film and television work. With his sense of fun and playful disposition he has starred in *The Fringe Dwellers* (1986), *Tudawali* (1987), and *A Walk Through the Hills* (1988).

Colin Friels 1953–

He graduated from NIDA, and had many starring roles in plays such as *Hamlet* and *The Caucasian Chalk Circle.* He also starred in the films *Monkey Grip* (1982), *Malcolm* (1986), *High Tide* (1987), and *Weekend with Kate* (1990) and *Dingo* (1992).

Mel Gibson 1956–

This sensational actor was the first Australian to be paid in excess of $1 million for a movie role. With his devil-may-care action performances he starred in the *Mad Max* and *Lethal Weapon* series and many more first-class action films.

John Hargreaves 1946–

This warm-hearted and popular actor played the lead roles in the films *The Removalist* (1975), *Don's Party* (1976), *My First Wife* (1984), *Emerald City* (1988), and *Country Life* (1994).

Chris Haywood 1949–

He arrived from London in 1970 and joined the Old Tote Theatre Company, where he had many roles to his credit. His films include *The Cars That Ate Paris* (1974), *In Search of Anna* (1978), and 'Janus' (TV) (1994).

Noni Hazelhurst 1954–

This fun-loving and sensitive actress, dancer and singer has notched up many successes in film and television. She is the 'face' of 'Play School' for many Australian children.

Paul Hogan ('Hoges') 1940–

From being a rigger on the Harbour Bridge, he became a multi-million dollar film producer when in the 1980s, in partnership with John Cornell, he produced *Crocodile Dundee* series.

Wendy Hughes 1950–

A film actress, internationally acclaimed for her performances in *Newsfront* (1978), *Careful, He Might Hear You* (1983), and *Boundaries of the Heart* (1988).

Bill Hunter 1939–

An able and sensitive character actor whose versatility allows him to portray a bent politician one day and an outback yobbo the next with equal conviction. Films include *Strictly Ballroom* (1993), *Priscilla, Queen of the Desert* and *Muriel's Wedding* (1994).

The father of the bride (Muriel's Wedding)

Nicole Kidman 1968–

She began her career at the age of fifteen, and among her many outstanding performances were the films *Dead Calm* (1988), *Emerald City* (1988), *Days of Thunder* (1990) and *Flirting* (1990). Now a movie star in Hollywood and has 'dinner with Tom Cruise' almost every night!

Sam Neill 1948–

An international actor of great ability who returns regularly to Australia to star in films such as

'Hoges' (Crocodile Dundee II)

The Piano (1992), *Sirens* and *Country Life* (1994).

An acclaimed actress, who has an impressive list of roles in film, stage and television. These include the films *Careful, He Might Hear You* (1983) and *Emerald City* (1988), and her stage performances in *A Street Car Named Desire* and *Who's Afraid of Virginia Woolf?*

Justine Saunders 1953–

She has become one of the most experienced and successful Aboriginal actresses since she came to notice in 1980 in the television series 'Pig in a Poke'. Her films include *Backlash* (1986) and *The Fringe Dwellers* (1986).

Jack Thompson 1941–

A popular and competent actor, he has appeared in the films *Sunday Too Far Away* (1975), *Breaker Morant* (1979), *The Man from Snowy River* (1983), *The Last Frontier* (1987), and *The Sum of Us* (1994).

Hugo Weaving 1960–

Experienced actor of theatre, television and film. He caused an enormous stir at 1991 Cannes Film Festival for his sensitive portrayal of a blind photographer in the film *Proof*. In 1994, to tremendous acclaim, he played Mitzi, the flamboyant and outrageous drag queen in

The Adventures of Priscilla, Queen of the Desert.

Weaving's outrageous Mitzi

Film-makers

Gillian Armstrong 1950–

Revered in the industry, her success in directing *My Brilliant Career* (1978) gained international recognition. Then followed *Starstruck* (1982), *Mrs Soffel* (made in Hollywood, 1984), *High Tide* (1986), *Fires Within* (USA, 1990), and the comedy-drama '*The Last Days of Chez Nous*' (1992), *Little Women* (1995).

Bruce Beresford 1940–

He has made more films and broken more ground, both artistically and commercially, than anyone else in the industry. He established himself in the 1970s with films such as *Barry McKenzie* (1972) and *Breaker Morant* (1979) and *Backlash* (1986). Has worked in Hollywood and has many notable films to his credit such as *Crimes of the Heart* (1986),

Driving Miss Daisy (1989) and *Black Robe* (1992).

A cinematographer, he has made some of the most famous Australian feature films, such as *Picnic at Hanging Rock* (1975), which won a British Oscar. This film captured the imagination of audiences worldwide, and set a mood for other films to follow. His later films were *Gallipoli* (1982), *Crocodile Dundee* (1986) and *Blood Oath* (1990).

Tim Burstall 1929–

He pioneered the 'new wave' films of the 1970s. His work includes *Alvin Purple* (1973), *Eliza Frazer* (1979) and *Attack Force Z* (1980) and a film version of D. H. Lawrence's novel *Kangaroo*.

Jane Campion 1954–

New Zealand film director with a most original talent. Her films have won international awards and *A Portrait of a Lady* (1993), *Sweetie* (1989) and *The Piano* (1993) illustrate her mastery of the visual image.

Charles Chauvel 1897–1959

The most accomplished film-maker of the 1920s and 30s. He made films with a distinctly Australian flavour, including *The Moth of Moonbi* (silent, 1926), *In the Wake of the Bounty* (1933) starring Errol Flynn, *Forty Thousand Horsemen* (1940) which is regarded as the first truly great Australian film, and *The Rats of Tobruk* (1949).

Byron Kennedy 1952–83 and George Miller 1949–

This was a highly successful production team, breaking new ground with the *Mad Max* series. *Mad Max* (1979) and *Mad Max 2* (1981) became the most imitated films of the 1980s. Kennedy Miller produced the television drama *The Dismissal* (1982), but tragically, in 1983, Kennedy was killed in a helicopter crash. Miller continued, and directed *Twilight Zone* in the USA in 1983, then *Mad Max 3* (1985), *Witches of Eastwick* (USA, 1987), *The Year My Voice Broke* (1987), *Dead Calm* (1988), and *Flirting* (1990).

Raymond Longford 1875–1959

Australia's most successful director of silent films, he independently developed the use of close-ups to great effect, particularly in *The Silence of Dean Maitland* (1914). He directed the silent cinema classics *Mutiny on the Bounty* (1916) and *The Sentimental Bloke* (1919).

Patricia Lovell c. 1932–

A dynamic film-producer and perfectionist who enjoys a challenge, she is responsible for three box-office hits: *Picnic at Hanging Rock* (1975), *Monkey Grip* (1982), and *Gallipoli* (1982).

He struck a new screen reality when he directed *Newsfront* (1978), where he moulded fictional footage with film of actual events from the 1950s. Others to his credit are *Heatwave* (1981), *Dead Calm* (1988), and for television *The Dismissal* (1983) and *Cowra Breakout* (1985). He became one of the 'Gum Leaf Mafia' (expatriates in Hollywood) where he made *Blind Frenzy* (1989).

Fred Schepisi 1940–

An acclaimed director, with a larrikin air and a rare wit. He left school at fifteen, and learnt his craft 'from the ground up'. He became a dynamic force in the film industry with films such as *The Devil's Playground* (1976) and *The Chant of Jimmie Blacksmith* (1978). He directed *Barbarossa* (USA, 1982), *Evil Angels* (1988), and *Russia House* (1990).

John Seale 1944–

He began his career in 1962 as a camera assistant, and is now a top cinematographer. In 1975 he assisted Russell Boyd with filming *Picnic at Hanging Rock*. His successes include *Careful, He Might Hear You* (1983) and *The Empty Beach* (1985). He moved to the USA, and filmed *Mosquito Coast, Children of a Lesser God* (1987), *Rain Man* (1988), and *Dead Poets Society* (1989).

Dean Semler 1943–

A cinematographer, whose pictures are distinguished by their sweeping vision of often unspoiled and unforgiving backgrounds. *Steam Train Passes* (1974) was his first, then his big break came with *Mad Max 2* (1981). From then on he had no shortage of work. He filmed *The Lighthorsemen* (1987), *Dead Calm* (1988), and he won an Oscar for his work on Kevin Costner's blockbuster movie *Dances with Wolves* (USA, 1991).

Peter Weir 1944–

He emerged from the 1970s as the country's leading director with films such as *The Cars that Ate Paris* (1974) and *Picnic at Hanging Rock* (1975). In 1982 he realised a burning ambition when he directed *Gallipoli*, which was a major success and won nine AFI awards. *The Year of Living Dangerously* (1982) was Weir's last Australian film of the 1980s. *Witness* (1984), *Mosquito Coast* (1986), *Dead Poets Society* (1989) and *Green Card* (1990) were all made in America.

Rock music

Popular rock 'n' roll is often transient. Overseas trends tend to demand that bands produce music which will attract huge audiences and in turn make huge profits. Australian bands on the whole, however, are noted for keeping to their own kind of individual music, regardless of fickle international markets.

AC DC

Considered to be Australia's loudest, hard rock band. Phenomenal worldwide success is due to hits such as 'Highway to Hell' (1975) and 'High Voltage Rock 'n' Roll' (1976). Their reputation for having a very Aussie sound still stands, with tracks such as 'Blow Up Your Video' (1988), 'Thunder Struck' (1990), 'Money Talks' and 'Big Guns' (1993).

Air Supply

One of Australia's biggest and earliest exports. They had seven hits on all world charts with their 'middle of the road' music, including 'The One That You Love' (1980), 'Lost in Love' (1981). Their greatest hit album including the single 'Without You' (1991), greatly influenced overseas artists like Mariah Carey.

Angels

With lead singer Doc Neeson,

Angels

their hard-rock athletic stage shows attracted large audiences. Hits are – 'Shadow Boxer' (1981), 'The Dogs Are Talking' (1990) and their album 'Evidence' (1994).

The Australian Crawl

One of the leading bands of the early 1980s with an Aussie beach-rock sound. James Reyne emerged from its ranks and has had success with singles like 'Motors Too Fast' (1991) and 'Way Out West' with James Blundell (1992).

Baby Animals

A hard rock band falling under the same influences as The Divinyls. Major success came with 'Baby Animals' album in 1991, and singles 'Early Warning' and 'Don't Tell Me What To Do' (1993). Hugely successful in USA touring with legends such as Van Halen and Robert Plant. 'Lights out at Eleven' was their 1994 album.

Jimmy Barnes 1946–

This screaming banshee was lead singer with Cold Chisel and has the well-earned title of 'wild man' of Australian rock. There are massive sales of anything that bears his name. His hits include 'Working Class Man' (1985), the albums 'Freight Train Heart' (1987), 'Two Fires' (1990), 'Soul Deep' (1992), 'Flesh and Wood' (1993) and the single 'Stone Cold' (1993).

Jimmy Barnes

Bee Gees

A highly successful trio of the 1960s. The group pioneered disco in the 1970s and broke new ground by writing the score for the film *Saturday Night Fever*, (1977).

Black Sorrows

A band of diversity and originality with a soulful sound, based around frontman Joe Cavaleri, (who in the 1970s and 80s was Jo Jo Zep and the Falcons). Their single 'You Got Me in the Shape I'm In' (1983) was a great hit. In 1988 they sold 175,000 copies of 'Hold Onto Me' followed in 1990 with 'Harley and Rose' and 'Better Times' (1991), 'The Chosen Ones' (1993), 'Last One Standing For You' (1994) and 'The Lucky Charm' album (1994).

Daryl Braithwaite 1949–

Lead singer with Sherbert until 1985, when he branched out on his own. In early 1989 he topped the charts with his legendary album 'Edge'. His 1991 singles were 'The Horses' and 'Don't Hold Back Your Love'. Latest are 'Six Moons' and 'How Can I Be Sure' (1994).

Kate Ceberano 1966–

Her sultry vocal ability which embodies a great natural style and range enabled her to branch into the jazz idiom especially in the UK. Her top hit singles are 'You've Always Got The Blues' and 'Bedroom Eyes' (1989), 'Every Little Thing' and 'See Right Through' (1991). She had a triple platinum album 'Brave' in 1989 and had colossal success with 'Everything's Alright' from the stage show 'Jesus Christ Superstar' (1992). Her latest is 'Kate Ceberano and Friends' (1994).

Cold Chisel

As the top rock 'n' roll band of the late 1970s, its music was considered to have the most typical Australian rock sound. 'Khe Sahn' (1973) and 'Cheap Wine' (1977) were prime examples of its blues-influenced, raunchy style. 'Gold Chisel – Greatest Hits' came out in 1993 followed by 'Teenage Love' (1994). Band member, Ian Moss had great success as a solo artist in 1989 with 'Tuckers Daughter'.

Crowded House

A Kiwi-Aussie group, reformed from the defunct Split Enz, which was an unparalleled creative force in the 1970–80s, topping the charts with 'I See Red' (1975) and 'I Got You' (1979). Now, the phenomenally popular Crowded House, with their easy anecdotal style and collective sense of humour has hit the top time and again with hits such as 'Chocolate Cake' (1991) and 'Together Alone' and 'Private Universe' (1994).

Daddy Cool – Mondo Rock

Under the leadership of the guitarist, Ross Wilson, Daddy Cool, with its energetic, jovial and post-hippy music, made a significant breakthrough in the 1970s. The most successful singles were 'Come Back Again' and 'Eagle Rock' (1975). Mondo Rock came from the skeleton of Daddy Cool. Popular singles are 'State of the Heart' (1981) and 'Come Said the Boy' (1984).

Diesel

As Johnny Diesel and the Injectors they appealed to younger audiences in the late 1980s with their blues-influenced guitar sound. The last single was 'Soul Revival' in 1989. Johnny dropped his first name and now goes under the name Diesel, touring extensively with Jimmy Barnes. Hits such as 'Love Junk', 'Come to Me' and 'Tip of my Tongue' come from his 1992 'Hepfidelity' album. The 'Lobbyist' (1993) is a set of live and studio tracks and his 1994 album is 'Solid State Rhyme'

Divinyls

This group topped the charts in the late 1970s and early 80s in the USA with Chrissy Amphlett renowned for her brazen and raunchy presentation of the songs. Hits include 'All The Boys in Town' (1981), 'Only Lonely', (1983), 'I Touch Myself' (1990), 'Love School' (1991), a new version of 'Wild Thing' (1993) and 'The Collection' (1994).

Easy Beats

One of Australia's earliest rock group exports, this strong, energetic band hit the Top 10 in the British charts, with 'Friday on my Mind' (1966) and 'Wedding Ring' (1967).

John Farnham 1949–

A 1960s solo artist, then a lead singer with Little River Band in the early 1980s. In 1986 he relaunched his solo career with 'Whispering Jack' album from which comes the hugely successful single 'You're the Voice'. His very powerful and technically capable vocal capacity dominates and he is now considered to be one of the best talents Australia has produced. Other albums are 'Age of Reason' (1988), 'Chain Reaction' (1990), 'Full House' (1991) and 'Then Again' (1993).

Hoodoo Gurus

A purely rock 'n' roll guitar band, with a folk, nearly hippy element. Hits are 'Miss Freelove' (1991), albums 'Stone Age Romeos' (1984), 'Kinky' (1991), 'Electric Soup' (1992) and 'Crank' (1994).

Hunters and Collectors

Lived in England during the 1980s where they opened the eyes and ears of the world with the musical diversity of their hugely successful rough-edged Australian rock style. Had outstanding success with 'Where Do You Go?' (1991), 'We the People' (1992) and the albums 'Cut' (1992) and 'Demon Flower' (1994).

Hunters and Collectors

Ice House (originally Flowers)

This was one of the first high-tech synthetic bands to be accepted as authentic Australian rock. Based around lead singer Iva Davis they took their present name from the 1980 album 'Ice House'. Singles include 'I Can't Help Myself' (1980), 'Hey, Little Girl' (1982), 'Man of Colours' (1987),

'Electric Blue' (1988), 'Touch the Fire' (1990) and 'Miss Divine' (1991), and the albums 'Master Files' (1992) and 'Big Wheel' (1993) followed, assuring their success.

INXS

Australia's biggest international act of all times. Fourteen years of globe-trotting at breakneck speed make it the hardest working and most successful band ever to emerge from Australia. Phenomenal successes include 'Shabooh Shoobah' (1982), 'Listen Like Thieves', (1985), 'Kick' (1988) and their singles 'What You Need' (1985), 'Suicide Blonde' (1988) 'Bitter Tears' and 'By My Side' (1990) and 'Heaven Sent' and 'Baby, Don't Cry' (1992). Their albums are 'Welcome to Wherever You Are' (1993) and 'Greatest Hits' (1994). Michael Hutchence, lead singer, is considered to be the Mick Jagger of the 90s.

Col Joye 1937–

The grandfather of Australian rock music has a career extending over three decades. He began with Johnny O'Keefe in 1958, and his hits were 'Sixteen Candles' (1959) and 'Bye Bye, Baby' (1959).

Paul Kelly 1958–

A multi-talented singer/songwriter who has written for many Aussie bands. Internationally acclaimed for his unique style of hypnotic music which reflects the darker side of street life and modern living. His albums 'Manila' (1992), 'Wanted Man' and 'Post' (1994), are chilling examples of his work.

Paul Kelly

Little River Band

With Glenn Shorrock as lead singer, the band was wildly successful in the USA, with well-produced, catchy, mainstream rock hits such as 'Help is on its Way' (1977) and 'Reminiscing' (1978).

Richard Lowenstein 1960–

Was amongst the new wave of young film makers of the 70s achieving astounding success internationally. He directed many feature films such as 'Strikebound' (1984), 'Dogs in Space' (1986) and 'Say a Little Prayer' (1992). In addition, he perfected the technique of video filming famous rock bands such as INXS, Cold Chisel and Split Enz.

Wendy Matthews 1960–

With her LP 'Emigre' (1990) and her huge album 'Lily' (1992), Wendy has become Australia's premier female artist. Her album 'Lily' went triple platinum in 1994 and her latest album is 'The Witness Tree' (1994).

Ian ('Molly') Meldrum 1945–

He produced Australia's first TV rock programme 'Countdown' (1975–87) and is considered to be the guru of the Australian rock scene. Many Australian bands owe their success to his promotion. He has his own record label Melodium, and his high profile worldwide, enables him to have *entre* to first class international performers.

Men At Work

World renowned good-humoured band with Aussie rock sound. Hits include 'Who Can it be Now' (1981), 'Be Good Johnny' (1982) and 'Down Under' which became the celebratory song for Australia's victory in the America's Cup in 1983. They disbanded in the late 1980s.

Mental as Anything

Internationally popular five-piece outfit with a quirky pop style, and a large dash of good humour. Hits are 'If You Leave Me Can I Come Too', (1981), 'Live It Up' (1985), the album 'Cyclone Raymond' (1990).

Midnight Oil

A forthright politically motivated band, with a powerful rhythm section. Songs such as 'Power and the Passion' and 'US Forces', (1983), '10 to 1' (1985), 'Diesel and Dust' (1987) and their album, 'Earth, Sun and Moon' (1993) ensured them mega success. In 1995 world renowned artists joined with them to produce an environmental single called 'Land'. Their politically active lead singer is Peter Garrett.

Kylie Minogue 1968–

Her meteoric rise to top international recording artist is phenomenal. 'Locomotion' (1987) became the biggest selling Australian single record of the 1980s. The songs 'I Should be so Lucky' (1988), 'What Do I Have to Do?' and 'Word of Mouth' (1991) and 'I Guess I Like It Like That' (1992) appealed to British teenagers. Latest album is '50 to 1, Kylie' (1994).

Jenny Morris 1957–

She has sung with many popular bands of the 1980s. Her meteoric rise to fame came when she was invited by the superstar Prince, to tour Europe in 1990. Her albums, 'Shiver' (1990) and 'Honey Child' (1991), are incredibly successful. Singles are 'Break in the Weather' (1991) 'Zero', 'Tears' and her latest album 'Story So Far' (1992).

Noiseworks

A band which played typical Australian 1980s rock, with a soulful sound, catering for a wide range of audiences. Singles were 'No Lies' (1986), 'Freedom' (1989), 'In My Youth' (1990), 'Miles And Miles', 'Hot Chilli Woman', 'R.I.P. Millie' (1991) and 'Let It Be' (1992). When they disbanded, lead singer Jon Stevens went solo and two other members formed The Electric Hippies. Their 1994 single was 'Greedy People'.

Kylie Minogue

Johnny O'Keefe 1935–78 (J O'K)

Known as the 'Boomerang Kid', his career began in 1956 with the volatile and action-packed TV show 'Six O'clock Rock'. 'She's My Baby', (1959) written for him by rock king Bill Haley, made the American charts. Other hits were 'Shout' (1959), 'I'm Counting on You' (1961) and 'Move Baby Move' (1963).

Archie Roach c1955–

Aboriginal singer/song writer. His 1990 debut album, 'Charcoal Lane', is widely regarded as one of the most compelling in Australian recording history. Then came 'Jamu Dreaming' (1993).

Archie Roach

Normie Rowe 1948–

At 17 he was crowned Australia's first king of pop but his career was interrupted by army service in Vietnam. He now performs in musicals and on the cabaret circuit.

The Screaming Jets

They hit instant fame in 1991 with smash hit 'Better' and albums 'One for All' and 'Tear of Thought'. The band has toured extensively in USA and UK and considered to be the new wild boys of Australian rock.

Sherbert

A hugely successful band of the 1970s with their solo single 'You're My World' (1975). 'Howzat' made it to the top in 1976, both here and in the UK and USA. Sherbert was known as Highway in the USA.

silverchair

Considered to be Australia's answer to Nirvana, these three 15-year-old Novocastrians took the rock scene by storm with their phenomenally successful single 'Tomorrow' (1994) which sold double platinum. Their 1995 new single is 'Pure Massacre'.

Skyhooks

With their two prominent characters. 'Shirley' Strachan and Red Simons, the band was recognised for its truly Australian flavour and powerful vocal and guitar style. Albums are 'Living in the Seventies' (1975) and 'Latest and Greatest' (1990).

Billy Thorpe and the Aztecs

A wild band of the 1970s. 'Over The Rainbow' was an Aussie classic and Thorpe was indisputably the rock 'n' roll hero of urban beer-swilling Aussie yobboes. He has now become a serious songwriter and recording performer in the USA. His ambitious albums 'Children of the Sun' (1980), 'Stimulation' (1981) and 'War of The Worlds' (1983) (a cartoon series) have won critical acclaim. Latest is 'Collector Box Set' (1994).

Billy Thorpe

Yothu Yindi

An award-winning Aboriginal band. Its traditional dance and contemporary hard-rock beat produces a powerful sound reflecting the passions and frustrations of the Aboriginal race. The hit album is 'Tribal Voice' from which comes the singles 'Treaty' (written in collaboration with Paul Kelly) and 'Djapana (Sunset Dreaming)' (1992). Then came 'Freedom' (1993).

Other bands of influence over the years were Boom Crash Opera, Choir Boys, Delltones, Models, Gangajang, The Church, Radiators, Spy vs Spy,

and other artists of influence were Marsha Hines and Richard Clapton.

Some very promising bands at present are: Frente!, Girl Friend, Cruel Sea, Caligula, Nick Cave and the Bad Seeds, Chocolate Star Fish, Southern Sons and Tiddas. Promising artists are: Peter Andre, (considered to be the Michael Jackson of Australia), Deborah Conway, Grace Knight, Danni Minogue and Tina Arena.

Popular music

Hundreds of talented musicians have contributed over the years to the popular music scene. Names such as Eric Bogle, June Bronhill, Peter Dawson, Smokey Dawson, Slim Dusty, Jon English, Rolf Harris, Kamahl, Reg Lindsay, Ricky May, Gladys Moncrieff, Olivia Newton-John and The Seekers always evoke memories of fantastic performances which have sometimes changed the direction of the music scene in Australia.

Peter Allen 1944–92

Born in Tenterfield, NSW, he was an internationally renowned songwriter and performer. His popular 'I Still Call Australia Home' became the catchcry of expatriate Aussies in the late 1970s. Other hits include 'Tenterfield Saddler' (1979), 'I

Go to Rio' (1974) and 'Don't Cry Out Loud' (1980). His last album was 'Making Every Moment Count' (1991).

Julie Anthony 1951–

One of Australia's favourite singers. In 1988 she sang a stirring rendition of 'Advance Australia Fair' on the steps of the new Parliament House, Canberra, at the opening ceremony.

James Blundell 1965–

In 1987 he was just a stockman who could sing. Now he is the hottest act in the country and western music scene. This smouldering young sex symbol has broken down urban barriers, attracting wide audiences with songs such as 'Kimberley Moon' (1990), 'Time on His Hands' (1991) and his albums 'Touch of Water' and 'Way Out West' (1993).

James Blundell

Don Burrows 1928–

A jazz musician, whose distinguished career spans more than thirty years, he excels with the flute, saxophone and clarinet. He was the associate director of jazz at the NSW Conservatorium until 1990. He is renowned for his interest in children's music, as well as Latin American music.

Debbie Byrne 1958–

One of the six original Young Talent Time team, this popular and versatile singer has made many memorable stage appearances, particularly in *Cats* and *Les Misérables*. Her albums are 'Caught in the Act' (1991), 'Sleeping Child' (1994), from which comes the hit song 'Hearts Filled with Anger'.

Nathan Cavaleri 1982–

This pocket-sized 13-year-old genius is a blues guitarist. His extraordinary first album was 'Jammin with The Cats' (1993) with Jimmy Barnes, Diesel and Gangajang. In 1994 he toured extensively in the USA and played with world-renowned blues guitarists.

Tommy Emmanuel 1955–

He is regarded as one of the world's finest guitarists. His music is an integration of blues ('Deep River Blues' (1987)), rock-a-billy ('Guitar Boogie' (1990)) and bluegrass rhythms ('Terry on the Turnpike' (1989)), interspersed with classical and wild Spanish flamenco music. His hits are 'Determination' (1991), 'The Journey' (1993), 'The Journey Continues' (1994) and 'Terra Firma' (Tom and Phil) (1995).

Tommy Emmanuel

Geoff Harvey 1935–

He was the musical director for the 'Midday Show' from 1986 to 1994. He is an accomplished musician and composer.

Gina Jeffreys 1968–

Her vocal talents cover country blues and folk music and she is the exciting star of the country-music scene. She hit the top when she toured in 1994 with Johnny Cash and Kris Kristofferson.

James Morrison 1963–

This world-famous jazz musician tours extensively. His natural sense of humour and his ability to play 16 instruments, excelling at trumpet and trombone, makes him a much sought after performer. His latest albums are 'Men are Dangerous' (1992) and 'Two the Max!' (1994).

Marina Pryor 1964–

A feisty young opera singer who went from busking in the street to lead role as Mabel in 'The Pirates of Penzance' (1983). Then came 'Camelot' (1984) and the prestigious female lead, Christine, in 'The Phantom of the Opera' (1992). She sang, to great acclaim, in concert with Jose Carreras in 1994.

Helen Reddy 1941–

In 1965 she was the most successful female vocalist in Australia. Her breakthrough in the USA came in 1972 with the single 'I Am Woman', which became the theme song for the women's liberation movement.

Tommy Tycho c. 1929–

A musical director, he migrated from Hungary in 1951, bringing with him the twin gifts of musical genius and excellent training. He has devoted his life to music, and is highly acclaimed as a superb conductor, composer, arranger and virtuoso pianist.

Anthony Warlow 1962–

He has a glorious baritone voice with a tenor reach. Had tremendous success in 'Les

Miserables' and was 'the voice' that gave 'The Phantom of the Opera' a spirit all of its own. His performances are a refreshing blend of sheer talent and amiability.

His perception and deep understanding of human nature allows this Aussie balladeer to write enormously popular songs, which strike a chord in most of us. 'Old Man Emu' was the first of many great hits. Others include 'True Blue', 'Cootamundra Wattle', 'Mallee Boy', 'Goodbye Blinky Bill', 'Rip, Rip, Woodchip' and 'Tubbo Station' which assure his continuing success.

John Williamson

Classical music

John Antill 1904–86

A composer, and former assistant musical director for the ABC. His ballet *Corroboree* is based on snatches of tunes gleaned from the music of the Aboriginals at La Pérouse, Sydney, and it has since been performed as a symphonic work by the London Symphony Orchestra.

Don Banks 1923–80

A leading Australian composer and teacher specialising in composition of electronic music. In the 1950s he established the Australian Music Association in London, which introduced Australian composers and performers to the international circuit.

Richard Bonynge 1930–

An opera conductor, he was the vocal coach for Joan Sutherland; they married in 1954. His conducting debut was with the Santa Cecilia Orchestra in Rome in 1962. He became the musical director of the Australian Opera in 1976, and is renowned for his interest in the lesser-known operas of the eighteenth and nineteenth centuries. (See also Opera.)

Nigel Butterley 1935–

A contemporary composer specialising in music for string quartets, he won the prestigious Italia Prize for *In the Head the Fire,* a musical work for radio. His music has often been inspired by poetry and architecture.

Stewart Challender 1948–91

A Tasmanian, he began his musical career at the age of five. He was guest conductor of many of the world's great orchestras, including the Chicago Symphony Orchestra, his greatest triumph. He was considered to be a master of the large symphony, and was chief conductor of the Sydney Symphony Orchestra.

Sir Eugene Goossens 1893–1962

An Englishman, he became the resident composer and conductor of the Sydney Symphony Orchestra and co-director of the NSW Conservatorium of Music in 1947. He was the SSO's greatest single influence, changing it from a city orchestra to one which was world class. He turned Sydney into a mecca for the world's finest artists.

Percy Grainger 1882–1961

A pianist and composer of world fame, he gave concerts as a child, and at the age of eleven continued his musical studies in Germany. His irreverent and uninhibited approach to the piano delighted his audiences everywhere. His most famous compositions were *Shepherd's Hey* and *Country Gardens* (c. 1907).

Sir Bernard Heinze 1894–1982

He was the most powerful musical administrator in Australia, and virtually controlled the classical musical scene in the 1940s and 50s. He was director of the NSW Conservatorium of Music and music advisor to the ABC, and he was responsible for all the states having their own symphony orchestras. He trained thousands of young musicians, and his music examination system is still used.

Eileen Joyce 1912–91

Born in the Tasmanian bush, she grew up in Kalgoorlie, and later became an international concert pianist. By 1950 she had the widest following of any concert pianist in England.

Sir Charles Mackerras 1925–

A renowned conductor with many successful postings to his credit, including one as the first conductor of the Hamburg State Opera, a position which he held until 1969. He is best known for his deeply sympathetic interpretation of Czechoslovakian music.

Joseph Post 1906–72

He was one of the most experienced and respected of Australia's musical conductors. His characteristic brisk and down-to-earth intensity was highly regarded. He was the original director of the Elizabethan Opera Company, an associate conductor of the Sydney Symphony Orchestra, and a director of the NSW Conservatorium of Music.

Peter Sculthorpe 1929–

A talented contemporary composer. From 1965 to 1967 he wrote *Sun Music I, II, III* and *IV*, all based on the Australian landscape. Other works include the operas *Rites of Passage* (1974) and *Quiros* (1982). In 1988 he composed the opera *Voss*, which was commissioned by the federal government for Australia's Bicentenary.

John Williams 1941–

One of the world's leading classical guitarists. His music possesses a distinctive clarity of tone. At the age of twelve he studied with the world-famous guitarist Andrés Segovia, after which he toured extensively. In 1979 he formed the jazz-oriented group Sky.

Malcolm Williamson 1931–

A prolific composer, he was appointed Master of the Queen's Music in 1975. His best-known works are the music for Sir Robert Helpmann's ballet *The Display* (1964), and his own opera *English Eccentrics*, which premiered at the Aldeburgh Festival in England.

Roger Woodward 1942–

An acclaimed pianist, he studied in London and Warsaw, and made his debut with the Warsaw National Philharmonic Orchestra in 1967. His wide repertoire ranges from Beethoven and Chopin to Australian contemporary music.

Simone Young 1962–

Regarded as one of the most highly talented conductors of her time making guest appearances conducting orchestras worldwide. She broke new ground in 1993 when she became the first female conductor of the all-male Berlin Philharmonic Orchestra.

Ballet

In 1938 Edouard Borovansky established his renowned ballet company in Melbourne. Before this, overseas companies enjoyed great success in Australia but the local artists were viewed with some degree of apathy. His company was a pioneering force for the next two decades, with local artists and productions of high quality. In 1961 a new national company was formed, the Australian Ballet (now the Australian Ballet Foundation), under the artistic direction of Peggy Van Praagh. This, together with subsidies from the federal government in the 1970s, enabled Australian ballet to at last become recognised worldwide.

Vicki Attard c. 1967–

An accomplished principal artist with the Australian Ballet whose inspired performances in the title roles of *Giselle* and Odette in *Swan Lake* have gained her much recognition. She dances regularly with the Sydney Dance Company and danced the title role with them in *Daphnis and Chloe* in USA.

Margaret Barr c. 1925–

A protégé of Martha Graham of New York. She is an imaginative and independent dancer, choeographer and teacher.

Edouard Borovansky 1902–59

Czech-born, he came to Australia as a dancer with Anna Pavlova in 1926. In 1938 he returned, and founded the Borovansky Ballet in Melbourne in 1939. This company was the nucleus of the present Australian Ballet.

Kelvin Coe 1946–92

A foundation member of the Australian Ballet, he and Marilyn Rowe-Maver were the first Australians to compete in the Moscow International Ballet Competition in 1973.

Miranda Coney 1966–

An extensive repertoire including the title roles in *Romeo and Juliet* and Princess Aurora in *The Sleeping Beauty* has placed this Perth-born artist at the top of her profession. She is a principal artist of the Australian Ballet, touring extensively overseas winning many awards.

Paul De Masson 1953–

This highly motivated dancer, choreographer, producer and actor has performed on many stages around the world. He is a principal artist of the Australian Ballet and his extremely varied repertoire includes leading roles in *Spartacus*, *The Pillar of Fire* and *The Rite of Spring*.

Maina Gielgud 1946–

Artistic director of the Australian Ballet since 1983 she has made an outstanding contribution to the Australian ballet scene.

Steven Heathcote 1965–

Born in Perth, he has toured extensively. He is presently a principal dancer with the Australian Ballet.

Steven Heathcote in the ballet Spartacus

Sir Robert Helpmann 1909–86

Born in Adelaide, he danced his way to fame in 1933, partnering Dame Margot Fonteyn at the Sadler's Wells Ballet. He created the first all-Australian ballet, *The Display*, in 1964.

Greg Horsman 1963–

Was a principal artist in the Australian Ballet. He is married to dancer Lisa Pavane and in 1994 they became senior principal dancers with the English National Ballet.

Marilyn Jones 1940–

She was widely considered to be Australia's prima ballerina. She danced with Marquis de Cuevas and Borovansky companies.

David McAllister 1963–

With guest appearances worldwide and an extensive repertoire, his performances are inspiring. He is a principal artist with the Australian Ballet and his outstanding soloist roles include those in *Equus* and *Don Quixote*.

Adam Marchant 1963–

A highly creative and competent dancer whose innovative approach has won great acclaim. He has performed many principal roles with the Australian Ballet including the title role in *Spartacus* and as Danilo in *The Merry Widow*.

Laurel Martyn 1916–

She has had a distinguished career spanning more than half a century. She danced with the famed Sadler's Wells Ballet, and for thirty years she was director of the Victoria Ballet Guild.

Graeme Murphy 1950–

Melbourne-born, he became the artistic and choreographer director of the Sydney Dance Company in 1976. The 1992 production of *Nutcracker* was amongst his most innovative productions.

Justine Summers, Damien Welch and Vicki Attard 'Divergence'

Garry Norman 1951–

An inspired dancer, his elevation to soloist and a principal dancer with the Australian Ballet was meteoric. He toured the world extensively, then became a faculty member of the Australian Ballet School in 1982.

Lisa Pavane 1962–

Born in Newcastle, she became a principal artist of the Australian Ballet in 1986. Her performances were breathtaking. She is now senior principal dancer with the English National Ballet.

Colin Peasley 1934–

His background in theatre, television, classical ballet and modern dance has flavoured his distinguished career. His extraordinary ability to re-create character roles has placed him at the top of his profession. He is the manager of educational programmes with the Australian Ballet.

Dame Peggy Van Praagh 1901–90

A dancer and ballet mistress with the Sadler's Wells Ballet School, she then became the founding director of the Australian Ballet which encouraged and established the careers of many young, talented dancers.

Marilyn Rowe-Maver 1946–

The first ballerina to reach the pinnacle of her profession having trained only with the Australian Ballet. In 1973 she, together with Kelvin Coe, won a silver medal in Moscow.

Dame Margaret Scott 1922–

She danced with the Sadler's Wells Ballet in London (1940–52). She became founding director of the Australian Ballet School in 1964, and retired in 1990 after more than fifty years' association with ballet.

Gailene Stock 1946–

In 1962, at the age of sixteen, she was the youngest member of the fledgling Australian Ballet. She toured extensively, and in 1990 she succeeded Dame Margaret Scott as the new director of the Australian Ballet School.

Roslyn Watson 1954–

A talented Aboriginal dancer who trained with the Australian Ballet, she joined the Australian Dance Theatre in 1979. In Paris in 1982 she produced a ballet, *Voyage at the End of a Dream*.

Garth Welch 1937–

A highly innovative teacher of abstract dance. He is now Dean of the Victorian College of Arts' School of Dance.

Opera

Opera has always been popular in Australia, and eisteddfods and aria competitions foster the aspirations of young singers. Tendency in the past had been to disregard local talent in favour of overseas singers and productions; singers were expected to have European training before they were recognised. Great Australian singers of the early part of the century were:

Florence Austral 1894–1968

She stood supreme amongst world sopranos. Her great vocal ability to evoke strong emotion enchanted audiences and was unparalleled. She battled for many years with multiple sclerosis.

'A Midsummer Night's Dream' (Australian Opera)

John Brownlee 1901–69

A world-famous operatic baritone who was encouraged by Dame Nellie Melba. He sang duets with her in the early 1900s.

Dorothy Helmrich 1889–1984

She was the first Australian to achieve worldwide recognition as a lieder singer. She founded the Arts Council movement in Australia in 1943 to enable the youth of the nation to experience music and the arts.

Gertrude Johnson c.1897–1973

A coloratura soprano, she was a pupil of Melba. She founded the Australian National Theatre Movement in 1934, which at last began to produce operas with all-Australian casts.

Marjorie Lawrence 1908–79

A brilliant soprano, she made operatic history in Europe by riding a horse into the flames on stage as Brunnhilde in *Der Ring des Nibelungen*, as Wagner intended. In 1941 she contracted poliomyelitis but made many wheelchair appearances.

Dame Nellie Melba 1861–1931

Her voice was acclaimed everywhere for its purity and silvery brilliance of tone. Gounod coached her in the role of Juliette in his opera *Romeo et Juliette*, and Puccini chose her to play Mimi in his opera *La Boheme* in 1900.

In 1934 the National Theatre Movement was established, and in 1951 Clarice Lorenz set up the National Opera of Australia.

The Australian Elizabethan Theatre Trust was formed in 1956, and with government and private funding, Australian opera is at last highly regarded internationally. Recent contemporary artists are:

Robert Allman 1929–

A principal baritone of world renown, his ability and sensitivity enables him to create wonderful dramatic characters such as Tonio in *Pagliacci*.

Heather Begg 1933–

A New Zealand-born mezzo soprano, with an international career spanning nearly 40 years. Well known for her extensive repertoire of character roles such as Flora in *La traviata* and Mother Marie in *Dialogues of the Carmelites*.

Joan Carden c. 1939–

A soprano, and one of the truly remarkable singers to emerge in Australia. Her international performances were highly acclaimed; in 1971 she returned and began a long association with national opera, with singing engagements all over Australia.

Marie Collier 1927–71

A dramatic and flamboyant soprano, her greatest triumph came in 1964 when she stood in for Maria Callas in *Tosca* at Covent Garden, taking fourteen curtain calls and twenty minutes of applause. She fell to her death in London in 1971.

Dame Joan Hammond 1912–

A soprano, she upheld the traditions of Nellie Melba and Florence Austral, and reigned supreme in prima donna roles. She toured the world extensively, and was noted for her superb singing of the role of Tosca.

Yvonne Kenny c. 1952–

A leading soprano, she appears regularly in operas around the world as well as performing with famous symphony and philharmonic orchestras in Europe. Recently topped the classical music charts with popular opera and song selections for ABC Classics.

Yvonne Kenny

Moffatt Oxenbould 1944–

He was appointed artistic director of The Australian Opera in 1984 after producing many operas over a thirty-year period.

Graham Pushee c. 1955–

Much sought after because of his unusual counter-tenor voice. He has appeared in most of the famous opera houses of the world to sell-out audiences. Has an extensive repertoire including title role in Handel's *Julius Caesar* and Andronicus in Handel's *Tambourlaine*.

Donald Shanks 1940–

A bass baritone from Brisbane, he has been singing professionally with the Australian Opera since he was twenty-four. His versatility spans dramatic, comic and *bel canto* styles, and his roles include many from the works of Wagner and Verdi. He is in great demand overseas.

John Shaw c. 1923–

A baritone, he began his international career as Rigoletto at Covent Garden in 1958. He is renowned for his roles as Iago in *Otello* and Scarpia in *Tosca*.

Donald Smith 1922–

A lyric tenor, he was born in Bundaberg, Qld. and spent most of his career in Australia. His greatest roles were Manrico in *Il Travatore* and Calaf in *Turandot*.

Dame Joan Sutherland 1926–

She is the foremost soprano of our age, and one of the greatest operatic artists of all time. Her husband and coach, conductor Richard Bonynge, recognised the potential of her voice, and together they resurrected some of the seldom-sung major 'bel canto' roles in opera. She retired in 1990.

Neil Warren-Smith 1929–81

He was a leading principal bass singer with a refreshing comic talent. Sang with the Australian Opera for twenty-five years.

DID YOU KNOW?
The Australian Opera begins preparation for future seasons five years in advance. In general terms a new production could cost between $500 000 and $900 000 (1995).

Art

The Dreaming is an Aboriginal philosophy explaining the origins of the universe. It embraces people, animals and landscape as part of a harmonious whole. Ancient Aboriginal art, spanning tens of thousands of years, reflects this religious theme, and there are many cave paintings and rock carvings of great significance still in existence. The modern resurgence of Aboriginal art, incorporating new forms, continues this rich tradition and philosophy.

For early European painters in Australia the new land was so strange that they found it difficult to reproduce a true likeness of their surroundings. Convict painters, such as Joseph Lycett, John Eyre and Thomas Watling, produced bland images more reminiscent of the gentler landscape of their homeland than the harsher landscape of Australia. Free settlers who had arrived by 1830 included professional artists, and they recorded the new colony in a more romantic way in drawings and watercolours.

Louis Buvelot 1814–88

A Swiss, who could depict the elusive colours of light, he brought to Australia the traditions of European landscape painting, and profoundly influenced young artists of the 1860s and 70s by encouraging them to paint outdoors.

Charles Conder 1868–1909

A surveyor, he met Tom Roberts in a Sydney wine bar in 1888, and returned with him to Melbourne where he spent two years painting at the artist's camp. His paintings include *The Departure of the S.S. Orient* (1888) and *A Holiday at Mentone* (1888).

John Glover 1767—1849

He arrived in Tasmania in 1831, aged sixty-four. He recognised the differences and subtleties of light in Australia, and this is evident in his paintings *Patterdale Farm* (c. 1840) and *Glover's House and Garden* (1840).

Sir Hans Heysen 1877–1968

His parents emigrated from Germany, and settled in Hahndorf, South Australia. He remained completely unaffected by the popular theories of the day, and had a single-minded devotion to the one ideal of capturing the beauty and majesty of the Australian landscape. A notable example is *Summer* (1909).

Frederick McCubbin 1855–1917

Inspired by the landscape around Melbourne, more than any painter before him, he understood the Australian bush. His paintings frequently told stories of the hardship of the pioneers: *Down on his Luck* (1889), *The Wallaby Track* (1896), and the three-panel work *The Pioneer* (1904).

Sir Bertram Mackennal 1863–1931

A prolific sculptor. In 1888 he completed the panelling for Government House in Melbourne. His most famous works are *Circe* (1893), and a marble bust of Dame Nellie Melba (1899).

Conrad Martens 1801–78

A watercolourist, he left England in 1832, and after sailing around the world for three years settled in Sydney. His main paintings were *Sydney* (1857) and The *Viaduct Lithgow* (1876).

Max Meldrum 1875–1955

A former pupil of McCubbin, he caused a sensation in art circles by challenging the Heidelberg school's theories. His ideas of strict tonal painting were promoted through his own art school, which he began in 1913. One of his most famous works showing tonal theory is *Portrait of the Artist's Mother* (1913).

Tom Roberts 1856–1931

The 'father' of Australian landscape painting. A pupil of Buvelot and influenced by French Impressionism, he recognised the subtle effects of the changing of light on colour. He and Frederick McCubbin started the now-famous painting camps outside Melbourne, and together with Arthur Streeton and Charles Conder were the first Australian painters to capture the spirit and colour of the Australian landscape; they became known as the Heidelberg School of Australian Impressionism. His paintings

The Sunny South *by Tom Roberts*

Shearing the Rams *by Tom Roberts*

include *Bailed Up* (1895), *Shearing the Rams* (1890) and *Breakaway* (1891).

Sir Arthur Streeton 1867–1943

He was revered as the painter who 'fixed the images of his country'. He was an official World War I artist, and his works are displayed in the Australian War Memorial in Canberra. His most noted paintings include *Fire's On, Lapstone Tunnel* (1891) and *The Purple Noon's Transparent Might* (1896).

During the first part of the twentieth century post-impressionism came to prominence. The many influences resulted in a kaleidoscope of differing styles, which gave rise to the Modern Movement in Australia: experiments with texture and colour allowed artists to be less restricted; they became aware of the vastness of the desolate landscape, the intimidatory nature of the urban scene, and the hostile character of war.

Arthur Boyd 1920–

Along with artists such as Albert Tucker, Sidney Nolan, John Perceval and Danila Vassilieff, he belonged to the 'Angry Decade' of 1937–47 which disliked the complacency of Australian society. Boyd's works include *The Butterfly Man* (1943), *Wimmera Landscape* (1950), *Figure in Landscape* (1961) and *Landscape at Murrumbeena* (1987).

Born in Vienna, she came to Australia as a refugee with her family after World War II. She is best known as a portrait painter in an abstract and impressionist style. Her portraits of the royal family were hung at the Royal Academy, London, in 1962.

Grace Cossington Smith 1892–1984

Together with Roland Wakelin and Roy de Maistre, she established the Modern Movement in Sydney. Her painting *The Sock Knitter* (1915) was the first modern painting to be exhibited in Australia by an Australian.

John Coburn 1925–

An abstract painter; among his works are *Power Game* (1968), and the design for the 'Moon and Sun' curtains for the Sydney Opera House in 1973.

Sir William Dobell 1899–1970

His finest works were portraits, such as *Margaret Olley* (1948) and *Dame Mary Gilmore* (1957). He won the Archibald Prize in 1943 with the controversial portrait *Joshua Smith*. His other work includes *The Boy at the Basin* (1932) and *The Billy Boy* (1943).

Sir Russell Drysdale 1912–81

He was born in England into a

The Rabbiters *by Russell Drysdale*

family whose members had been among the pioneer pastoralists of Australia. *Two Children* (1946), *The Rabbiters* (1947) and *Sofala* (1947) are among his well-known works which capture the desolation and colour of the outback.

Sam Fullbrook 1922–

He is recognised as a supreme colourist, and is one of Australia's best draughtsmen. A maverick in the art world, he lives in Ohio, USA. His works include *Girl and Fruit* (1967) and *The White Heifer* (1985).

Sali Herman 1898–1993

Swiss-born, he migrated to Australia in 1937. He was best known for his paintings of the early slums and tenements of Sydney, particularly the areas of Paddington, Kings Cross and Woolloomooloo. Typical of his works are *Potts Point* (1957) and *Colonial Castle* (1958).

Robert Klippel 1920–

He is considered to be Australia's greatest modern contemporary sculptor. His *Steel and Bronze* sculpture (1961) is exhibited in the Art Gallery of New South Wales.

Colin Lanceley 1938–

He tries to produce in his collage paintings a deep sense of belonging, and melds sculpture and painting into one poetic art form. His *Pianist,* *Pianist* (1965), *The Fall of Icarus* (1985) and *The Song of a Summer Night – Lynn's Garden* (1985), are among his well-known works.

Norman Lindsay 1879–1969

He was a controversial and multi-talented artist, and his works included woodcuts, watercolours and etchings. Well-known works are *Pollice Verso* (1907) and *The Crucified Venus* (1907). He wrote and illustrated the children's book *The Magic Pudding* (1918).

Sally Morgan 1951–

She was inspired to paint when she met a near-blind relative on the edge of the desert who drew stories of his people. Her paintings deal with the history of Aboriginal people in Western Australia.

Albert Namatjira 1902–59

A full-blooded member of the Arunta tribe, his watercolours of Central Australia became very popular in the 1950s and 60s. He handled European techniques with great skill.

Trevor Nicholls 1949–

A painter of considerable experience, he has lectured in art in most states of Australia. He has held many individual exhibitions, and was chosen to represent Australia at the 1990 Venice Biennale.

He was perhaps the most distinguished Australian painter of the century. He often painted series which together captured a changing mood or action. *Paradise Gardens*, consisting of 1320 paintings, was given by Sir Sidney to the Victorian Arts Centre, and is permanently housed there. Other examples are *Pretty Polly Mine* (1948) and the *Ned Kelly* series (1956).

John Olsen 1928–

A landscape painter who depicts the emotions. His *Salute to Five Bells* (1973) is in the Sydney Opera House.

Margaret Preston 1883–1963

A prolific painter, she was a forthright modernist who had an instinctive feel for colour. Later in her career she was influenced by Aboriginal art and carvings. Her works include *Implement Blue* (1927) and *Gum Blossoms* (1927).

Lloyd Rees 1895–1988

He was a fine draughtsman with a unique vision of the Australian landscape, and his works recall the dreamlike quality of the light and colour of Tuscany. Among his paintings are *The Road to Berry* (1946) and *A Tribute to France* (1968).

Ron Robertson-Swann 1941–87

He is a contemporary surrealistic sculptor who works with unemotional objects. His machine-like sculpture *Big Red* was completed in 1962.

Dick Roughsey c. 1920–87

A member of the Lardil tribe from the Gulf of Carpentaria, he was encouraged to paint by a charter pilot, Percy Trezise. He received considerable acclaim Australia-wide, and his paintings include selections from his book *The Rainbow Serpent* (1976).

Tim Storrier 1949–

A contemporary abstract painter, he is an exponent of still life. His works include *Moonstick, Box and Berry – Still Life with Fire* (1976) and *Isolation* (1977).

Clifford Possum Tjapaltjarri c. 1943– and Tim Leurah Tjapaltjarri c. 1930–84

Members of the Anmatjera clan of the Northern Territory, in the 1960s and 70s they learnt to use the mediums of acrylic paints and canvas. Their paintings still reflected traditional symbols and imagery, but were painted in a contemporary way. Their *Paint on Canvas – Warlugulong* (1976) hangs in the Art Gallery of New South Wales.

Brett Whiteley 1939–92

He was an uninhibited and polished draughtsman who tried to express in his paintings 'life force and its insoluble conflicts'. His works include *The Christie Series* (1964), *The Big Orange –*

Sunset (1974) and *The Balcony* (1975).

He was born in Melbourne, and in his works he simplified and abstracted the Australian landscape. Examples include *Sapling Forest* (1962) and *Waterfall Polyptych* (1979).

Sporting highlights

1901   Australia wins cricket test match against England. In one game M. A. Noble takes 7 wickets for 17 runs, and Hugh Trumble a hat-trick. England all out for 61, Australia wins by 229 runs.

1903   First car race in Australia. Dick Cavill wins every men's freestyle event at Australian swimming championships.

1904   First Australian Open golf championship held at Botany, NSW.

1905   First Davis Cup entry by Australasia. Norman Brookes reaches the tennis finals at Wimbledon.

1906   Bondi Surf Bathers' Life Saving Club is formed.

1907   First Davis Cup win to Australasia. Norman Brookes is the first non-British tennis player to win at Wimbledon (singles, doubles and mixed doubles). Rugby League begins.

1908   First Australian Surf Carnival held at Manly, NSW. H. D. McIntosh builds Sydney Stadium to promote world boxing. Australia wins gold at London Olympics for Rugby Union. Davis Cup final here for first time. Australasia beats USA 3–2.

1909   Australian Rugby Union team, called Wallabies for first time, beats England 25 to 5 games, 2 drawn.

1910   Frank Beaurepaire tours Europe, winning all 48 swimming races in which he competes.

1911   Second Kangaroo Rugby League team tours England and wins test, a feat not repeated until 1963. Australian Pro Golf Association formed.

1912   The all-round sportsman 'Snowy' Baker buys Sydney Stadium and establishes championship conditions, rules and standardisation in Australian boxing. Australia wins two gold medals at Stockholm Olympics: Fanny Durack (swimming), and men's swimming team.

1913   Dally Messenger, 'master of Australian Rugby League', retires. Middleweight Jerry Jerome becomes first Aboriginal to hold the title of national boxing champion.

1914	Norman Brookes wins men's singles tennis title at Wimbledon.
1916	Les Darcy becomes Australian heavyweight boxing champion.
1917	Annette Kellerman makes world record dive of 28 metres. Les Darcy dies in the United States.
1918	A cricket over is increased from 6 to 8 balls.
1919	Australian Imperial Force rowing team wins Royal Henley Peace Regatta; the trophy becomes the King's Cup.
1922	Gerald Patterson wins men's singles tennis title at Wimbledon.
1924	Australia wins three gold medals at Paris Olympics: Andrew 'Boy' Charlton (swimming), Dick Eve (high dive) and Anthony Winter (triple jump). Speedway racing is inaugurated at Maitland, NSW.
1926	Sydney Showground speedway opens. Roy Cazaly becomes folk-hero of Australian Rules football. The cry 'Up there Cazaly' passes into the language.
1927	First meeting of 'electric hare racing' at Epping, NSW. Fred Cavill, who experimented and developed new swimming techniques, dies.
1928	H. R. Pearce wins gold medal at Amsterdam Olympics for single sculls rowing. Don Bradman plays in his first cricket test match. Hubert Opperman wins French Bol d'Or 24-hour cycling event.
1929	Sydney–Perth Trans-Continental Air Race – de Havilland makes fastest time in *Gypsy Moth.*
1930	Phar Lap wins Melbourne Cup, at 11/8 on, being the shortest odds in history of Cup. Bradman sets world record in first-class cricket for a single innings with a score of 452 runs. Bradman's aggregate of 974 runs in five tests against England sets world record (still stands) of 139.14.
1932	Phar Lap dies in the United States in controversial circumstances. Walter Lindrum sets world record in billiards. 'Bodyline' cricket test series begins. Australia wins three gold medals at Los Angeles Olympics: Claire Dennis (breaststroke), Duncan Gray (cycling), H. R. Pearce (rowing).
1933	England regains the Ashes after controversial 'bodyline' cricket tour. Jack Crawford wins men's singles at Wimbledon.
1934	C. W. A. Scott and T. Campbell Black win Melbourne Centenary England–Australia Air Race. Australia wins the Ashes in England.

1935   Adrian Quist and Jack Crawford win Wimbledon doubles
        title.
1936   Don Bradman appointed Australian cricket captain. Lionel
        van Praag wins first world speedway title. Water-skiing
        begins in Australia.
1937   First Australian women cricket team tours England.
1938   Bathurst's Mt Panaroma racing circuit completed. Peter
        Whitehead of England wins Grand Prix at Bathurst, NSW.
1939   Australia wins Davis Cup for first time.
1945   First Sydney–Hobart yacht race.
1946   Sydney Turf Club introduces photo-finish cameras. Horace
        Lindrum wins world snooker championship.
1947   Jim Ferrier wins US professional golf champion title. John
        Marshall wins every Australian men's freestyle champion-
        ship.
1948   Australia wins two gold medals in London Olympics: John
        Winter (high jump), Mervyn Wood (single sculls). Don
        Bradman retires from test cricket with an aggregate of 6996
        runs made in 52 tests (av. 99.94).
1949   Don Bradman is knighted. David Sands wins Empire
        middleweight boxing title.

The Melbourne Cup

1950   Jockey Rae 'Togo' Johnstone wins four of the five England classic horse races in one season. Adrian Quist and John Bromwich win Wimbledon doubles title. John Marshall's sensational swimming establishes four world freestyle records in US national championships. Clive Churchill captains Australia's Rugby League team's victory against England.

1951   Frank Sedgman wins US men's singles tennis title.

1952   Australia wins six gold medals at Helsinki Olympics: Marjorie Jackson (running, 2), Shirley Strickland (hurdles), Russell Mockridge (cycling), Mockridge/Lionel Cox (tandem). Ken Rosewall and Lew Hoad (both 17) win Wimbledon doubles tennis. Jimmy Carruthers is Australia's first world boxing champion.

1953   Lew Hoad and Ken Rosewall retain Davis Cup.

1954   Golfers Peter Thompson and Kel Nagle win Canada Cup. Peter Thompson wins the British Open golf tournament. Jimmy Carruthers retires undefeated from world boxing. John Landy becomes the second man to break the four-minute mile, a few weeks after Roger Bannister of England. Bannister beats Landy at Vancouver Commonwealth Games (the first race where two men break the four-minute mile). Clive Churchill captains Australia's World Cup Rugby League team in France. 'Gelignite' Jack Murray wins Redex Motor Trial.

1955   Arthur 'Scobie' Breasley begins a horse-racing record of 100 winners each season.

1956   The first Olympic Games held in the Southern Hemisphere are held in Melbourne. Australia wins 13 gold medals: Betty Cuthbert (sprinting, 2), Shirley Strickland (hurdles), women's relay, Ian Brown and Anthony Marchant (cycling), Jon Hendricks (freestyle), Murray Rose (freestyle, 2), David Thiele (backstroke), men's swimming relay, Dawn Fraser (freestyle), Lorraine Crapp (freestyle, beats 18 world swimming records), and women's swimming relay. Lew Hoad beats Ken Rosewall for men's singles tennis title at Wimbledon. Peter Thompson wins the British Open golf tournament, the first to win the event three years in succession.

DID YOU KNOW?

The racecourse Automatic Totalizator (tote) was invented by George Julius of Sydney in 1913.

Aussie Rules Football

1957   Ian Craig captains Australia's cricket team in Johannesburg. John Marshall, the swimmer, is killed in a car crash. Ron Barassi kicks five goals in Australian Rules grand final match between Melbourne and Essendon.

1958   Herb Elliott runs his first sub-four-minute mile in 3 minutes 59.9 seconds. Marlene Matthews sets world records for running 90 metres and 200 metres. Richard (Richie) Benaud, great all-rounder, captains Australian cricket team from 1958 to 1963.

1959   Racing driver Jack Brabham becomes world Grand Prix champion. Reg Gasnier begins his career in Rugby League. John Konrads wins all men's freestyle swimming events in the Australian championships.

1960   Australia wins eight gold medals at the Rome Olympics: Herb Elliott (running), Dawn Fraser (freestyle), Murray Rose (freestyle), David Thiele (backstroke), John Devitt (freestyle), John Konrads (freestyle), and two in the equestrian events. Neale Frazer beats Rod Laver at Wimbledon. Australia plays the West Indies in the only cricket test ever tied. Kel Nagle wins British Open golf championship in its centenary year.

1961   Heather Blundell McKay is national squash champion.

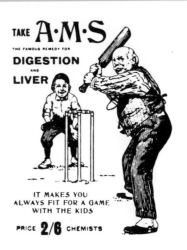

TAKE **A·M·S**

THE FAMOUS REMEDY FOR

DIGESTION

AND

LIVER

IT MAKES YOU
ALWAYS FIT FOR A GAME
WITH THE KIDS

PRICE **2/6** CHEMISTS

1962   Australia wins 17 gold medals in the Perth Commonwealth Games. Dawn Fraser becomes the first woman swimmer to break 60 seconds for 100 metres freestyle. Rod Laver wins 'Grand Slam' of world tennis (Australian, French, Wimbledon and US titles – second man to do so). Stewart McKenzie wins Henley Diamond Sculls for the sixth time. Reg Gasnier is appointed Australia's youngest-ever Rugby League test captain (aged 23).

1963   Margaret Smith Court is first Australian to win Wimbledon women's singles title. Ken Hiscoe wins all world squash titles. Australian netball team wins world championship in London.

1964   Lake Eyre, SA, is venue for world land and water speed records (Donald Campbell). The first official world surfing championship held at Manly, won by Midget Farrelly. Australia wins six gold medals at the Tokyo Olympics: Betty Cuthbert (sprinting), Dawn Fraser (freestyle), Kevin Berry (butterfly), Ian O'Brien (breaststroke), Robert Windle (freestyle), and the 5.5 metre class yachting. Dawn Fraser becomes the only swimmer ever to win gold medals in three successive Olympic Games (still stands, 1995).

1965   Linda McGill is the first Australian to swim the English Channel. Long-distance runner Ron Clarke breaks 11 world records. Bill Lance sails single-handed around Cape Horn. Geoff Hunt is national squash champion at 17 years of age.

Peter Thompson wins the British Open golf tournament for the fifth time (second only to H. Vardon, six times).

1966   First-ever lawn bowls world championships held in Sydney; Australia wins.

1967   Australia wins Admiral's Cup for yachting. Roy Emerson becomes Australian singles tennis champion. *Dame Pattie* loses America's Cup challenge. George Moore wins the English Derby on Royal Palace. Australia wins Davis Cup for fourth successive time.

1968   Australia wins five gold medals at the Mexico Olympics: Ralph Doubell (sprinting), Maureen Caird (hurdles), Michael Wenden (freestyle, 2), Lynette McClements (butterfly). Annual Iron Man surfing championships introduced: Barry Rogers wins first three. Boxer Lionel Rose wins world bantamweight title. Rod Laver becomes the first player to win two 'Grand Slams' in world tennis. Nat Young wins world surfboard championship.

1969   Boxer Johnny Famechon wins world featherweight title. Margaret Court wins 'Grand Slam' of tennis (second woman to do so).

1970   Australia loses third America's Cup challenge. John Newcombe wins men's singles at Wimbledon. Judy Trim wins world championship in ladies' standard pistol shooting. Bill Lawry retires from test cricket after scoring a total of 13 centuries. Ken Rosewall wins USA open tennis championship.

1971   Wayne Jones is the first Australian to waterski over 160 km/h. Ken Rosewall wins world tennis championship in Dallas, Texas. Roy Emerson and Rod Laver win men's doubles at Wimbledon. Evonne Goolagong, the first Aboriginal to play at Wimbledon, wins the women's singles championship. Australian netball team wins the world championship in Kingston, Jamaica. Gunsynd, the 'Goondiwindi grey', wins the 'grand slam' of four top mile events in Australian horse racing (the Epsom, Toorak, George Adams and Doncaster handicaps).

1972   Australia wins eight gold medals at Munich Olympics: Brad Cooper (freestyle), Shane Gould (medley; freestyle, 2), Beverley Whitfield (breaststroke), Gail Neall (medley), John Cuneo and David Forbes (yachting). Shane Gould becomes the first woman to hold all world freestyle swimming records at once (five). Joe Meissner, from Sydney, becomes the first non-Japanese world karate champion.

1973 Margaret Court wins her fifth US tennis singles championship. Heather McKay wins her fourteenth Australian women's squash title.

1974 Evonne Goolagong wins Australian women's open tennis title. Australia qualifies for World Soccer Cup final for first time.

1975 John Newcombe beats Jimmy Conners for Australian men's open tennis title. Des Renford becomes 'King of the Channel' with his tenth English Channel crossing between 1970 and 1975. Australian netball team wins world championship in Auckland, NZ.

1976 Controversy over Raylene Boyle's disqualification for two 'false' starts at Montreal Olympics.

1977 Women's bowls team wins a gold medal in world bowls titles. Rocky Mattioli wins the world junior middleweight boxing championship. Trainer Bart Cummings has his sixth Melbourne Cup win with the horse Gold and Black. World Series Cricket is launched. Australia and England commemorate 100 years of test cricket. Heather McKay wins her sixteenth British squash championship. Wayne Bartholomew wins world surfing championship.

1978 Tracey Wickham takes the only world record set at the Commonwealth Games. Australian women's cricket team wins the second World Cup tournament in India. Ken Warby sets world's water speed record. Edwina Kennedy, 19, of Sydney, becomes British women's amateur golf champion.

1979 Jack Newton wins Australian Open golf tournament. Greg Norman wins Hong Kong Open golf tournament. Australian Netball team shares win in World Championship in Spain.

1980 Australia wins two gold medals at the Moscow Olympic Games: Michelle Ford (freestyle) and the men's medley swimming relay. Jeff Hunt wins his seventh Australian Open squash title. Greg Norman wins Australian Open golf tournament. Allan Jones wins World's Formula One driver championship. Grant Kenny wins both junior and senior Iron Man titles (aged 16). Des Renford swims English Channel three times in ten days to regain title of 'King of the Channel' (16 crossings in all). Gary Sutton wins world amateur point score for 50 kilometre cycling (the most prolific winner of national titles, 41).

1981　David Graham wins US Open golf championship. Australian women's cricket team wins third World Cup tournament in New Zealand. Jan Stephenson wins the women's world golfing championship in Japan.

1982　Australia wins three gold medals at Commonwealth Games in Brisbane. Bob Shearer wins Australian Open golf tournament. Kangaroo Rugby League team wins all matches against British Isles and France, for the first time.

1983　Jeanette Baker wins Tenpin Bowling World Cup. Greg Chappell retires; he was Australia's highest run-getter (displacing Bradman) with 7110 runs in his career; played in 88 tests. Dennis Lillee retires, one of the greatest fast bowlers in world test cricket. Rodney Marsh retires as one of the greatest wicketkeepers of all time. *Australia II* wins the America's Cup for 12 metre class yachts, after America had held it for 132 years. Eddie Charlton considered Australia's top snooker player. Davis Cup victory for Australia. Greg Norman wins Hong Kong Open again. Grant Kenny wins fourth Iron Man title. Australian Netball team wins world championship in Singapore.

1984　Australia wins four gold medals at the Los Angeles Olympics: Dean Lukin (weightlifting, super heavyweight), Glynis Nunn (heptathlon), Jon Sieben (butterfly), and men's pursuit cycling. Peter Brock wins Bathurst 1000 car race for eighth time. Kim Hughes, captain of Australia's test cricket team, resigns over criticism. The Wallabies Rugby Union team is undefeated and complete a 'grand slam' by defeating England, Scotland, Wales and Ireland in four tests. Mark Ella is the first Aboriginal to become captain of Australian Rugby Union team; on tour of United Kingdom he scores tries against England, Wales, Scotland and Ireland in the one season (a record). Darren Gauci becomes champion apprentice jockey of the year. Bret Wing becomes fastest man in world for barefoot water skiing. His brother Robert becomes fastest man in world for backward barefoot water skiing.

1985   Inaugural Australia Games held. Jeff Fenech (20) wins IBF world junior bantamweight title. Barry Michael wins IBF world junior lightweight title from Lester Ellis. An Australian rebel cricket team tours South Africa. The Australian women's bowls team wins three gold medals at world bowls titles held in Melbourne (Merle Richardson, captain). World Formula One Grand Prix first held in Adelaide.

1986   Robert de Castella wins Boston Marathon. Australia wins 40 gold medals in the Edinburgh Commonwealth Games; these include Lisa Martin's win in the inaugural women's marathon and Gail Martin's first Australian win in the women's discus and shot putt. For the second time running, the Kangaroo Rugby League team is undefeated in tour of British Isles and France. Men's eights win world championship rowing. Australia wins men's world cup hockey. Kerry Saxby sets world record in Moscow for walking (10 km track). The World Cup, played in India and Pakistan, was won by an Australian cricket team for the first time.

1987   Greg Norman wins British Open Golf championship. Jeff Fenech successfully defends his EBC World Super Bantamweight Boxing Championship. Wayne Gardner wins the World 500 cc Motorcycle Championship. Pat Cash becomes the first Australian to win Wimbledon in 17 years. Maree Lyndon becomes the first woman jockey to ride in the Melbourne Cup. Martin Vinnicombe wins the world amateur 1000 metres cycling championship.

1988   Yacht designer Ben Lexcen dies. Kay Cottee becomes the first woman sailor to circumnavigate the globe, solo and non-stop (190 days). Australia wins three gold medals at Seoul Olympics: Duncan Armstrong (freestyle), Debbie Flintoff-King (hurdles), and women's hockey team. Jeff Fenech wins the IBF world bantamweight, the WBC world super bantamweight and the WBC world featherweight boxing titles, becoming the first boxer in history to win three world titles without a defeat on his record.

1989   Australian cricket team regains the Ashes in England. Clifford Bertram (68) oldest man to ever swim the English Channel. Wayne Gardner wins inaugural 500 cc motorcycle Grand Prix at Phillip Island. Barton Lynch wins world surfing championship. Stephen Pate wins world professional cycling championship. Ian Dipple wins world water ski championship. Kerry Saxby sets world record for 3 kilometre indoor walk. Jeff Fenech successfuly defends his WBC World Featherweight boxing crown for 3rd time. Jeff 'Hitman' Harding takes WBC world light heavyweight title.

1990   Vicki Roycroft is world champion lady show jumper. Susie Maroney (15) becomes the youngest and fastest Australian to swim the English Channel. Trevor Hendy wins Iron Man. Stephen McGlede wins world 50 kilometre amateur cycling point score. Jeff Harding successfully defends his boxing title, then loses it in a sensational knockout.

1991   Inaugural Gold Coast Indianapolis car race. Australian equestrian team wins Nations Cup in Hungary. Shelley Taylor-Smith world marathon swimming champion. Richard Marsh wins inaugural AA rated Australian Surf Professional Open championship. Craig Parry wins Italian open golf championship. Susie Maroney swims record breaking double crossing of English Channel. Ian Baker-Finch wins British Open Golf Championship. Simon Fairweather is first Australian to win world's archery title. Australian women's netball team wins world championship. Australian women's hockey team wins World Cup. Wallabies historic win in Rugby Union World Cup. David O'Brien becomes men's professional world swimming champion and premier marathon swimmer.

1992   Rugby League Ashes won against Great Britain. Australia wins 7 gold at Barcelona Olympics. Australian disabled skiers win gold for first time in Winter Paralympics. 37 gold medals won in Summer Paralympics. Wallabies defeated Ireland, Wales and Barbarians. Jeff Harding regains WBC world light/heavyweight title. AFL flag won by West Coast Eagles. Mark Woodford and Tod Woodbridge win World Doubles Championship. Wayne Gardner retires from 500 cc motor cycle racing. Famous spin bowler, Bill (Tiger) O'Reilly dies. Scott Sunderland wins Mazda Alpine Tour (cycling). Steve Elkington wins Australian Open Golf Championship.

DID YOU KNOW?

The first rail service in Australia ran from Flinders Street to Port Melbourne in 1854. The Sydney–Parramatta rail service began in 1855.

1993   Famous cricketer Lindsay Hassett dies. Greg Norman wins British Open Golf. Australia retains the Ashes. Allan Border holds world records for runs, catches, playing in Test matches and being captain for his country. Wallabies beat Springboks in historic Rugby Test series. Jeff Harding holds WBC title. Lester Ellis wins WBF world welterweight title. Women's hockey team wins The Champions Trophy. Men's hockey team wins The Champions Trophy for 6th time. Michellie Jones becomes world champion triathalon.

1994   Jeff Malcolm wins WBF welterweight championship. Grahame (Spike) Cheney retains WBC welterweight title. Garry Parsons breaks world record for 1000 mile track run. Rebecca Brown breaks world record for 200 m breast stroke. Australia wins World Series cricket defeating South Africa in finals. Allan Border retires from international cricket. Miles Stewart wins men's and Rina Bradshaw wins women's worlds indoor triathalon championships. Mick Doohan wins World 500 cc Motorcycle Championship. Australian Women's Hockey team wins World Cup. Kangaroos win Rugby League Ashes against England. Australia wins World Series Cricket. Craig Parry wins Australian Masters Golf for second time. Susie Maroney wins round-Manhattan marathon swim. Australia wins 71 gold medals at Commonwealth Games in Canada. Lew Hoad dies. Gary Pemberton to head Year 2000 Olympic Committee. Mal Meninga retires. Wallabies beat the All Blacks – retain Bledisloe Cup. Robert Allenby is Australian Open Golf Champion.

1995   Australia retains the Ashes. Kostya Tszyu wins junior welterweight IBF boxing championship. Super league controversy splits rugby league clubs. Australian cricketers beat West Indies and win Frank Worrell trophy after 20 years. Mick Doohan wins for second time World 500cc Motorcycle Championship. Steve Elkington wins USA Golf Championship. Canterbury (NSW) wins last Rugby League Winfield Cup – Terry Lamb (captain) retires.

DID YOU KNOW?
Marble Bar, Western Australia, recorded the longest period of extreme heat of above 37.7°C, for 160 days from October 1923 to April 1924.

Books

This is a selection of much-loved Australian books. Many have won national and international literary awards and so deserve to be included. Others are great favourites which many Australians have on their bookshelves, and regard as old friends.

Title	Author	Publisher	Year 1st/current

Non-fiction

Title	Author	Publisher	Year 1st/current
An Aboriginal Mother Tells of the Old and the New	Labumore: Elsie Roughsey	Penguin	1984
The Anzacs	Patsy Adam-Smith	Penguin	1978/91
Damned Whores and God's Police	Anne Summers	Penguin	1975
Unreliable Memoirs	Clive James	Picador	1980
The Female Eunuch	Germaine Greer	Paladin	1970
Flaws in the Glass	Patrick White	Penguin	1980
A Fortunate Life	A. B. Facey	Penguin	1981/88
Georgiana	Brenda Niall	Miegunyah	1994
Growing Up in ... (series)	A. T. Yarwood	Kangaroo Press	1984
The Letters of Rachel Henning	David Adams (ed.)	Penguin	1979/88
The Lucky Country	Donald Horne	Penguin	1976
Lyrebird Rising	Jim Davidson	Miegunyah	1994
The Macquarie Dictionary	–	Macquarie Library	1981
A Million Wild Acres	Eric Rolls	Penguin	1984
Mother Stayed at Home	Toni Mackenzie	Pan	1985
My Place	Sally Morgan	Fremantle Arts Centre Press	1988
My Wife, My Daughter and Poor Mary Anne	B. Kingston	Hale & Iremonger	1977
One Man's War	Stan Arnell	Sun Mac	1978
The Oxford Anthology of Australian Literature	Leonie Kramer & Adrian Mitchell (eds)	Oxford University Press	1985
The Oxford History of Australia (several volumes)	–	Oxford University Press	1986 onwards

Patrick White Letters	David Marr	Random	1994
The Penguin Leunig	Michael Leunig	Penguin	1974
The Real Matilda	Miriam Dixson	Penguin	1976/84
The Rise and Rise of Kerry Packer	Paul Barry	Bantam	1993
The Road from Coorain	Jill Ker Conway	Heinemann	1989
A Short History of Australia	Manning Clark	Penguin	1963/87
Snow on the Saltbush	Geoffrey Dutton	Penguin	1985
Kings in Grass Castles	Mary Durack	Constable	1959/85
Triumph of the Nomads	Geoffrey Blainey	Macmillan	1975
True North	Jill Ker Conway	Random	1993
The Tyranny of Distance	Geoffrey Blainey	Sun Books	1966
The War Diaries of Weary Dunlop	E. E. Dunlop	Penguin	1990
The Watcher on the Cast-iron Balcony	Hal Porter	Faber	1971
Weevils in the Flour	Wendy Lowenstein	Hyland House	1978
What Bird is That?	N. W. Cayley	Angus & Robertson	1931/73

Fiction

All the Rivers Run	Nancy Cato	New English Library	1978
Battlers	Kylie Tennant	Penguin	1941
The Bellarmine Jug	Nicholas Hasluck	Penguin	1984
But the Dead Are Many;	Frank Hardy	Bodley Head	1975
Power Without Glory	Frank Hardy	Angus & Robertson	1950/82
Capricornia;	Xavier Herbert	Shillington House	1938/81
Poor Fellow My Country	Xavier Herbert	Fontana	1975
Cassidy	Morris West	Hodder & Stoughton	1986

The Chant of Jimmy Blacksmith;	Thomas Keneally	Penguin	1972/87
Schindler's Ark	Thomas Keneally	Coronet	1983
Coonardoo	Katharine Susannah Prichard	Angus & Robertson	1975
Drift	Brian Castro	Heinemann	1994
The Empty Beach	Peter Corris	Unwin	1983
The Americans, Baby	Frank Moorhouse	Angus & Robertson	1972
For the Term of His Natural Life	Marcus Clarke	Angus & Robertson	1874/ 1981
The Fortunes of Richard Mahony	Henry Handel Richardson	Penguin	1917/82
The Harp in the South	Ruth Park	Penguin	1948
Tomorrow and Tomorrow and Tomorrow	M. Barnard Eldershaw	Virago	1983
Illywhacker;	Peter Carey	University of Queensland Press	1985
Oscar and Lucinda	Peter Carey	University of Queensland Press	1988
The Unusual Life of Tristan Smith	Peter Carey	University of Queensland	1994
It's Raining in Mango	Thea Astley	Penguin	1987/89
Remembering Babylon	David Malouf	Random	1993
An Imaginary Life	David Malouf	Picador	1980
Just Relations	Rodney Hall	Penguin	1982
Lilian's Story	Kate Grenville	Macmillan	1992
Dark Places	Kate Grenville	Macmillan	1994
The Man Who Loved Children	Christina Stead	Penguin	1979
The Mango Tree	Ronald McKie	Collins	1974
Miss Peabody's Inheritance;	Elizabeth Jolley	University of Queensland Press	1983
The Well	Elizabeth Jolley	Penguin	1987
Monkey Grip	Helen Garner	Penguin	1978
My Brilliant Career	Miles Franklin	Angus & Robertson	1901/79
My Brother Jack	George Johnston	Collins	1964/81
On Our Selection	Steele Rudd	Angus & Robertson	1899/ 1973

The Orchard	Drusilla Modjeska	Macmillan	1994
The Overlanders	Dora Birtles	Shakespeare (U.K.)	1946
The Power of One	Bryce Courtenay	Mandarin	1992
Riders	Tim Winton	Pan Macmillan	1994
Picnic at Hanging Rock	Joan Lindsay	Penguin	1967/75
Robbery Under Arms	Rolf Boldrewood	Angus & Robertson	1882/ 1980
Sara Dane	Catherine Gaskin	Collins	1955
The Shiralee	D'Arcy Niland	Penguin	1955/88
The Sundowners	Jon Cleary	Angus & Robertson	1954/80
The Thorn Birds	Colleen McCullough	Harper	1977
The Timeless Land	Eleanor Dark	Angus & Robertson	1947/80
A Town Like Alice	Neville Shute	Heinemann	1950
The Transit of Venus	Shirley Hazzard	Penguin	1980
The Twyborn Affair	Patrick White	Penguin	1979/81
While the Billy Boils	Henry Lawson	Angus & Robertson	1896/ 1980
A Woman of the Future	David Ireland	Penguin	1979
The Year of Living Dangerously	Christopher·Koch	Sphere	1979

Poetry

Around the Boree Log	John O'Brien	Angus & Robertson	1921
Collected Poems	A. D. Hope	Angus & Robertson	1975
Collected Poems	James McAuley	Angus & Robertson	1971
Collected Verse	A. B. ('Banjo'.) Paterson	Angus & Robertson	1982
Collected Poems	Judith Wright	Angus & Robertson	1971
Daylight Moon	Les Murray	Angus & Robertson	1987
Dimensions	Bruce Dawe (ed.)	McGraw-Hill	1974
From the Midnight Courtyard	Elizabeth Riddell	Angus & Robertson	1988
Joe Wilson's Mates	Henry Lawson	Angus & Robertson	1901/80

The Man from Snowy River and Other Verses	A. B. ('Banjo') Paterson	Angus & Robertson	1895/ 1982
My People	Oodgeroo Noonuccal (Kath Walker)	Jacaranda Wiley	1970/81
Passionate Heart and Other Poems	Dame Mary Gilmore	Angus & Robertson	1918/79
The Penguin Book of Australian Verse	H. Heseltine (ed.)	Penguin	1982
The Poetic Works of Henry Lawson	Henry Lawson	Angus & Robertson	1900/81
Selected Poems	Rosemary Dobson	Angus & Robertson	1975
Selected Poems	Gwen Harwood	Angus & Robertson	1975
Selected Poems	Kenneth Slessor	Angus & Robertson	1975
Selected Poems	Douglas Stewart	Angus & Robertson	1937
The Sentimental Bloke	C. J. Dennis	Angus & Robertson	1915/77
The Treasury of Colonial Poetry	–	Currawong Press	1982
The Vernacular Republic	Les Murray	Angus & Robertson	1976

Drama

Eden House	Hal Porter	Angus & Robertson	1969
The Elocution of Benjamin Franklin	Steve J. Spears	Currency Press	1977
The Fire on the Snow	Douglas Stewart	Angus & Robertson	1941/76
A Hard God	Peter Kenna	Currency Press	1974
Kullark (Home) and The Dreamers	Jack Davis	Currency Press	1982
Norm and Ahmed	Alexander Buzo	Currency Press	1968/76
The One Day of the Year	Alan Seymour	Angus & Robertson	1976
Inside the Island and Precious Women	Louis Nowra	Currency Press	1977

The Removalist;	David Williamson	Currency Press	1972
The Club;	David Williamson	Currency Press	1978
Don's Party	David Williamson	Currency Press	1973
Rusty Bugles	Sumner Locke Elliott	Currency Press	1949/80
The Shifting Heart	R. Benyon	Angus & Robertson	1957/76
Summer of the Seventeenth Doll	Ray Lawler	Currency Press	1955/78
Too Young for Ghosts	Janus Balodis	Currency Press	1982

Books for children

Alex's Outing	Pamela Allen	Viking	1993
Belinda	Pamela Allen	Viking	1992
Amy's Place	M. Stafford	Penguin	1980/89
Ash Road	Ivan Southall	Penguin	1985
Bananas in Pyjamas Series	Various	ABC Enterprises	1989–95
Cairo Jim & the Sunken Sarcophagus of Sekheret	Geoffrey McSkimming	Hodder	1989–94
Chai	Pam Blashki & Clifton Pugh	Heinemann	1985
Cole's Funny Picture Book	W. Cole	Collins	1879/ 1984
Come the Terrible Tiger	Kim Gamble	Allen & Unwin	1993
The Complete Adventures of Blinky Bill	Dorothy Wall	Angus & Robertson	1939/85
The Complete Adventures of Snugglepot and Cuddlepie	May Gibbs	Angus & Robertson	1918/63
Dot and the Kangaroo	Ethel Pedley	Angus & Robertson	1978
Duck for Cover	Paul Jennings Ted Greenwood Terry Denton	Viking	1994
Fast Forward	Jimmy Pausacker	Angus & Robertson	1989
The Gathering	Isobelle Carmody	Viking	1993
Gulpilil's Stories of the Dreamtime	H. Rule & S. Goodman	Collins	1979

Title	Author	Publisher	Year
Imagine	Alison Lester	Little Ark	1989
My Farm	Alison Lester	Allen & Unwin	1992
I Went Walking	Sue Machin	Omnibus	1989
Jeremy's Tail	Duncan Ball & Donna Rawling	Ashton Scholastic	1990
Little Brother	Allan Baillie	Magnet	1988
A Little Bush Maid	Mary Grant Bruce	Ward Lock	1930/74
Love Me, Love Me Not	Libby Gleeson	Viking	1993
The Magic Pudding	Norman Lindsay	Angus & Robertson	1918/77
My Place	Nadia Wheatley & Donna Rawlings	Collins Dove	1987
The Paw Thing	Paul Jennings	Puffin	1989
Undone	Paul Jennings	Puffin	1993
The Gizmo	Paul Jennings	Puffin	1994
Playing Beatie Bow	Ruth Park	Penguin	1980/82
Selby's Secret	Duncan Ball	Angus & Robertson	1985
Seven Little Australians	Ethel Turner	Lansdowne	1894/ 1983
So Much to Tell You	John Marsden	Walter McVitty Books	1987
Sticky Beak	Morris Gleitzman	Pan Macmillan	1992
Storm Boy;	Colin Thiele	Weldon	1963/81
Blue Fin	Collin Thiele	Rigby	1982
Thunderwith	Libby Hathorn	Heinemann	1989
Blabber Mouth	Morris Gleitzman	Pan Macmillan	1992
Waltzing Matilda	A. B. ('Banjo') Paterson	Collins	1917/70
We of the Never Never	Mrs Aeneas Gunn	Angus & Robertson	1908/82
Where the Forest Meets the Sea	Jeannie Baker	Julia MacRae	1987
The Wild Colonial Boy	J. A. King	Collins	1985

DID YOU KNOW?
Up until 1902 there were laws in force preventing bathing in the daytime on inner city beaches.

Films

Since 1970 we have experienced an extraordinary upsurge of world-wide interest in Australian films. However, our film industry dates back to the late 1890s.

Here is a brief selection of films from some producers and directors who pioneered the industry in those early days. They helped to engender a spirit of cohesiveness and nationalism in the people of a vast and scattered land.

Date	Film title	Producer or director
1898	*Our Social Triumphs*	Salvation Army Films
1900	*Soldiers of the Cross*	Salvation Army Films
1906	*The Story of the Kelly Gang*	J. & N. Tait
1907	*Robbery Under Arms*	J. & N. Tait
1911	*Captain Midnight*	Charles Cozens Spencer
1916	*Mutiny on the Bounty*	Raymond Longford
1919	*The Sentimental Bloke*	Raymond Longford
1920	*On Our Selection*	Raymond Longford
1926	*The Moth of Moonbi*	Charles Chauvel
1927	*The Kid Stakes*	Tal Ordell
	For the Term of His Natural Life	Norman Dawn

Take II: The talkies

For thirty years the Australian film industry was in eclipse, and Australians, like other people all over the world, flocked to see the products of Hollywood. However, some Australian films had popular success.

Date	Film title	Producer or director
1933	*The Squatter's Daughter*	Ken Hall
	In the Wake of the Bounty	Charles Chauvel
1940	*Forty Thousand Horsemen*	Charles Chauvel
1949	*The Rats of Tobruk*	Charles Chauvel
	Sons of Matthew	Charles Chauvel
	Eureka Stockade	Harry Watt
1951	*Captain Thunderbolt*	Cecil Holmes
1955	*Jedda*	Charles Chauvel
1958	*Smiley*	Anthony Kimmins
1966	*They're A Weird Mob*	Michael Powell
1969	*Age of Consent*	Michael Powell

Take III: The 1970s surge

During the 1970s the Australian film industry expanded greatly, and produced a number of films which won international acclaim. Here is a selection of the most successful box-office hits.

Key: P = producer, D = director, A = actor

Date	Film title	Producer, Directors, Actors
1971	*Wake in Fright*	George Willoughby (P), Ted Kotcheff (D), Garry Bond (A)
1972	*The Adventures of Barry McKenzie*	Phillip Adams (P), Barry Crocker (A)
1973	*Alvin Purple*	Tim Burstall (D), Graeme Blundell (A)
1974	*The Cars that Ate Paris*	Peter Weir (D), Terri Camilleri (A)
1975	*Picnic at Hanging Rock*	Pat Lovell (P), Anne Lambert (A)
	The Removalists	Margaret Fink (P), John Hargreaves (A)
	Sunday Too Far Away	Gil Brealey (P), Jack Thompson (A)
1976	*Caddie*	Donald Crombie (P), Helen Morse (A)
	Don's Party	Phillip Adams (P), John Hargreaves (A)
	The Devil's Playground	Fred Schepisi (D), Arthur Dignam (A)
	Storm Boy	Matt Carroll (P), Greg Rowe (A), Henri Safran (D)
	The Fourth Wish (TV)	Don Chaffey (D), John Meillon (A)
1977	*The Getting of Wisdom*	Phillip Adams (P), Susannah Fowler (A)
1978	*My Brilliant Career*	Gillian Armstrong (D), Sam Neill (A), Judy Davis (A)
	Newsfront	Phillip Noyce (D), David Elfick (P), Bill Hunter (A)
	The Chant of Jimmie Blacksmith	Fred Schepisi (D), Tommy Lewis (A)
1979	*Mad Max*	Byron Kennedy and George Miller (P), Mel Gibson (A)
	Breaker Morant	Bruce Beresford (D), Bryan Brown (A), Jack Thompson (A)

Take IV: Films of the 1980s

Investors in films in the early 1980s were allowed generous tax concessions. This resulted in a spate of people entering the industry with very little knowledge of how it worked. At times creativity was compromised in the great quest for monetary gains. Although many films of quality were made, some were of dubious value.

Date	Film title	Producer, Directors, Actors
1981	*Mad Max 2*	Byron Kennedy and George Miller (P), Mel Gibson (A), Bruce Spence (A)
	Monkey Grip	Ken Cameron (D), Noni Hazlehurst (A), Colin Friels (A)
	Puberty Blues	Bruce Beresford (D), Jad Capelja (A), Nell Schofield (A)
	Winter of Our Dreams	John Duigan (D), Richard Mason (P), Judy Davis (A), Bryan Brown (A)
1982	*Gallipoli*	Pat Lovell (P), Peter Weir (D), Mel Gibson (A), Mark Lee (A)
	The Man from Snowy River	George Miller (D), Tom Burlinson (A), Kirk Douglas (A)
	The Year of Living Dangerously	Peter Weir (D), Mel Gibson (A), Linda Hunt (A)
1983	*Careful He Might Hear You*	Jill Robb (P), Wendy Hughes (A), John Hargreaves (A)
	Phar Lap	Simon Wincer (D), Tom Burlinson (A)
1984	*Annie's Coming Out*	Gil Brealey (D), Tina Arhondis (A), Drew Forsythe (A), Angela Punch-McGregor (A)
	My First Wife	Paul Cox (P & D), John Hargreaves (A), Wendy Hughes (A)
	Robbery Under Arms	Donald Crombie & Ken Hannam (D), Sam Neill (A)
1985	*Bliss*	Ray Lawrence (D), Barry Otto (A), Lynette Curran (A)
	Burke & Wills	Graeme Clifford (P & D), Jack Thompson (A), Nigel Havers (A)
	Devil in the Flesh	Scott Murray (D), Katia Caballero (A), Keith Smith (A)
	Empty Beach	Chris Thomson (D), Bryan Brown (A)
1986	*Backlash*	Bill Bennet (P & D), David Argue (A), Gia Carides (A), Justine Saunders (A)
	Crocodile Dundee	Peter Faiman (D), Paul Hogan (A), Linda Kozlowski (A)
	The Fringe Dwellers	Bruce Beresford (D), Kristina Nehm (A), Justine Saunders (A)
	The More Things Change	Robyn Nevin (D), Judy Morris (A), Victoria Longley (A), Barry Otto (A)
1987	*Boundaries of the Heart*	Lex Marinos (D), Wendy Hughes (A), John Hargreaves (A)
	High Tide	Gillian Armstrong (D), Judy Davis (A), Colin Friels (A)
	The Lighthorsemen	Simon Wincer (P & D), Peter Philps (A), Jon Blake (A)

	The Year My Voice Broke	John Duigan (D), Noah Taylor (A), Loene Carmen (A)
1988	Crocodile Dundee II	John Cornell (D), Paul Hogan (A), Linda Kozlowski (A)
	Dead Calm	Phillip Noyce (D), Sam Neill (A), Nicole Kidman (A)
	Evil Angels	Fred Schepisi (D), Sam Neill (A), Meryl Streep (A)
1989	Boys in the Island	Geoffrey Bennett (D), Yves Stening (A), Jane Stephens (A)
	The Delinquents	Chris Thomson (D), Kylie Minogue (A), Charlie Schlatter (A)
	Jig Saw	Marc Gracie (D), Rebecca Gibney (A), Dominic Sweeney (A)
	Sweetie	Jane Campion (P & D), Genevieve Lemon (A), Karen Colston (A)

Take V: Films of the 1990s

The period pieces and costume dramas of the 70s and 80s which explored our origins made way for very different and volatile films in the 90s. Diverse, urban, smart, irreverent, witty and sometimes shocking, they captured the imagination of the box office crowd, who left the theatres clamouring for more.

Date	Film title	Producer, Directors, Actors
1990	The Crossing	George Ogilvie (D), Russell Crowe (A), Robert Mammone (A)
	Flirting	John Duligan (D), Noah Taylor (A), Tandy Newton (A)
1991	Death in Brunswick	John Ruane (D), Sam Neill (A), Zoe Carides (A), John Clarke (A)
	Waiting	Jackie McKimmie (D), Noni Hazlehurst (A), John Hargreaves (A)
1992	Dingo	Rolf de Heer (D), Colin Friels (A)
	Spotswood	Mark Joffe (D), Anthony Hopkins (A), Alwyn Kurts (A), Ben Mendlesohn (A)
	Fern Gully animation	Wayne Young and Peter Faiman (Ds), Dianna Young (Story)
	The Last Days of Chez Nous	Gillian Armstrong (D), Lisa Harrow (A), Bruno Ganz (A)
	Strictly Ballroom	Baz Luhrmann (D), Paul Mercurio (A), Tara Morice (A)
	Romper Stomper	Geoffrey Wright (D), Russell Crowe (A), Daniel Pollock (A)
1993	Reckless Kelly	Yahoo Serious (D), Yahoo Serious (A), Melora Hardin (A)

	The Nostradamus Kid	Bob Ellis (D), Noah Taylor (A), Miranda Otto (A)
	Gross Misconduct	Jimmy Smits (A), Sarah Chadwick (A), Naomi Watts (A)
	The Piano	Jane Campion (W/D), Holly Hunter (A), Anna Paquin (A), Harvey Keitel (A)
1994	*The Adventures of Priscilla, Queen of the Desert*	Hugo Weaving (A), Terence Stamp (A), Guy Pearce (A), Lizzy Gardner and Jim Chappel (Costumes), Stephan Elliott (W/D)
	Sirens	Sam Neill (A), Elle McPherson (A), John Duigan (W/D)
	The Sum of Us	David Stevens (W), Jack Thompson (A), Russell Crowe (A)
	Bad Boy Bubby	Rolf De Heer (D/W), Nicholas Hope (A)
	Muriel's Wedding	Toni Collette (A), Rachel Griffiths (A), Bill Hunter (A), P.J. Hogan (W/D)
	Country Life	John Hargreaves (A), Sam Neill (A), Kerry Fox (A), Greta Scacchi (A)
1995	*Little Women*	Gillian Armstrong (D)
	Lilian's Story	Ruth Cracknell (A), Toni Collette (A), Barry Otto (A)
	The Seedling	Alex Morcos (W/P/D/A), Bill Hunter (A), Deborah Kennedy (A).

The Adventures of Priscilla, Queen of the Desert

Muriel's Wedding

Songs and poems

Advance Australia Fair

The original words and music were supposedly written and composed by Peter Dodds McCormick about 1878. In 1983 a new version of the song was adopted by the Australian government as the national anthem.

Australians all let us rejoice,
For we are young and free,
We've golden soil and wealth
for toil;
Our home is girt by sea;
Our land abounds in nature's
gifts
Of beauty rich and rare;
In history's page, let every
stage
Advance Australia Fair.

Beneath our radiant Southern
Cross,
We'll toil with hearts and
hands;

To make this Commonwealth
of ours
Renowned of all the lands;
For those who've come across
the seas
We've boundless plains to
share;
With courage let us all
combine
To Advance Australia Fair.
In joyful strains then let us
sing,
Advance Australia Fair.

Kookaburra Sits on the Old Gum Tree

This song is widely known overseas. It is one of many songs about Australia which is taught in schools in other countries. For information about kookaburras, see p 224.

Kookaburra sits on the old
gum tree,
Merry, merry king of the bush
is he,
Laugh! kookaburra, laugh!
kookaburra,
Gay your life must be.
Kookaburra sits on the old
gum tree,
Eating all the gum nuts he
can see,
Stop! kookaburra, stop!
kookaburra,
Please leave some for me.

My Country
Dorothea Mackellar

This poem, written in 1908, epitomises for most Australians the deep feelings of pride and love they have for their country. Although the young poet was born in England, she came to Australia as a young child. It was then that she began to love this 'sunburnt country'. that she began to love 'this sunburnt country .

The love of field and coppice,
Of green and shaded lanes,
Of ordered woods and gardens
Is running in your veins;
Strong love of grey-blue distance,
Brown streams and soft,
    dim skies –
I know, but cannot share it,
My love is otherwise.

I love a sunburnt country,
A land of sweeping plains,
Of ragged mountain ranges,
Of droughts and flooding rains;
I love her far horizons,
I love her jewel-sea,
Her beauty and her terror –
The wide brown land for me!

The stark white ring-barked
    forests,
All tragic to the moon,
The sapphire-misted
    mountains,
The hot gold hush of noon,
Green tangle of the brushes
Where lithe lianas coil,
And orchids deck the tree-tops,
And ferns the warm dark soil.

Core of my heart, my country!
Her pitiless blue sky,
When, sick at heart, around us
We see the cattle die –
But then the grey clouds
    gather,
And we can bless again
The drumming of an army,
The steady soaking rain.

Core of my heart, my country!
Land of the rainbow gold,
For flood and fire and famine
She pays us back threefold.
Over the thirsty paddocks,
Watch, after many days,
The filmy veil of greenness
That thickens as we gaze . . .

An opal-hearted country,
A wilful, lavish land –
All you who have not
    loved her,
You will not understand –
Though Earth holds many
    splendours,
Wherever I may die,
I know to what brown country
My homing thoughts will fly.

DID YOU KNOW?
Sydney Harbour, or Port Jackson, extends over 55 square kilometres.

Waltzing Matilda
A.B. ('Banjo') Paterson

This song was written at Dagworth Station near Winton in
Queensland at the turn of the century by one of Australia's favourite
poets. It depicts a crafty wanderer of the outback, a swagman,
whose only comfort against his harsh life is his 'Matilda', his blanket
roll. He is caught for sheep stealing but before the troopers can
arrest him, he defiantly jumps into the billabong (water-hole),
making it clear that he would rather drown than be taken prisoner.

However, 'Waltzing Matilda' is far more than a song about a
crafty swaggie. It universally marks us as Australian, and is a song
which seems to embody the rebellious spirit of early Australia,
reminding us of the harsh beginnings of white settlement. It is a
song which evokes great emotion and which lives in the hearts of
most Australians.

*Once a jolly swagman camped
by a billabong,
Under the shade of a coolabah
tree,
And he sang as he watched
and waited till his billy
boiled,
'Who'll come a-waltzing
Matilda with me?'*

Chorus
*'Waltzing Matilda, waltzing
Matilda,
'Who'll come a-waltzing
Matilda with me?'
And he sang as he watched
and waited till his billy
boiled,
'Who'll come a-waltzing
Matilda with me?'*

*Down came a jumbuck to
drink at the billabong,
Up jumped the swagman and
grabbed him with glee,*

*And he sang as he shoved
that jumbuck in his ·
tuckerbag,
'You'll come a-waltzing
Matilda with me.'*

*Up rode the squatter mounted
on his thoroughbred,
Down came the troopers, one,
two, three,
'Where's that jolly jumbuck
you've got in your
tuckberbag?
'You'll come a-waltzing
Matilda with me.'*

*Up jumped the swagman and
jumped into that billabong,
'You'll never take me alive',
said he.
And his ghost may be heard
as you pass by that
billabong:
'Who'll come a-waltzing
Matilda with me?'*

Click go the Shears

There is great camaraderie in shearing sheds. It is back-breaking work and the champion shearer (the ringer) is continually challenged by his mates, especially the old men of the shed (snaggers), who are well past their prime. To get an easy sheep to shear, with no belly wool, and beat the ringer, would be a feather in their caps. But shoddy workmanship is frowned upon and the snagger has to be quite crafty. At the end of the run the shearers gather to quench their thirst at the nearest pub. Their philosophy is – work hard, drink hard and die hard.

Out on the board the old
   shearer stands,
Grasping his shears in his
   long, bony hands;
Fixed is his gaze on a bare-
   bellied ewe,
Glory if he gets her, won't he
   make the ringer go!

Chorus
Click go the shears boys,
   click, click, click;
Wide is his blow and his hands
move quick,
The ringer looks around and is
   beaten by a blow,
And curses the old snagger
   with the bare-bellied ewe.

In the middle of the floor, in
   his cane-bottomed chair,
Sits the boss of the board,
   with eyes everywhere;
Notes well each fleece as it
   comes to the screen,
Paying strict attention if it's
   taken off clean.

The tar-boy is there, awaiting
   in demand,
With his blackened tar-pot,
   and his tarry hand,

Sees one old sheep with a cut
   upon its back,
Hears what he's waiting for,
   'Tar here, Jack!'

Shearing is all over and we've
   all got our cheques.
Roll up your swag boys, we're
   off on the tracks;
The first pub we come to, it's
   there we'll have a spree,
And everyone that comes
   along, it's 'Have a drink
   with me!'

Down by the bar the old
   shearer stands,
Grasping his glass in his thin
   bony hands;
Fixed is his gaze on the
   green-painted keg,
Glory, he'll get down on it, ere
   he stirs a peg.

There we leave him standing,
   shouting for all hands,
Whilst all around him every
   drinker stands:
His eyes are on the keg,
   which is now lowering fast,
He works hard, he drinks
   hard, and goes to hell at last!

The Man from Snowy River
A. B. ('Banjo') Paterson

One of the best-known story/poems in Australian literature.

There was movement at the
   station, for the word had
   passed around
     That the colt from old Regret
     had got away,
And had joined the wild bush
   horses – he was worth a
   thousand pound,
     So all the cracks had
     gathered to the fray.
All the tried and noted riders
   from the stations near and far
     Had mustered at the
     homestead overnight,
For the bushmen love hard
   riding where the wild bush
   horses are,
     And the stock-horse snuffs
     the battle with delight.

There was Harrison, who
   made his pile when Pardon
   won the cup,
     The old man with his hair as
     white as snow;
But few could ride beside him
   when his blood was
   fairly up –
     He would go wherever
     horse and man could go.
And Clancy of the Overflow
   came down to lend a hand,
     No better horseman ever
     held the reins;
For never horse could throw
   him while the saddle-girths
   would stand –
     He learnt to ride while
     droving on the plains.

And one was there, a stripling
   on a small and weedy
   beast;
     He was something like a
     racehorse undersized,
With a touch of Timor pony –
   three parts thoroughbred
   at least –
     And such as are by
     mountain horsemen
     prized.
He was hard and tough and
   wiry – just the sort that
   won't say die –
     There was courage in his
     quick impatient tread;
And he bore the badge of
   gameness in his bright and
   fiery eye,
     And the proud and lofty
     carriage of his head.

But still so slight and weedy;
   one would doubt his power
   to stay,
     And the old man said, 'That
     horse will never do
'For a long and tiring gallop –
   lad, you'd better stop away,
     Those hills are far too
     rough for such as you'.
So he waited, sad and
   wistful – only Clancy stood
   his friend –
     'I think we ought to let him
     come,' he said:
'I warrant he'll be with us
   when he's wanted at
   the end,

*For both his horse and he
are mountain bred.
'He hails from Snowy River,
up by Kosciusko's side,
Where the hills are twice as
steep and twice as rough;
'Where a horse's hoofs strike
firelight from the flint stones
every stride,
The man that holds his own
is good enough.
'And the Snowy River riders
on the mountains make
their home,
Where the river runs those
giant hills between;
'I have seen full many
horsemen since I first
commenced to roam,
But nowhere yet such
horsemen have I seen.'*

*So he went; they found the
horses by the big mimosa
clump,
They raced away towards
the mountain's brow,
And the old man gave his
orders, 'Boys, go at them
from the jump,
No use to try for fancy
riding now,
'And, Clancy, you must wheel
them, try and wheel them to
the right.
Ride boldly, lad, and never
fear the spills,
'For never yet was rider that
could keep the mob
in sight,
If once they gain the shelter
of those hills.'*

So Clancy rode to wheel

*them – he was racing
on the wing
Where the best and boldest
riders take their place,
And he raced his stock-horse
past them, and he made the
ranges ring
With the stockwhip, as he
met them face to face.
Then they halted for a
moment, while he swung
the dreaded lash,
But they saw their well-
loved mountain full in view,
And they charged beneath
the stockwhip with a sharp
and sudden dash,
And off into the mountain
scrub they flew.*

*Then fast the horsemen
followed, where the gorges
deep and black
Resounded to the thunder
of their tread,
And the stockwhips woke the
echoes, and they fiercely
answered back
From cliffs and crags that
beetled overhead.
And upward, ever upward, the
wild horses held their way,
Where mountain ash and
kurrajong grew wide;
And the old man muttered
fiercely, 'We may bid the
mob good day,
No man can hold them
down the other side.'*

*When they reached the
mountain's summit, even
Clancy took a pull –
It well might make the*

boldest hold their breath:
The wild hop scrub grew
    thickly, and the hidden
    ground was full
    Of Wombat holes, and any
    slip was death.
But the man from Snowy
    River let the pony have
    his head,
    And he swung his
    stockwhip round and gave
    a cheer,
And he raced him down the
    mountain like a torrent
    down its bed,
    While the others stood and
    watched in very fear.

He sent the flint-stones flying,
    but the pony kept his feet,
    He cleared the fallen timber
    in his stride,
And the man from Snowy
    River never shifted
    in his seat –
    It was grand to see that
    mountain horseman ride.
Through the stringy barks and
    saplings, on the rough and
    broken ground,
    Down the hillside at a
    racing pace he went;
And he never drew the bridle
    till he landed safe
    and sound
    At the bottom of that
    terrible descent.

He was right among the
    horses as they climbed the
    farther hill,
    And the watchers on the
    mountain, standing mute,
Saw him ply the stockwhip

fiercely; he was right
    among them still
    As he raced across the
    clearing in pursuit.
Then they lost him for a
    moment, where two
    mountain gullies met
    In the ranges – but a final
    glimpse reveals
On a dim and distant hillside
    the wild horses racing yet,
    With the man from Snowy
    River at their heels.

And he ran them single-
    handed till their sides were
    white with foam
    He followed like a
    bloodhound on their track,
Till they halted, cowed and
    beaten; then he turned their
    heads for home,
    And alone and unassisted
    brought them back.
But his hardy mountain pony
    he could scarcely raise a
    trot,
    He was blood from hip to
    shoulder from the spur;
But his pluck was still
    undaunted, and his
    courage fiery hot,
    For never yet was mountain
    horse a cur.

And down by Kosciusko,
    where the pine-clad ridges
    raise
    Their torn and rugged
    battlements on high,
Where the air is clear as
    crystal, and the white stars
    fairly blaze
    At midnight in the cold and

frosty sky,
And where around the
  Overflow the reed-beds
  sweep and sway
  To the breezes, and the

rolling plains are wide,
The Man from Snowy River is
  a household word today,
And the stockmen tell the
  story of his ride.

Ballad of the Drover
Henry Lawson

Lawson is one of Australia's best-loved writers. His vivid
descriptions of the self-reliant bush folk of the turn of the century,
are legendary. His poems depict the 'hard time' endured by
people employed in the pastoral industry and praise the courage
with which they faced adversity. There is a gentle humour which
sets his work apart, while his sympathy for the 'common man'
reflects the feeling of 'mateship' which is familiar to most
Australians.

Across the stony ridges,
  Across the rolling plain,
Young Harry Dale, the drover,
  Comes riding home again,
And well his stock-horse bears
  him,
  And light of heart is he,
And stoutly his old packhorse
  Is trotting by his knee.

Up Queensland way with cattle
  He's travelled regions vast,
And many months have
  vanished
  Since home-folks saw him
  last.
He hums a song of someone
  He hopes to marry soon;
And hobble-chains and camp-
  ware
  Keep jingling to the tune.

An hour has filled the heavens
  With storm-clouds inky
  black;
At times the lightning trickles
  Around the drover's track;

But Harry pushes onward,
  His horses' strength he tries,
In hope to reach the river
  Before the flood shall rise.

When flashes next the
  lightning,
  The flood's grey breast is
  blank;
A cattle-dog and packhorse
  Are struggling up the bank,
But in the lonely homestead
  The girl shall wait in vain –
He'll never pass the stations
  In charge of stock again.

Across the flooded lowlands
  And slopes of sodden loam
The packhorse struggles
  bravely
  To take dumb tidings home;
And mud-stained, wet, and
  weary,
  He goes by rock and tree,
With clanging chains and
  tinware
  All sounding eerily.

The Man from Ironbark
A. B. ('Banjo') Paterson

As sophistication developed among city-dwellers, at the end of the nineteenth century, there was a growing tendency to regard the bushman as a rural clown. This is a whimsical glimpse of the way one such 'clown' dealt with the situation.

tote   – a record and distribution of a bet
yokel – a country bumpkin
peeler – a policeman

It was the man from Ironbark
    who struck the Sydney town,
He wandered over street and
    park, he wandered up and
    down.
He loitered here, he loitered
    there, till he was
    like to drop,
Until at last in sheer despair
    he sought a barber's shop.
''Ere! shave my beard and
    whiskers off, I'll be a man of
    mark,
I'll go and do the Sydney toff
    up home in Ironbark.'

The barber man was small
    and flash, as barbers
    mostly are,
He wore a strike-your-fancy
    sash, he smoked a huge cigar:
He was a humorist of note
    and keen at repartee,
He laid the odds and kept a
    'tote', whatever that may be.
And when he saw our friend
    arrive, he whispered 'Here's
    a lark!
'Just watch me catch him all
    alive, this man from
    Ironbark.'

There were some gilded
    youths that sat along the
    barber's wall,
Their eyes were dull, their
    heads were flat, they had no
    brains at all;
To them the barber passed the
    wink, his dexter eyelid shut,
'I'll make this bloomin' yokel
    think his bloomin' throat is
    cut.'
And as he soaped and rubbed
    it in he made a rude remark.
'I s'pose the flats is pretty
    green up there in Ironbark.'

A grunt was all reply he got;
    he shaved the bushman's
    chin,
Then made the water boiling
    hot and dipped the razor in.
He raised his hand, his brow
    grew black, he paused a
    while to gloat,
Then slashed the red-hot
    razor-back across his
    victim's throat;
Upon the newly shaven chin it
    made a livid mark –
No doubt it fairly took him
    in – the man from
    Ironbark.

He fetched a wild up-country
yell might wake the dead
to hear,
And though his throat, he
knew full well, was cut from
ear to ear,
He struggled gamely to his
feet, and faced the
murderous foe.
'You've done for me! you dog,
I'm beat! one hit before I go!
'I only wish I had a knife, you
blessed murdering shark!
'But you'll remember all your
life the man from Ironbark.'

He lifted up his hairy paw,
with one tremendous clout
And landed on the barber's
jaw, and knocked the
barber out.
He set to work with tooth and
nail, he made the place a
wreck;
He grabbed the nearest
gilded youth, and tried to
break his neck.
And all the while his throat
he held to save his vital
spark,
And 'Murder! Bloody Murder!'
yelled the man from
Ironbark.

A peeler man who heard the
din came in to
see the show!
He tried to run the bushman
in, but he refused to go.
And when at last the barber
spoke, and said ''Twas all
in fun –
''Twas just a harmless little
joke, a trifle overdone.'
'A joke!' he cried, 'By George,
that's fine; a lively sort of
lark;
'I'd like to catch that
murdering swine some
night in Ironbark.'

And now while round the
shearing-floor the listening
shearers gape,
He tells the story o'er and
o'er, and brags of his
escape.
'Them barber chaps what
keeps a tote, by George,
I've had enough,
'One tried to cut my bloomin'
throat, but thank the Lord
it's tough.'
And whether he's believed or
no, there's one thing to
remark,
That flowing beards are all the
go way up in Ironbark.

From Bell-birds'
Henry Kendall

A poem written in the 1880s capturing the rhythm of the cascading waterfalls in the forest, the home of the bellbirds (see page 223).

By channels of coolness the
*   echoes are calling*
And down the dim gorges I
*   hear the creek falling;*
It lives in the mountain
*   where moss and the sedges*
Touch with their beauty
*   the banks and the ledges;*
Through breaks of the cedar
*   and sycamore bowers*
Struggles the light – that is
*   love to the flowers*
And softer than slumber, and
*   sweeter than singing*
The notes of the bell-bird are
*   running and ringing.*

Tranquil Margaret River area: Western Australia

DID YOU KNOW?

The oldest daily newspaper in the southern hemisphere is the *Sydney Morning Herald* (1831).

Platypuses, plants, parrots

For millions of years the fauna of Australia evolved in isolation, and many different forms came from relatively few ancestral types. As a result, Australia has some of nature's strangest creatures, which draw enthusiastic zoologists and tourists to study them at first hand.

Mammals

Australia has about 230 species of mammals and almost half are marsupials, the pouched mammal. The balance consists of placental mammals (having a placenta which nourishes the embryo), and the monotremes, the lowest order of egg-laying mammals (having one opening for digestive, urinary and genital organs).

Marsupials

Most of the world's marsupials are found in Australia.

Australia's wildlife reserves (over 20 000 ha)

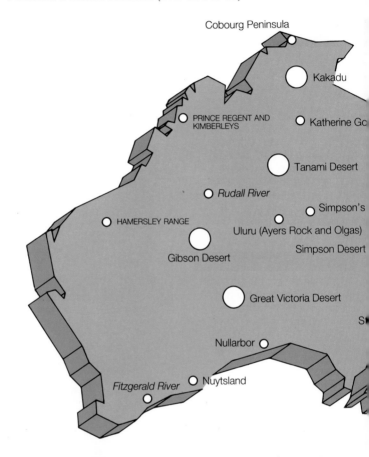

Cobourg Peninsula

Kakadu

PRINCE REGENT AND KIMBERLEYS

Katherine Go

Tanami Desert

Rudall River

Simpson's

HAMERSLEY RANGE

Uluru (Ayers Rock and Olgas)

Gibson Desert

Simpson Desert

Great Victoria Desert

S

Nullarbor

Fitzgerald River   Nuytsland

DID YOU KNOW?

There are 2987 wildlife reserves in Australia, with a total area of 30 304 378 hectares, equivalent to 3.9% of the area of the continent. In addition, there is an area of 34 380 000 hectares of the Great Barrier Reef Marine Park offshore from the Queensland coast.

Cape York Peninsula

Lakefield

Hinchinbrook Island

Cape Cleveland

Eungella

Great Barrier Reef

Fraser Island

ake Eyre

Northern Tablelands

Wollemi   Ku-ring-gai

Blue Mountains
National Park

Sunset Country   Morton

Wadbilliga

Desert

KOSCIUSKO AND
SOUTHERN ALPS

Wilson's Promontory

FOLK RANGE   Cape Barren Island

CENTRAL HIGHLANDS

Freycinet Peninsula

n-west
mania

Bandicoot

This small rat-like marsupial of the Peramelidae family is interesting because of its zoological likeness to the kangaroo and possum families, and yet it is insectivorous (insect-eating) and resembles the flesh-eating native cat. Bandicoots are found in most parts of Australia.

Koala

Phascolarctos cinereus
This enchanting little animal is unique to Australia. It is not a member of the bear family, but a marsupial; it has a pouch which opens downwards.
The koala is a tree-dweller, drowsing during the daytime and becoming more active in the evening, and feeding on vast quantities of gum leaves which have a high oil content. This enables it to go without water for long periods of time. The koala is Queensland's animal emblem.

Kangaroos

Kangaroos are represented in Australia by three subfamilies. The most primitive is the rat-kangaroo, Hypsiprymnodontinae, which is thought to be the connecting link between the possum and kangaroo families. The second sub-family, the Potoroinae, is represented by the more advanced typical rat-kangaroo, and the third and most varied sub-family, the Macropodinae, embraces the most advanced herbivorous (plant-eating) kind. This includes small scrub and rock wallabies, the large or brush wallabies and the typical large kangaroos.

The kangaroo is a marsupial whose pouch opens upwards, unlike the koala's. It has a unique continuous flow of reproduction, with one joey outside the pouch which will still suckle, one inside suckling, and one embryo 'on hold'. Thus the female can produce offspring long after the male has disappeared. The kangaroo is also capable of limiting reproduction during drought.

There are 45 species of kangaroo in Australia. They are bipedal (two-footed), having a remarkable hopping action which prevents them from easily moving backwards. The kangaroo represents the world's only marsupial group to become entirely dependent on this specialised form of locomotion.

The kangaroo is Australia's animal emblem.

The 'Queensland' tree kangaroo, *Dendrolagus lumholtzi*, is a unique animal which lives in the trees of the rainforests. It has evolved because of pressure on the ground food supplies. Over millions of years it has undergone a reversal of development, returning to the tree haunts of its primitive possum-like ancestors.

The red kangaroo, *Macropus rufus*, and the great grey kangaroo, *M. giganteus*, are the largest marsupials. A height of 2.92 metres and a weight of more than 100 kilograms has been recorded. The red kangaroo is the Northern Territory's animal emblem.

The musk rat-kangaroo, *Hypsiprymnodon moschatus*, is the smallest of the kangaroos and lives in the Atherton Tableland of the north coast of Queensland. It is less then 300 millimetres long.

Marsupial mole

Notoryctes typhlops
This small animal lives in desert regions of southern and western Australia. It is eyeless and has no claws, unlike the true mole. It tunnels with its fleshy feet through loose sand, and is rarely found because it stays underground.

Numbat

Myrmecobius fasciatus
This unique-striped marsupial is

DID YOU KNOW?
The mature Karri tree of Western Australia can yield more than 250 kilograms of honey from its estimated 500 000 blossoms.

found only in Western Australia. It is considered to be an endangered species as it is widely hunted by feral animals. It has sharp front claws and a sticky tongue with which it attacks ant and termite nests. However, it can open only the weakest nest, but is unable to completely destroy it as it can't burrow in too far. Although it is a marsupial, strangely it has no pouch. Instead the young (usually four), cling with their mouths to the mother's underside until old enough to fend for themselves. The numbat is Western Australia's animal emblem.

Possums

Australian possums, or phalangers, are herbivorous marsupials which live in trees. They belong to four main families: ringtails and large gliders; brushtails and cuscus; feathertail and pygmy possums and honey possums. They are shy nocturnal creatures. Some are capable of gliding, but it is not considered true flight. They have a pouch, but also carry their young on their backs.

The greater glider possum, *Petauroides volans*, is an elusive creature which usually finds a home in the hollow of a gum tree. It is capable of gliding or volplaning from one tree to another by an extension of skin along the sides of the body and limbs, which when extended forms a sort of parachute.

Leadbeater's possum, *Gymnobelideus leadbeateri*, is a tiny possum which lives only in Victoria over an area of 100 square kilometres extending from Marysville, north-west of Melbourne, to Tanjil Bren. After 1909 it was thought to be extinct but was re-discovered in 1961, again at Marysville. It is the animal emblem of Victoria.

Tasmanian devil
Sarcophilus harrisii
The Tasmanian devil is the largest surviving carnivorous (meat-eating) marsupial. It is nocturnal and very shy, belying its name. It is the size of a fox terrier but has strength enough in its teeth to consume a whole sheep, including the skull. Usually there are litters of four which remain in the pouch for several months.

Tasmanian tiger
Thylacinus cynocephalus
Also known as the thylacine, this is the largest carnivorous marsupial in the world. It is presumed extinct, although there are many unconfirmed sightings. Thylacines were at one time very common, but a bounty placed upon them caused widespread destruction. The last one was caught in 1933, and died in Melbourne in 1936. They are wolf-like but are not related to the canine family.

Tasmanian Devil

As a rule the litter numbers four, the young remaining in the pouch for perhaps three months before they are ready to leave the 'nursery'.

Wombats

The wombat is a powerful, thickset, burrowing marsupial found only in Australia. The common wombat, *Vombatus ursinus*, is a forest dweller and the hairy-nosed wombats, *Lasiorhinus latifrons* and *L. krefftii*, are plains dwellers. Because of loss of habitat, the northern *L. krefftii* is considered an endangered species. It is not a very sociable animal. The wombat has a bony plate in its rump, which can be used to kill any predator which might follow the wombat down its burrow by crushing it against the roof of the burrow. Because of their instinct to go through things rather than go around, wombats are often considered stupid and destructive. However, they have a brain proportionally larger than any other marsupial, indicating high intelligence. The hairy-nosed wombat is South Australia's animal emblem.

Placental mammals

Australia's placental mammals comprise bats, the dingo, marine mammals and rodents. Placental mammals produce fully developed young.

Bats

Bats are the only true flying mammal. They are warm-blooded and are covered in fur. They nourish their young with milk. They can fly long distances, using echo location to find their way. As a result they have a highly developed sense of smell and hearing. Bats are represented in Australia by fifty-eight species including the fruit bat, *Chiroptera pteropodidae*, as well as the rare ghost bat, *Macroderma gigas*, of central Australia, which is a cannibal bat living on smaller species of its own kind and other animals.

Dingo
Canis familiaris dingo
This dog is regarded as indigenous to Australia, and is presumed to have evolved from dogs brought from Asia 3000 to 8000 years ago by the ancestors of the Australian Aboriginals. They are stealthy nocturnal hunters, and often set up a continual chorus of dismal howls, much like the northern hemisphere wolf.

Marine mammals
Sea lions, of the family Otariidae, and seals, of the family Phocidae, are ocean mammals which are found on Australia's southern coastline. Seals have limited mobility on land as they have to drag their hind limbs; sea lions, with more use of their hind limbs, are more mobile.

Dugongs, *Dugong dugon*, are completely herbivorous. They

Dingo

graze on the sea grasses on the ocean bottom as sheep graze in a paddock.

Rodents

There are numerous species of native Australian rodents. They are not as prolific in breeding habits as introduced species so they are not as widespread, nor are they considered a pest.

Monotremes

Echidna

Tachyglossus aculeatus

These bizarre creatures, together with the platypus, are the world's only egg-laying mammals. The echidna, or spiny ant-eater, has sharp claws and a long sticky ribbon-like tongue with which it gathers up ants and termites at lightning speed. It has no teeth, and relies on its stiff spines for protection. It lays a single egg which is carried and hatched in a temporary but commodious pouch formed from folds of skin. The female has no teats. The milk is exuded into the pouch and is licked up.

Platypus

Ornithorhynchus anatinus

This animal, unique to Australia, is the world's strangest aquatic mammal. It has often been considered a living fossil and may be the missing link between reptiles and mammals. It has webbed clawed feet and a duck-like bill, which is fleshy and sensitive, for foraging food. It has beaver-like fur and tail, lays eggs and suckles its young, and, just to make things more complicated, the male has a poison spur behind its back leg, the reason for which is not known. It inhabits the eastern watercourses, making its burrow entrance above the water-line. The platypus is the animal emblem of New South Wales.

Introduced species

Australia has many introduced species of mammal which have gone wild (feral). These include the rabbit, hare, horse, donkey, deer, camel, fox, pig, goat, sheep, cow, rat, mouse, dog, cat, and water buffalo. Some are regarded as pests, and cause considerable damage to agriculture and to native plants and animals.

Reptiles and amphibians

Australia has about 140 species of snake, 360 species of lizard,

---

DID YOU KNOW?

Because of its suitability to immersion in water, timber from the Satinay tree was shipped to Egypt from Fraser Island in 1925 to prop up the walls of the Suez Canal.

2 species of crocodile, 15 species of freshwater tortoise and 6 species of marine turtle.

Crocodiles

Both species of Australian crocodiles are found in our northern waters. The freshwater crocodile, *Crocodylus johnstoni*, is not dangerous to people; however, the saltwater species, *C. porosus*, which can grow to 7 metres long, is dangerous. Both are protected, as it is felt that they are endangered. Not only are they hunted for their skins, but it is believed low-flying aircraft disturb the females, so that they leave their eggs unprotected to be eaten by predators.

Frogs

There are approximately 130 species of frog in Australia, but no salamanders. Australia's native frogs include a diverse array of tree frogs, marsh frogs and burrowing frogs.

The golden swamp frog, from the genus *Limnodynastes*, is the most widely distributed frog in Australia.

The gastric-brooding frog, *Rheobatrachus silus*, was first discovered in 1973. It is unique in the animal world because the female inhibits its gastric juices and turns its stomach into a uterus. It swallows the fertile eggs, which turn into fully developed young in the temporary nursery. The young then emerge through the frog's mouth.

The water-holding frog of Australia, *Cyclorana platy-cephalus*, appears above ground only after rain. As it is a desert creature, it has long spells in its cocoon-like chamber below ground. During wet times, it fills the chamber with water, and then sits in the water till the drought is over.

The corroboree frog, *Pseudophryne corroboree*, grows to 3 centimetres long, and is pale green with black markings.

The cane toad, *Bufo marinus*, of South America was introduced into Australia in 1935 to control cane-borer beetles. It failed to do this, and since then it has spread in plague proportions along the east coast.

Lizards

Australian lizards range in size from 55 millimetres to 2.4 metres long. The great perentie or goanna, *Varanus giganteus*, is the second-largest lizard in the world.

The most popular lizard is the frill-necked lizard, , *Chlamydosaurus kingii*. It has a vivid frill of skin which is normally folded back. Under attack, it unfolds the frill, sways to and fro, opens its mouth wide and hisses. However, it does not readily attack, and if in doubt runs at great speed on its back legs. (In other words it knows when to quit!)

The blue-tongue lizard, of which *Tiliqua scincoides* is the most common, belongs to the skink family of lizards. They are the most prevalent in Australia.

The moloch or thorny devil, *Moloch horridus*, is well protected from predators by its ability to camouflage itself. It also has skin armour so sharp that no animal could eat it without injuring itself.

Snakes

Only about 140 species of snake are found in Australia, and of these approximately 100 are venomous. The non-venomous snakes include pythons, blind snakes, file snakes and some colubrid snakes. The largest is the amethystine or scrub python, *Liasis amethystina*, which grows to about 7 metres and the smallest the carpet python, *Morelia spilota variegata*, and diamond python, *Morelia spilota spilotes*, both of which reach a length of 2–4 metres.

Among the venomous snakes is the death adder, *Acanthophis*. It grows to a length of about 60 centimetres, and its venom is more potent than that of the Indian cobra. It has a broad, flat, constricted head, and a short, thin tail.

The tiger snake of the genus *Notechis* is distributed throughout the southern part of the continent. This aggressive and dangerous snake does not grow more than 2 metres in length. The venom is more powerful than that of any other land snake. It is coloured from tan to olive, with dark bands across the body.

The 3.4 metre taipan, *Oxyuranus scutellatus*, of Queensland, is one of the world's most venomous land snakes. It carries enough venom to kill 23 000 mice. It is brown and is Australia's largest venomous species.

There are over thirty species of sea snakes found in our northern waters, the most common of which is the yellow-bellied sea snake, *Pelamis platurus*.

Earthworms

The world's largest earth-worm, *Megascolides australis*, is found in Gippsland in Victoria. It grows to 3.56 metres long and 1.9 centimetres in diameter.

Insects

Australia has over 50 000 species of insects. There are about 350 species of butterflies, 7600 species of moths, 18 000 species of beetles and 900 species of ants.

Cicadas

There are over 200 species of Australian cicadas, having such fanciful names as double drummer, *Thopha saccata*, cherry nose, *Macrotristria angularis*, red eye, *Psaltoda moerens*, black prince, *P. plaga*, and yellow Monday and green Monday (or greengrocer), *Cyclochila australasiae*. The nymphs (the young) live beneath the ground for several years before hatching, living on sap tapped from the roots of trees. They finally emerge, and within weeks they mate and die.

It is only the male cicada which sings so deafeningly. A collection of them can produce a noise in excess of 120 decibels, equal to the noise produced by a very loud rock band.

Arachnids

The funnel-web spider, *Atrax robustus*, is the most poisonous spider in Australia. The male is five times more toxic than the female. It is found only in a small area of coastal New South Wales.

The male red-back spider, *Latrodectus mactans*, is one third the size of the female and is reputed to be non-poisonous. The female, on the other hand, is highly venomous.

Termites

Australia's magnetic termite, *Amitermes meridionalis*, builds a nest approximately 4 metres high, 3 metres long and 1 metre wide. The narrow ends point north-south, and so the nest is called a meridional or compass nest. They have been used as direction finders by lost travellers.

Marine organisms

The Great Barrier Reef

The Great Barrier Reef, the largest and most intricate expanse of coral reefs in the world, extends along the Queensland coast for more than 2000 kilometres, covering a total area of almost 260 000 square kilometres.

The earth's largest structure created by living creatures, this reef began forming more than 10 000 years ago. It is a complex ecological maze of fortress-like structures composed of dead coral, over which the living coral forms a mantle. The living coral, made up of millions of coral polyps, produces a limestone secretion for support and protection. These tiny marine animals,

---

DID YOU KNOW?
Sharks have caused more deaths in Australia than anywhere else. Even so, since 1791 fewer than a hundred people have been killed.

whose growth and reproduction build on to the remains of their ancestors, in turn create a still larger and more complex coral colony.

Between the outer Barrier Reef and the coast, ridges of small reefs have developed. Here corals of brilliant colours and fantastic designs live in the sheltered waters: mushroom coral; brain-like coral with intricate cerebral engravings; organ-pipe and gorgonian corals; delicate traceries of lace in the shapes of fans and ferns. There are 'table-tops', and many-pointed antlers and sturdy stag-horn branches. Brightly-hued fish dart about the coral, clams open to display their velvet-soft linings of many hues, and anemones, with decoy fish cradled in their tentacles, feed on anything that comes within reach.

Blue-ringed octopus
Hapalochlaena maculosa
These small octopuses are found over vast areas, from inter-tidal waters to about 40 to 50 metres deep. Often they take the colour of their background, but when irritated they light up electric-blue rings around their body. Normally they are not aggressive, although if they are handled and they sting, the sting can prove fatal. The first recorded death was in 1956. The octopus's body is about the size of a 20c piece, and the tentacles are 7–8 centimetres long. They can live up to one year.

In the north-west corner of the continent, a slightly larger version of the species occurs, *H. lunulosa*. It has not been proved yet whether the sting is poisonous.

Crown-of-thorns starfish
Acanthaster planci
This starfish, approximately 30 centimetres in diameter, is widespread in the Pacific region. It is not deadly, but because the spines are quite toxic it is hard to handle. In recent years, abnormal growth in numbers has occurred, not only in Australian coral reefs, but as far afield as East Africa to Guam, giving rise to the belief that the increase is more a result of natural phenomena than the result of pollutants in our seas. The starfish attacks only living coral, and there is a widely held opinion that, because the reefs mainly comprise dead coral, the relatively small amounts of living coral destroyed are no great threat to the vastness of the

---

DID YOU KNOW?
Monkey Mia, Shark Bay, WA, is the only place on earth where dolphins regularly seek to associate with people.

reef. Layers of spines of the starfish have been found in calcified coral set down over hundreds of years, indicating, perhaps, that outbreaks may come in cycles.

Sea wasp
Chironex fleckeri
This creature is found in Australian tropical waters during summer months. It is often referred to as the box jellyfish because of its cubic shape. Roughly the size of a wine cask, it has a simple branched tentacle, flowing from each corner of the cube, which is extremely dangerous. In fact, it is considered to be the most poisonous creature in our seas. A sting can cause death within minutes. Radio warnings are given when sea wasps are sighted, and intending swimmers are well advised to change their plans.

Birds

Australia is richer in birdlife than most other countries. There are over seven hundred different kinds, including the bower-builders, the lyrebirds, magpies, butcherbirds and song larks.

Bell-bird
Manorina melanophrys
Bell-birds are found in open forests and sheltered dells on the eastern coast. They have a loud bell-like note, and can often be heard by travellers at sharp bends in a road where the bushland drops away into a gully. In contrast to their beautiful song they are small and nondescript.

Black swan
Cygnus atratus
The black swan is unique to Australia and is the only species of swan on the continent. It is distributed throughout the country, building its nest, about a metre in diameter, among reeds in swamps; it feeds on aquatic plants and animals. It has a trumpet-like call. It is Western Australia's bird emblem.

Bower bird

The satin bower bird, *Ptilonorhynchus violaceus*, is found only in Australia and New Guinea. The male builds a decorated bower with a series of archways, and fills the area with objects to attract the female to a mating dance. She in turn builds her nest in the trees, where she lays her eggs.

DID YOU KNOW?
No part of Australia is further than 1000 kilometres from the sea.

Brolga

Grus rubicunda

The brolga or native companion is the only Australian crane. It is a swamp dweller, found mostly on the inland plains. Flocks of brolgas perform a stately mating dance, using their long legs to perfect the formal routine of the dance.

Emu

Dromaius novaehollandiae

The emu is the unofficial bird emblem of Australia. It is flightless, and stands about 1.5 metres high and is Australia's largest bird. It is closely related to the cassowary, and next in size to the ostrich. The dark-green eggs average nearly a kilogram in weight. These are hatched by the male who sits on them for eight weeks before the chicks appear.

Despite its name, the mallee emu wren, *Stipiturus malachurus*, is Australia's smallest bird. It gets its name because its tiny tail is similar in shape to an emu feather.

Honeyeater

The helmeted honeyeater, *Meliphaga cassidix*, is one of the rarest birds in the world. It is only found in southern Victoria, east of Port Phillip. This is the only bird species restricted to that state, although it belongs to the larger group of over eighty species of honeyeater. The honeyeater has a yellow crest or helmet, and a yellow tuft behind each ear with a distinctive black face. The helmeted honeyeater is the bird emblem of Victoria.

Kookaburra

Unique to Australia, these birds are the largest of the kingfishers. There are two types, the laughing jackass of the eastern states, *Dacelo gigas*, and the blue-winged kookaburra, *D. leachi*, of the north and north-west. They breed in families, so the older offspring help raise the fledglings. They 'laugh' raucously in chorus, marking out their territory. They live on reptiles, small mammals, mice and sometimes fish. The kookaburra is the bird emblem of New South Wales. A well-known song about it is on p. 202.

Lyrebird

The male lyrebirds, *Menura novae hollandiae* and *M. alberti*, have a fancy gauze-like tail giving this unique bird its name. The female is nondescript in appearance. Lyrebirds are ground feeders, and build

---

DID YOU KNOW?
The flightless wood hens of Mt Gower, Lord Howe Island, are amongst the rarest birds on earth.

Kookaburra

incubation mounds for nests which keep the interior at 30°C. They have a wide vocal range and are splendid mimics.

Parrot

There are more than fifty species of Australian parrots. Among them are galahs, *Cacatua roseicapilla*, sulphur-crested cockatoos, *Cacatua galerita*, rosellas, of the genus *Platycercus*, lorikeets, of the genera *Trichoglossus* and *Glossopsitta*, and budgerigars, *Melopsittacus undulatus*. They are usually found in semi-arid areas, gathered together in large flocks.

Penguin

The only penguin species residing in Australian waters is the fairy or little penguin, *Eudyptula minor*. Phillip Island, near Melbourne, is the home of the best-known colony. In summer, tourists flock to Phillip Island to watch the penguin parade, as the birds waddle back to their nests after a day's fishing.

Swift and swallow

The migratory spine-tailed swift, *Hirundapus caudacutus*, is known as the storm-bird. It is seen soaring high in the sky before and after a storm, feeding on the insects trapped in the turbulence. It rarely lands, and spends much of its life in the sky.

The welcome swallow, *Hirundo neoxena* spends long hours soaring. These birds can feed their young without alighting on the nest. They hover

over the fledglings and drop the food.

Wedge-tailed eagle
Aquila audax

With an average wingspan of 2.5 metres, this bird is Australia's largest raptor. It is clearly recognisable by its huge broad wings and the long wedge-shaped tail. The general colour is dark brown, with a chestnut neck. The legs are feathered right down to the feet. Its hooked beak and strong talons clearly mark the wedge-tailed eagle as a bird of prey. It is found throughout Australia, and is more common in the arid centre than on coastal plains. It is the Northern Territory's bird emblem.

Plants

Although Australia is predominantly arid, with vast desert areas, there are many other vegetation regions such as rainforests, savanna grasslands, scrub, mallee, heath and alpine areas.

Australian plants in general are characterised by their drought-resistant qualities. They have tough spiny leaves and thick bark to resist evaporation. They are also very fire-resistant, and many of these plants need a fierce fire to germinate seeds and rejuvenate.

The Australian land flora comprises over 12 000 species of flowering plants, and is dominated by *Eucalyptus* (over 550 recognised species), *Melaleuca* (paperbark), *Leptospermum* (tea-tree), *Callistemon* (bottlebrush), *Banksia* (honeysuckle), *Acacia* (wattle), *Casuarina* (she-oak) and *Xanthorrhoea* (blackboy). The eucalypt is the most dominant tree in Australia, and has tough, durable wood. It is able to resist the ravages of fire by sending out shoots from the trunk, which keep the tree alive until the branches recover. The bark, leaves and branches are constantly shed, which creates fuel for a bushfire. As well, eucalyptus oil is highly flammable. During a bushfire, the oil creates a gas which forms fireballs. This is nature's way of keeping the fire alive so as to burn and then rejuvenate the Australian bush.

The Ku-ring-gai Chase national park, north of Sydney, was named after the Gurringai Aboriginal tribe who had lived there over 20 000 years before white settlement. It is one of the oldest national parks in Australia, and contains more species of plants than are found in the whole of the UK. The park is 14 656 hectares.

Forests

On the northern and eastern coastlines of the Australian continent are vast areas of forest which experience rainfall ranging from 1000 to 2500 millimetres per year.

In the broad-leaved rainforests of the north buttressing fig trees, interlacing lianas, cabbage fan palms, *Livistona australia*, entanglements of lawyer vines, *Smilax australis*, eucalypts, nettle trees of the family *Urticaceae*, and fungi predominate to create a dank brooding atmosphere.

The open forests around the top end of the Northern Territory and on the east coast are less formidable and dense. Here eucalyptus such as mountain ash, *Eucalyptus regnans*, spotted gum, *E. maculata* and hoop pine, *Araucaria cunninghamii*, dominate the landscape, with the perennial plants, like prickly Moses, *Acacia ulicifolia,* and purple coral-pea, *Hardenbergia violacea*, flowering in spring. In the New South Wales and Tasmanian forests the waratah, *Telopea speciosissima*, blooms with its crimson composite flower, 10 centimetres wide, on a single straight stem. The waratah is the floral emblem of New South Wales.

Golden wattle, *Acacia pycnantha*, is Australia's floral emblem. It is one of 850 species of Australian acacia also found in scrublands. The bark is a source of gum arabic used in tanning. Wattle has fragrant golden yellow flowers.

The common pink heath, *Epacris impressa labill*, is Victoria's floral emblem. It occurs mainly in the southern part of Victoria, chiefly in the wetter foothill country, the coastal heathlands, the Grampians and the Little Desert scrub. It grows to about 1200 metres above sea level.

The Cooktown orchid, *Dendrobium bigibbum*, is native to tropical Queensland, and has been chosen as the floral emblem of that state. It has purple flowers about 4 centimetres across; the orchid grows in rocks and trees in well-watered areas of Cape York Peninsula.

Grasses and woodlands

These areas of Australia are to be found mainly 200 to 300 kilometres inland from the north and eastern coast. There is a greater distance between the trees than in the forests, and the tree crowns are quite large. Here the eucalypt abounds, and varieties such as yellow box, *Eucalyptus melliodora*,

---

DID YOU KNOW?
The world's first green ban was placed on Kelly's Bush, Hunters Hill, Sydney, in 1972 by Jack Mundey of the Builders' Workers' Union.

white cypress pine, *Callitris columellaris*, Darwin stringybark, *E. tetrodonta*, and river red gum, *E. camaldulensis*, flower in spring and summer.

The gradual blending of woodland into grassland produces a more sporadic grouping of trees intermingled with varieties of grasses such as kangaroo grass, *Themeda australis*, and blue devil, *Eryngium rostratum*.

An unusual plant of the grasslands is the subterranean orchid, *Rhizanthella gardneri*. It is found in the wheat-belt of south-east Western Australia. It exists wholly beneath the soil and does not disturb the surface. Farmers found this elusive plant while ploughing. It is thought that it could become extinct because of loss of natural habitat.

Scrub and mallee

This is a diverse community of shrubby plants where the most dominant, the Mallee eucalyptus, is no more than 8 metres high. It is restricted to the south-eastern and south western regions of the country where many Australian wildflowers grow. The saw banksia, *Banksia serrata*, grows in this area. It was named after Sir Joseph Banks, the botanist who came with Captain Cook on the *Endeavour*.

Banksia species (bottle-brushes) are considered to be the honeysuckle trees of Australia. Like most Australian plants they need an extremely hot fire to germinate their seeds. May Gibbs, the Australian author of children's books, immortalised this tree by creating the Bad Banksia Men characters in *Snugglepot and Cuddlepie*.

Deserts

The true desert prevails over vast regions of the inland. Here the land receives unpredictable and extremely low rainfall, temperatures are extreme, and the evaporation exceeds precipitation. These adverse conditions not only create a variety of dry salt lakes and dry riverbeds but produce a complex mosaic of plant communities. Plants adapt by growing spindly leaves and tough bark to stop evaporation in the extreme heat. Again the eucalypts, coolabah, *E. microtheca*, and ghost gum, *E. papuana*, dominate the desert trees. The unusual bottle

DID YOU KNOW?
Cocklebiddy Cave, Western Australia, a few miles from the Great Australian Bight, contains the world's longest underwater passages.

trees, for example *Brachychiton rupestre*, derive their name from their bottle-shaped trunk. The branches look like the roots of the tree, which resulted in an Aboriginal myth that the tree lives upside down. It has adapted well to desert conditions by storing water in its trunk.

Porcupine grass, such as *Triodia irritans*, and saltbush, *Atriplex vesicaria*, are the dominant plants in Australian desert areas. They are tough grasses of rounded tussocks and sharp pointed leaves. Being drought-resistant, the seeds are dispersed by the dried plant tumbling in the wind.

Sturt's desert rose, *Gossypium sturtianum*, is a small bushy plant, growing to a height of 1.5 metres, with dark green leaves. The petals of the flowers are mauve, with deep red markings at the base. Sturt's desert rose is an arid-zone plant found in the southern part of the Northern Territory, and it was adopted for the territory's emblem in 1974. It was named for Captain Charles Sturt, an explorer (see p. 14).

Sturt's desert pea, *Clianthus formosus*, is South Australia's floral emblem. It is a creeper with brilliant scarlet and black flowers, growing only in dry, sandy country.

A desert boab tree

Lambertia formosa

DID YOU KNOW?
Fifty per cent of the continent has less than 300 millimetres annual rainfall.

In the early days of the colony the precarious food supplies resulted in a staple diet of meat and cheese, tempered with some vegetables and wheat products. It was mainly based on English fare, and by 1900, regardless of our long hot summers, the preference for hot meals with plenty of meat still persisted. In fact, Australians were recognised as the greatest meat-eaters in the world. Even the middle class rarely ate fresh fruit or salads and Australia's wonderful variety of sea food was largely unrecognised.

There was little change in dietary habits until the post-war immigration years, when the introduction of cuisines from many lands widened Australians' culinary horizons.

While there is now a more cosmopolitan attitude to the selection of food, many traditional recipes from the early days remain popular.

Lamingtons

These small cakes were popularised by Queenslanders in the early 1990s.

¾ cup butter
¾ cup castor sugar
3 eggs
½ teaspoon vanilla
1 cup self-raising flour
½ cup plain flour
½ cup milk
chocolate icing and desiccated coconut

Beat butter and sugar until creamy. Add 2 eggs, one at a time and beat well.

Add the vanilla and half the sifted flour. Mix well. Add milk, the remaining flour and the third egg, and mix until smooth.

Place in a well-greased lamington tin (or baking-dish), and bake for 30 minutes in a pre-heated moderate to slow oven. Cool and cut into small squares.

Spear each square on a carving fork, dip in chocolate icing, drain, and toss in desiccated coconut.

Famous cornflour sponge cake

A Royal Show special.

3 eggs, separated
pinch of salt
½ cup castor sugar
¼ teaspoon vanilla
⅔ cup cornflour
1 slightly rounded tablespoon plain flour
1 level teaspoon baking powder

Pre-heat oven to 190°C (375°F). Beat egg whites with salt until soft peaks form. Gradually beat in sugar, a little at a time, then continue beating until the whites are stiff.

Add egg yolks and vanilla. Beat until combined. Sift together, three times, the cornflour, plain flour and baking powder. Add to egg mixture. Carefully and lightly fold into mixture with wooden spoon. Do not stir.

Divide batter evenly between two greased and lightly floured 20 centimetre, round sandwich pans. Bake for 18–20 minutes.

Pumpkin scones

These moist delicious scones are old favourites.

1 level tablespoon butter
3 level tablespoons sugar
1 egg
¾ cup cooked mashed pumpkin
2 cups self-raising flour
pinch salt
¼ cup milk

Cream the butter and sugar, add the egg, and mix. Fold in the pumpkin.

Sift the flour and salt, and fold in with beaten egg and milk.

Knead well. Roll out the dough, and cut it into circles with a scone-cutter. Bake in a hot oven for 15 minutes.

Queensland Blue pumpkin soup

The Queensland Blue is a variety of pumpkin which is noted for its flavour and keeping qualities. The quantities given will serve six people.

¾ cup butter
4½ cups peeled chopped pumpkin
½ cup chopped onion
2 cups water
3 tablespoons plain flour
1 cup milk
1 egg yolk

Melt ½ cup butter in heavy pan, add pumpkin and onion. Cook for 10 minutes with the lid on, stirring occasionally. Add water, and simmer until the pumpkin is very tender.

Press through a sieve, or puree in a blender with a little milk.

Melt the rest of the butter, and stir in the flour. Gradually add the puree of pumpkin and the remaining milk, stirring constantly. Simmer for 20 minutes.

Just before serving, combine egg yolk with a little of the pumpkin mixture, then stir it into the pumpkin soup.

DID YOU KNOW?

The average Australian can expect to eat during his or her lifetime: 17 beef cattle, 92 sheep, 4 005 loaves of bread, 165 000 eggs, half a tonne of cheese, 8 tonnes of fruit, and 10 tonnes of vegetables.

Billy tea

To be found where old mates yarn.

Place a billycan of fresh stream water onto the hot coals of a fire. When the water is boiling, sprinkle in a handful of tea leaves and allow to boil one minute. Drop in a green gum leaf or two for flavour. Allow the brew to stand by the fire for two minutes. Tap sides with stick to settle the tea leaves, and pour tea into mugs. Some old-timers 'swing the billy' of boiling tea around their heads. This is a sure way of making a good brew.

Peach Melba

This dessert was named for the famous singer, Dame Nellie Melba.

3 large peaches
vanilla icecream
whipped cream
raspberry syrup

Cook the peaches carefully so that they do not break. Drain them, cut them in half, and chill. Place them, cut side up, in individual dishes. Fill each with a scoop of icecream, and top with whipped cream. Pour raspberry syrup around peaches.

Pavlova

The pavlova was created in 1935 by chef Bert Sachse, while he was working at Perth's Esplanade Hotel. He made it in honour of the hotel's most distinguished guest of previous years, the great prima ballerina, Anna Pavlova. It is now considered to be a national dish.

This popular party dessert consists of a shell of meringue, filled with whipped cream and fresh fruit.

4 egg whites
pinch salt
1¼ cups castor sugar
1 teaspoon vinegar
2 teaspoons cornflour
whipped cream
fruit to decorate

Heat oven to moderate. Mark a 20 centimetre circle on greaseproof paper. Brush paper with oil, and place on a greased oven tray.

Beat egg whites and salt at high speed until they are stiff but not dry. Gradually add sugar, a tablespoon at a time, beating well after each addition. The meringue should be smooth and glossy, and hold firm peaks.

Remove beaters and sprinkle vinegar and cornflour over top of mixture, and fold in lightly.

Spoon mixture onto the greased paper circle, and spread evenly. Make a depression in the middle with the back of a spoon.

Place in bottom half of oven, and immediately reduce heat to low. Bake for 1½ hours. Turn off heat, and allow pavlova shell to cool in the oven.

When cool, fill the shell with whipped cream and decorate with strawberries, sliced kiwi fruit and passionfruit.

DID YOU KNOW?

In an election at the Waverley Municipal Council in 1859, Elizabeth Cadman, the wife of ex-convict John Cadman, the superintendent of government boats, was the first woman in Australia to demand to be allowed to vote.

Vegemite pinwheels

These are made from the famous Kraft product Vegemite, a favourite of many Australians. The quantities given will make about 4½ dozen.

2 cups self-raising flour
1 good pinch of cayenne pepper
1 teaspoon of dry mustard
2 tablespoons butter
1½ cups grated cheese
⅓ cup water
Vegemite

Sift the dry ingredients together. Rub in the butter, and add cheese. Mix to a firm dough with water.

Turn out onto a floured board, and knead well. Roll pastry into a rectangle. Spread with Vegemite, and roll it into a long coil.

Cut into pinwheel slices, and place them flat on a greased tray. Bake in hot oven for 15–20 minutes.

Bush brownie

A stockman's stand-by.

1½ cups self-raising flour
1 teaspoon each of ginger, all-spice, nutmeg
¾ cup butter
½ cup brown sugar
2 cups mixed fruit
1 egg
1 cup milk

Sift dry ingredients in a bowl. Rub in butter. Add fruit. Mix in egg and milk, beaten well together.

Pour into greased tin, and bake for 30–40 minutes in moderate oven. Serve sliced and buttered.

Anzac biscuits

A crisp tasty treat with good keeping qualities. Often sent to
Australian soldiers at Gallipoli by loving families. The quantities given
will make about 5 dozen biscuits.

½ cup butter
1 tablespoon golden syrup
½ teaspoon bicarbonate of soda
2 tablespoons boiling water
1 cup uncooked rolled oats
1 cup desiccated coconut
1 cup plain flour
1 cup brown sugar
2 teaspoons ground ginger

Melt butter and golden syrup in a large pan over a low heat. Add
bicarbonate of soda mixed with boiling water.

Combine dry ingredients in a mixing bowl, then pour melted
mixture into the centre, and mix to a moist but firm consistency.

Drop slightly rounded teaspoonfuls of mixture onto a cold
greased tray. Cook for about 15 minutes in a moderate oven. Cool
on a wire rack.

Drover's damper

Traditionally made by bushmen, damper can be cooked in the hot
ashes of a fire. The outside will be burnt; the damper is broken open
and only the centre eaten. Here is a sophisticated version of the
basic recipe. It is excellent with pumpkin soup.

2 cups self-raising flour
½ teaspoon salt
2 teaspoons sugar
1 tablespoon butter
1 cup milk

Sift flour and salt. Add the sugar. Rub in butter. Mix in milk to
make medium soft dough. Knead lightly on board until smooth. Pat
into round shape. Place in tin and glaze with milk. Bake in hot oven,
reducing heat until cooked (20 minutes). Turn out onto tea towel,
wrap and cool. Serve with butter and golden syrup (cocky's joy) or
jam.

Variations: to make fruit or grated cheese damper use 1 cup of
either ingredient, added to basic recipe. Beer damper can be made
by substituting beer instead of milk.

TINDALE, Norman, & GEORGE, B. *Australian Aborigines*. Lloyd O'Neil, 1983.

Touring Australia. Gregory's Publishing, 1987.

UNITED NATIONS. *Demographic Yearbook*. 1987.

VEITCH, Margot. *Australia's Entertainers*. Child & Associates, 1990.

WALKER, Clinton. *Inner City Sounds*. Globe Press, 1982.

WALKER, Clinton. *The Next Thing*. Kangaroo Press, 1984.

WALLACE, D. L. et. al. *Focus on Government*. Pitman, 1979.

WATSON, Eric. *Country Music Australia*. Angus & Robertson, 1983.

WEBBER, Graeme. *Australian Rock Folio*. Pentacle Press, 1976.

WILLIAMS, Mike. *The Australian Jazz Explosion*. Angus & Robertson, 1981.

WRITER, Larry. *Australia: The Moments that Mattered*. Lester Townsend, 1990.

Demographic statistics are the estimated resident population for local government areas at September 1992 compiled by the Australian Bureau of Statistics.

A census is taken every five years, and the preliminary results of the 1991 census were released in June 1992.

Facts and figures on the economy are from the Australian Bureau of Statistics and the Australian Stock Exchange.

Phrases

English is spoken in many countries, but the Australian brand is unmistakable. To the British our 'G'day, mate' will be curious, to the American it will be delightful, and to a home-sick Aussie it will be music to the ears.

Here is a guide to some of the most common Aussie expressions and their meanings.

ace – excellent

'ang on' – wait a moment

arvo – afternoon

'avago – have a go (usually 'ya mug' – you fool – is added)' try harder

back teeth treading water – badly need a comfort stop

barbie – short for barbecue

bewdy or bewdy bottler – good; the best

beyond the Black Stump – far from the city; the outback

bingle – minor car accident

bluey – a swag or a blanket roll

bombed out – unsuccessful; *also* drunk

bushed – lost; *also* tired

by crikey – an expression of surprise

cark it – to die

cashed up – having plenty of ready money

cheesed (off) – bored; fed up

chewy – chewing gum

chicka – usually the name of a mate down the road

chook – a domestic fowl

chook raffle – a lottery in which the prize is a chicken; usually held in a 'pub' (hotel)

chuck a willy (wobbly) – go berserk

cobber – friend

cobberdobber – a person who informs on a friend

cocky – know-all; *also* a small farmer

come a gutser (cropper) – to fall heavily

cot case – a drunk or exhausted person, fit only for bed

could eat a bullock stuffed with rabbits – extremely hungry

deadhead – a stupid person

dead marine – an empty beer bottle

dead set – certain; assured; used as an exclamation meaning 'really!'

dead set against it – unco-operative

dinky-di – genuine

do a Norm – to act foolishly

do the lolly (melon; nana; loaf) – to get very angry

dob in – to betray or report someone to the authorities; *also* to nominate someone for an unpleasant task

doing a Melba (or Melba's farewell) – saying goodbye time and time again

don't get off your bike – calm down

doughy – stupid

drongo – stupid person

dry as a drover's dog – extremely thirsty

dunny – an outside toilet

esky – a portable icebox (brand name)

fair crack of the whip – ease up

fair dinkum – honest; genuine

fair enough – all right; acceptable

DID YOU KNOW?
Sir Donald Bradman made his first century in cricket at the age of twelve at Bowral High School.

fair go – a chance; *also* an appeal for fairness

five-finger discount – shoplifting

flake (out) – to collapse; to fall asleep

flat out like a lizard drinking – lying prone; *also* rushed, extremely busy

flush – having plenty of money

fossick – to search for something

freak out – to have an extreme reaction (good or bad) to something

full as a goog (tick; boot) – drunk

game as Ned Kelly – very brave (Ned Kelly was a daring Australian bushranger (robber) in 1878)

garbage! – an exclamation meaning 'What rubbish, I don't believe you!'

go off like a bucket of prawns in the sun – to create a commotion

good one – an exclamation of approval

goodo – yes, all right!

gutful – more than enough

have tickets on oneself – to be conceited

hit the deck – to duck; to put one's head down

hit the tin – to put money in the kitty; to contribute to a collection of cash

hoon – a stupid or uncultivated person

hooroo – goodbye

jigging – playing truant from school

kick in – to help out with money

knock – to criticise, find fault

knocker – a person who makes derogatory remarks

like a hornet in a bottle – furious

like a possum up a gum tree – moving fast

like a rat up a drainpipe – moving even faster

lingo – language

loaded – extremely wealthy; *also* very drunk

mate – good or best friend; *also* used to greet someone as in 'G'day mate'

matilda – a blanket roll carried by a swagman

m'oath – my oath; on my oath mug' – you fool – is added);

mulga – rough country

no-hoper – an incompetent person; a social misfit

nosh-up – a good meal

nick – to steal

nick off – to go away; expression meaning 'lose yourself!'

get nicked – to be caught

nifty – stylish; clever; shrewd to the point of dishonesty

ocker – the archetypal uncultivated Australian man

'ooroo – goodbye

outback – the inland country far away from the cities

prang – minor car accident

rack off – to go away; expression meaning 'lose yourself!'

ring-in – a substitute

sangers – sandwiches

scungies – swimsuit worn for surfboard riding

shonky – poor quality; shoddy

sickie – a day taken off work, but not necessarily because of illness

skip – Australian-born (from Skippy the Kangaroo)

skite – a bragger

stinker – an objectionable person

stone the crows – exclamation of astonishment

swag – a blanket roll of light bedding

swagman – a man who travels around the country on foot and takes odd jobs

ratbag – a rogue; an eccentric person

rubbish – to criticise; to mock

ta ta – bye bye

tax – to steal; to nick

tinnie – a can of beer

too right – an exclamation meaning 'I quite agree'

top drop – a good beer

true blue – genuine

twit – a fool

up-ta-putty – terrible

vegie – a silly person

veg-out – to do something foolish

wag it – to play truant

wheelie – a noisy skidding turn while driving

whinge – to complain

whopper – something surprisingly big

wowser – a killjoy; a prudish teetotaller

write-off – a total loss

yakka – hard or heavy work

yobbo – a stupid or uncultivated person

zonked (out) – tired out; exhausted

TRUE BLUE

DID YOU KNOW?

The first point in Australia which is touched by the morning sun is Mount Warning near Murwillumbah in New South Wales, and the last touching point in the evening is Dirk Hartog Island near Exmouth in Western Australia.

T-SHOO

BANG-ER-OO

KON·KA·ROO

"DRINKO"

Smokettes

BONSER

BLUEE

EASO

BILLY BLUEGUM

R.I.P.A.

DID YOU KNOW?

The name 'gum tree' was first used by Sir Joseph Banks at Botany Bay in 1770, when he recorded a tree having gum exudations (later known as Eucalyptus gum).

Acknowledgements

This book has evolved from numerous sources and I wish to sincerely thank the many people who helped me gather material.

I thank the staffs of the following organisations: Antarctic Division, Kingston, Tasmania; Australian Ballet; Australian Bureau of Statistics; Australian Cotton Foundation; Australian Cycling Association; Australian Information Service; Australian National Library; Australian Opera; Australian Stock Exchange; Capella Bookshop, and Children's Bookshop, Beecroft; Confederation of Australian Broadcasters; Department of Aboriginal Affairs; Department of Foreign Affairs; Department of Immigration; Department of the Navy; Department of the Prime Minister and Cabinet; Education Bookshop 2000, Toronto; Honours Secretariat; Institute of Aboriginal Studies; Maritime Services Board; Mitchell Library; Museum of New South Wales; New South Wales Fire Department; New South Wales Government Information Service; Parliament House Construction Authority, Australian Capital Territory; Parliament House Education Resources, Australian Capital Territory; Peat Marwick; Pennant Hills Library; Premier's Department of each state; Reserve Bank; Roads & Traffic Authority, New South Wales; Sister Cities Association of Australia; St Vincent's Hospital; State Protocol Departments; Sydney Opera House Library; Toukley Library; Tourist Commissions of each state; Water Resources Commission.

I am indebted to the following people: Russell Best, flora and fauna; Ross Dundas, cricket; Craig Hilliard, athletics; Evelyn Klopser, performing arts; Don Matthews, radio; Ray Mitchell, sport; Melissa Ortlepp, music; Gerard Patterson, music; Des Renford, swimming; Jill Rivers, ballet; Jeff Rushton, radio; Tim McLean, Brash's Music Store, Kotara; John Williamson,

foreword; Pat Yardley, art.

For permission to include copyright material I thank: Australian Ballet for the photographs of Steven Heathcote (*Spartacus*), Justine Summers, Damien Welch, Vicki Attard (*Divergence*); Australian Opera for the photograph of their 1994 production of *A Mid-Summer Night's Dream* and photograph of Yvonne Kenny; Brian Brownscombe for the photograph of a waratah; Dennis Warren for photograph of boom-netting Great Barrier Reef; Mimmo Cozzolino for symbols reproduced from *Symbols of Australia*; Department of the Special Minister of State for the Commonwealth flag and coat of arms; Department of the Premier and Cabinet in Victoria, South Australia and Western Australia, the Premier's Department in New South Wales, Queensland and Tasmania, and the Department of the Chief Minister in the Northern Territory, for the state flags and coats of arms; EMI Records for the photograph of James Blundell; Festival Records for the photographs of Jimmy Barnes, The Angels, (photographer Chrystene Carroll) Hunters and Collectors, Paul Kelly, Archie Roach, Billy Thorpe and Kylie Minogue; Government Printer, Sydney, for the engraving *Arrival of the first railway train at Parramatta, from Sydney*; David Harcourt-Norton of the Australian Democrats; Kraft Foods Ltd for the Vegemite label; Mitchell Library for the engraving *The Settlement at Sydney Cove 1788*; National Gallery of Victoria for *The Rabbiters* by Russell Drysdale, *Shearing the Rams* and *The Sunny South* by Tom Roberts, and *Landing of Captain Cook at Botany Bay 1770* by E. Phillips Fox; National Library of Australia for the engravings *Sturt's party threatened by blacks . . .*, by J. Macfarlane, and 'Attempted escape of prisoners from Darlinghurst Gaol' from *Illustrated Sydney News* 1864; Northern Territory Tourist Bureau for the photographs of Katherine Gorge; Chris Ortlepp for the photograph of the author; Radio 2UE for the photograph of John Laws; Radio 2GB for photograph of Clive Robertson; Reserve Bank of Australia and the Australian Mint, Canberra for permission to reproduce facsimile currency; Retuse Ltd; Rimfire Films for the still from *Crocodile Dundee II*; Roadshow Film Distributors for the photographs of *Muriel's Wedding* (photography by Robert McFarlane) and *The Adventures of Priscilla, Queen of the Desert* (photography by Elsie Lockwood); Sony Music Australia for photograph of Tommy Emmanuel; Thévenot's Map of 1663 of Terra australis

List of sources

The author acknowledges indebtedness to the following books, which were consulted for reference.

ADAMS, Brian. *La Stupenda*. Hutchinson, 1980.
ADAMS, K. M. *Australia: Colonies to Commonwealth 1850–1900*. Angus & Robertson, 1971.
AITKEN, Don, & JINKS, Brian. *Australian Political Institutions*. Pitman, 1985.
ALEXANDER, Fred. *Australia Since Federation*. Nelson, 1980.
ART GALLERY OF NEW SOUTH WALES. *Aspects of Australian Art*. Art Gallery of New South Wales, 1968.
AUSTRALIA, DEPARTMENT OF ABORIGINAL AFFAIRS. *Background Notes 1981*. 1981.
AUSTRALIAN MUSEUM. *Complete Book of Australian Mammals*. Angus & Robertson, 1983.
AUSTRALIAN NEWS AND INFORMATION BUREAU. *Australians in the Antarctic*. 1961.
Australia's Yesterdays. Reader's Digest, 1974.
BEAVAN, B., & BOGDAN, H. *A Sunburnt Country*. Rigby, 1978.
BEAZEL, Mitchell. *The Great Geographical Atlas*. Rigby, 1984.
BLANCH, John. *Ampol Australian Sporting Records*. John Pollard, 1973.
BISSETT, Andrew. *Black Roots, White Flowers*. Golden Press, 1979.
BRIDGES, Nancye. *The Wonderful Wireless*. Methuen, 1983.
CARGHER, John. *Opera and Ballet in Australia*. Cassell, 1977.
CAYLEY, N. W. *What Bird Is That?* Angus & Robertson, 1973.
CLARK, Manning. *A Short History of Australia*. Macmillan, 1981.
COVELL, Roger. *Australia's Music*. Sun Books, 1967.
DIRECTORY OF AUSTRALIAN AUTHORS, National Book Council, 1989.

DRAPER, W.J. (ed.). *Who's Who in Australia*. Herald & Weekly Times, 1984.

DUNLOP E.E. *The War Diaries of Weary Dunlop*, Penguin, 1990.

FRASER, Bryce (ed.). *The Macquarie Book of Events*. Macquarie Library, 1983.

GIBSON, Mike, & CHAPPELL, Ian. *Australian Sporting Hall of Fame*. Angus & Robertson, 1984.

GLEESON, James. *Australian Painters*. Lansdowne, 1971.

GLENNON, James. *Australia's Music and Musicians*. Rigby, 1968.

GREENFIELD, Edward. *Joan Sutherland*. Ian Allan, 1972.

HETHERINGTON, John. *Melba*. Cheshire, 1967.

HUGHES, Robert. *The Art of Australia*. Pelican, 1966.

McGRATH, Noel. *Australian Encyclopaedia of Rock*. Outback Press, 1978.

McKENZIE, Valerie. *A Look at Yesteryear*. Centennial, 1980.

The Macquarie Dictionary. Macquarie Library, 1981.

Merit Student's Encyclopaedia. Macmillan, 1978.

MILLAR, Ann. *I See No End to Travelling*. Bay Books, 1986.

NEWBY, Eric. *The World Atlas of Exploration*. Colporteur Press, 1982.

One Thousand Famous Australians. Rigby, 1978.

ORCHARD, A. Arundel. *Music in Australia*. Georgian House, 1952.

O'SHAUGHNESSY, Peter. *The Restless Years*. Jacaranda, 1968.

The Pictorial Atlas of Australia. Rigby, 1977.

PORT, Leo. *Australian Inventors*. Ure Smith, 1979.

RASMUSSEN, Carolyn. *Early Colonial Society*. Nelson, 1984.

RAYMOND, Robert and MORRISON, Reg. *Australia, the Greatest Island*. Lansdowne, 1981.

RICHARDSON, Michael, & NEWMAN, Robin. *Australia's Natural Wonders*. Golden Press, 1984.

READERS' GUIDE TO AUSTRALIAN FICTION, THE, Oxford, 1992.

ROBERTS, J. *The Bold Atlas of Australia*. Ashton Scholastic, 1984.

ROGERS, Bob. *Rock 'n' Roll Australia*. Cassell, 1975.

RUSSELL, Elaine. *Australian Wildlife 1984*. Bay Books, 1983.

SADIE, Stanley (ed.). *The New Grove Dictionary of Music and Musicians*. Macmillan, 1980.

SHAW, John. *Australian Encyclopaedia*. Collins, 1984.

SHEPHERD, Jim. *Encyclopaedia of Australian Sport*. Rigby, 1980.

SPLATT, William, & BURTON, Barbara. *A Treasury of Australian Painting*. John Curry O'Neil, 1986.

STRATTON, David. *The Avocado Plantation*. Pan Macmillan, 1990.

STRATTON, David. *The Last New Wave*. Angus & Robertson, 1980.